The author

Harry Nicholson now lives nea
Yorkshire. He grew up in Hartl
family have fished since the 16^{t}

CW00922764

He had a first career as a radi
navy. A second career followed
retirement, he has taken up art, story-telling, poetry and
meditation.

By the same author:

Tom Fleck – historical novel of Cleveland and Flodden.

The Black Caravel – sequel to Tom Fleck.

Wandering About – poems of land and sea.

Green Linnet – short stories and poems (eBook only).

The Beveren Rabbit – a study of the breed.

One Jump Ahead --- SS Vyner Brooke escapes from Singapore

The Best of Days

A memoir of the sea

By Harry Nicholson

For Beryl with love

She also sailed the seas.

Contents

1

Gates of Weeping

None of us enjoy this passage down the Red Sea from Suez to Aden. This drowned extension of Africa's Great Rift Valley is a furnace of a place; never a cloud, never a breeze save the morsel stirred up by the old steamer as she plods south. I'm aged nineteen and second radio officer on a merchant ship. She's *SS Mahanada*, 9,000 tons, owned by T&J Brocklebank Steam Navigation Co. of Liverpool. It is early August 1957. I've been at sea for eighteen months, since I qualified at South Shields Marine College at seventeen. This is my fourth voyage to the Far East and I've been through this sweltering place before.

Off watch; content to be free of warbling headphones for four hours, I'm at the desk in my cabin, stark naked but for a towel. Sweat drips off my forehead onto the pad of lightweight Basildon Bond as I write letters ready for the post at Aden. I suspect even the cockroaches are panting. A chuntering electric fan, bolted to the steel bulkhead, alternately whirs and rattles; it blows a stream of hot air across my bare shoulders. For extra relief, I roll a can of chilled lager across my face and over my chest. That chest, I'm pleased to note, has lately sprouted a few hairs. I crack open the can of Tennent's and gulp it down – it runs straight out of my pores and soon I crave another. All this time the turbines throb. Vibrations run through the oiled steel deck plates, through the masts, through the halyards, through my bones.

Though my parents have vicariously travelled this route via my letters, I tell them again about the seascape that slides past the ship:

Today, it being so hot, I long for November rain on the Manchester Ship Canal. This Red Sea is like … a mirror. Because the sun is almost overhead at noon – the sea flares blinding white, splashed across with the colours of molten brass. When our bow wave subsides it turns from white to glowing mazarine blue. Now and then a shoal of flying fish break surface; they shoot up like a volley of arrows and flash across the water. They flee from something nasty below; jaws that gape and pursue them. As they fly they shed water droplets that gleam in the sun like quicksilver. We trail turmoil astern as the phosphor-bronze propeller thuds down in an endless rhythm and smashes up the vivid colours. Our white wake stretches for two hundred yards before it subsides into quiet, parallel undulations that fan outwards, and the scar is healed.

Mother might touch her own scar as she reads this. When she was a little girl her dress caught fire. Her damaged fingers and twisted nails might move down from her left eyebrow, across the tight skin of her cheek, down to that hurt corner of her lips.

In that quiet house, Mam and Dad have only the old valve wireless. They cherish my letters, so I write a bit more:

In our radio room, years of varnish soften; layers of it creep down the mahogany bulkheads (In Calcutta, the chief will likely have me sand it all down and do a re-varnish). Miles away, on either side of the ship, yellow and red cliffs bake in the heat. To starboard, in the far distance, the oven deserts of the Sudan quiver along a milk-white horizon. The Red Sea begins to narrow here. Desiccated and tortured, the mountains of Eritrea rise off the starboard bow. Away to port the town of Mocha huddles on the coast of ancient Sheba. Her yellow headlands creep nearer. Ahead, like the hulls of upturned ships, a string of low islands appear. Nothing green; just brown twisted pinnacles that rise out of black flows of ancient lava. In this glare, with its shimmering mirages, those rocks look like salamanders dancing in a furnace. The islands guard Bab el Mandeb, the straits that lead to the Arabian Sea; the name is Arabic and means: The Gates of Weeping. I've been reading 'The Burning Coast' by John Doody and learn that it was across these narrows that centuries of slaves were shipped in chains out of Africa to the markets of Arabia. I shudder. What a beautiful, but brutal place this is.

As I sign off, fold the pages and slip them into the airmail envelope, Mother might be on Hartlepool Headland. I imagine her shivering on the promenade as she peers through the rain, into a gale, across the charging white horses of the cold North Sea. She tells me later that she turned away with a prayer, 'Dear God, please don't let our Harry be out in all this.'

Writing in 2017, at ease in my study in Eskdale, I feel in communion with those long gone. But are the thoughts I set down today, real events, the true experiences of a nineteen year old chap, all earnest and bright-eyed, or are they the distortions of a *seen-a-bit* seventy-nine year old who peers backwards into the gloom? On my desk, between the computer screen and the onyx head of the serene Buddha I bought in Delhi, sits a china milk jug. It's

3

in the form of a black cat with open mouth and startled eyes that would intrigue my childhood mind as it stared down from the sideboard. My mother said it was her mother's, and might go back even further. I rescued the little jug when the sad day came to clear the family home. Unblinking, it gazes at me while I insert this poem into the text:

Pot Cat
It means a lot that black cat pot
staring at me from my desk
with lime-green eyes and pricked up ears.
Mam said it was long in years, that it
was her mother's, she who baited
lines and mended nets, delivered
bairns, washed down the dead
and could not read nor write.
I recall just a small brown face,
deep-wrinkled on the bed,
the smells of cabbage and old clothes,
and black damp climbing up the walls.
It sits between my PC screen
and the Buddha on the desk;
apart from Grandma's genes, it's all I've got,
that old-fashioned black cat pot.

From the rich layers of Mother's stories, I know something of her parents' character. Many years later, research gives the date and place of her own mother's wedding: 30th June 1884. The terraced house of the Catherine family in the colliery village of Haswell, County Durham. I imagine this:

Dorothy Ann Catherine glides downstairs in her white frock.

She sees her mother struggle with the iron fire-dog, sees how she lifts it from the blazing coals to send more heat into the side-oven. Outside, her dad is inspecting his leeks. Alice Catherine lowers the fire-dog onto the hearth and stands up, puts her hands onto the small of her back where it hurts, and stretches. She yells through the window to her husband, 'Come in from that garden, Dick; it's the lass's wedding day. We need coal on this grate, I've still got baking to do.'

'Oh, Mam, save your breath. I'll fetch him,' says Dorothy.

'Well, divn't get that frock all black. And tell him to get out of them pit clothes, his bath watter's ready. I have to scrub his back.'

From the mantel-piece the black cat's ceramic green eyes watch her walk lightly through the back door. She flounces up to her stoop-shouldered father and touches his elbow. He turns so that his quiet blue eyes can watch her lips form the words.

'Come in, Dad – your bath's in front of the fire.'

Richard Catherine, in his silent world, crunches along the cinder path to the back door. It will be another ten years before he fails to hear the coal train as he crosses the tracks to the mineshaft.

Dorothy pulls open the coal-house door and, minding her wedding dress, fills a bucket.

Later that day, George Horsley signs the register of St. Saviour's Church; his slight, seventeen-year-old bride makes her mark with a cross. They walk arm-in-arm from the coolness of arched stone into sunlight. George is big for his nineteen years and fills his Sunday suit. His brothers, Francis and John, known in Hartlepool as Bass and Smokey Hossler, with some of his mates from that fishing and ship-building town, are in the crowd. Even though they have heads *bad with the beer*, the men call out: 'Hooray for Mush Hossler. Yon's got his-sen a bonny lass and she'll be Dolly Mush Hossler from noo on.' Dorothy tosses her head, gives the young rowdies one of her vivacious smiles, takes George's hand and leads him to where her family stand, by the lichened headstones of miners.

Winter 1904, Hartlepool.
'I'm just gannin out, hinny. I won't be long. I'll be down the street at Clogger's; their bairn's due any time. Divn't get that pinny all black, you'll not be getting another for a bit.' Dolly Mush pulls her shawl off the peg, pulls open the door and, taking care not to mark the donkey-stone whitened door-step with her clog, goes out into Sussex Street.

Her little daughter, six-year-old Dorothy Ann Horsley, is full of joy over the gift of a delicate muslin pinafore. She stretches on tip-toe on the clip mat in front of the fire, to see how she looks in the mirror that hangs on the chimney-breast. *Yes*, she thinks, *It's a lovely pinny*. She stands, turning this way and that – admiring. The pot cat stares back, wide-eyed from the mantel-piece. Dorothy is flushed with excitement and says to the cat, 'I'll show the neighbours.' She rushes into the mossy back-yard, out onto the cobbled lane and into the neighbours' yard, closing the gate so as not to let the dog out. She reaches the back door just as it opens, but collides with the daughter of the house as she carries out a shovelful of hot fire ashes. Glowing ashes spill across her pinafore. It ignites. A gust of wind lifts the burning muslin into Dorothy's face. She shrieks and slaps at the flames with her bare hands. Then her eyebrows are burning – and her long hair. The girl with the shovel is screaming.

Dorothy falls to the floor, her arms unaccountably pinned to her sides. It goes dark and she swallows the reek of singed wool and burnt hair. She is suffocating. The light returns as a man unrolls her from his tattered coat. It's the old tramp who often begs at the door for scraps. Her skin feels sticky. It hurts.

The man's eyes bulge as he coughs, then gasps out his words, 'Now then, hunny. There-there. I've smothered the flames. It's all over. By Heck! I took that gate at a leap – so much for auld age.' His chest whistles and he coughs again. 'It's a good job I was in the back lane. Now, you'll be all right. Lay there and stay still while I fetch help.'

She sobs with shock for long minutes until dimly aware of someone kneeling by her, peering into her face.

'Aw! Little Dot, what's happened?' It's Mrs Pounder and her lad. 'Fred, don't just stand there, go and fetch her mam. She's at Clogger's.'

Now that help has arrived, the beggar slips away without waiting to be thanked. In hospital little Dorothy Ann is placed under an oil drip for weeks – a treatment now deemed the wrong way to treat burns. Through her life, she'll carry the scars of the burning on her hands and to one side of her face. She will take care to show only her undamaged side for the rare photograph. Despite the scars, she'll grow into a strong, vivacious young woman, with an intelligent and inquisitive mind, full of personality.

8am. Wednesday, 16th. December 1914. Hartlepool.
It is a cold morning on the Heugh, at the farthest extremity of the cliff-hung headland. Dorothy's mother, Dolly Mush Horsley, pulls her shawl tighter against the chill. In light mist on a calm sea a dozen cobles, a half-mile off-shore, drift in pairs. She recognises the blue-striped

coble of her husband's brothers, Bass and Smokey, working the flow from the Tees, netting for salmon.

A slight, north-westerly breeze pulls black smoke from both funnels of a distant ship, to send it slowly across the bay towards Redcar. A cluster of flashes and great hacking coughs erupt from the grey hull, followed by bursts of smoke. The first shells pass overhead; they shriek like a railway train with the brakes half-on. She sees them, and for an instant they seem to hang in the air before vanishing. She jerks around at the ear-splitting explosions behind her. Then silence. She can hear her heartbeat – until there comes a clamour from the gulls, then a distant hiss as a rain of roof slates descends from the sky to clatter on the cobbled streets. The town's dogs begin to bark. She twists back to the sea and shrinks deeper into her shawl. The mist is lifting and now there are three grey hulls, each with two funnels and a dark tower.

Dolly Mush is in her forty-eighth year and enjoys the sight of rare sailing ships and commonplace steamers. But those huge vessels are strange; she narrows her eyes. She cannot know she is watching the first salvos in a bombardment of her hometown by the German Vice-Admiral Hipper's heavy-cruisers, *Moltke, Blucher,* and *Seydlitz.*

The 25,000-ton *Seydlitz* fires again, then the *Blucher,* followed by the *Moltke.* She strains her eyes to see if she can follow the path of the shells. There will be more than a thousand shells in the next forty minutes and over one hundred folk will die. My great uncles, Bass and Smokey, raise sail and, helped by oars, flee across the bay to beach their fishing coble on the shore at Redcar. A schoolteacher volunteer, Private Theophilus Jones, on guard at the Heugh Battery, will be the first soldier to die on British soil in this war. Dolly cannot know that the *Seydlitz,* and those same eleven-inch guns, will help to kill John, her burnt daughter's young man. In eighteen months' time, nineteen-year-old stoker John Thomas Broom will die in blazing anthracite and steam in the stokehold of an exploding British battle-cruiser, the *Queen Mary,* at Jutland.

1916. Glasgow Railway Station.
Dolly Mush hands a scrap of paper to the policeman. 'Can you help me, mister? I've come to see our Dick. He's a soldier. He's been sent back from Belgium. He's in Glasgow hospital. I'm to bide with the Sutherans. I divn't read.'

He looks down at the little woman. She has bright blue eyes that twinkle. She's dressed in matching navy-blue coat and straw hat. He smiles, then reads the note aloud: '*This is Mrs Horsley who will be staying with Mrs Sutheran in Crawford Street. Please give her directions.*'

'Me son's called Dick Horsley and he's wounded. I've come up from Hartlepool, but I've nae reading.'

'Well, Glasgow is a giant of a place; but as it happens, I ken the Sutherans – they're on my beat. Come along and I'll take you there now.'

No. 3 Alfred Street, Hartlepool: One week later.
Dorothy Ann looks up from her sewing. 'Oh, you're back, Mam. How's our Dick?'

'His leg's a bit mangled. They've took his foot off, but he'll be all right. They'll fit him with a special boot. I expect he'll have a limp. But he'll not be gannin back to the trenches, and that's a good thing. Where's your dad?'

'At work, doing extra time in the yards. You'll be worn out, Mam, I'll put the kettle on.'

'Nae, divn't bother.' Dolly Mush hangs up her best hat and coat and pulls her shawl off its peg. 'I'm straight out again, there's summat on at the pictures I want to see.'

Young Dorothy brushes a curl from the taut, shiny skin of her brow, smiles and shakes her head as the door closes, and goes back to her dressmaking.

1942, Winterbottom Avenue, Hartlepool.

At the top of the road where the fields begin, we climb the silver steps of the shuddering, red *United* bus. It pulls away with a lurch so that Mam almost falls as she helps me climb onto the seat. The blue-patterned cloth is mucky and tickles my bare legs.

'What's that funny stink, Mam?'

'Somebody's smoking a foreign cigarette. Probably a Pasha,' she whispers.

The ticket woman comes up, grabbing at the seat backs as the bus sways. She has a black uniform on, with leather straps. She winks at me, then looks at Mam and I see her eyes change.

'Where to?'

'One and a half to Trinity Church, please.' Mam holds out some coppers.

The conductress takes the money, puts it into her leather bag and pulls two tickets out of the slotted thing that hangs on her straps.

'There you are, missus.' She glances at Mam's fingers. She can see the twisted nails. People seem to notice Mam's been burnt, but I hardly ever do . . . 'cos she's my Mam and she's always kind.

We rattle down Warren Road, past the gap where two houses were flattened by a bomb one night. All these houses are new, only four years old, same as me, but the bombs, just a hundred yards away, have cracked our upstairs ceilings and covered the beds with dust and flakes of white-wash.

In the first years of the war, we had many warnings. Everyone hurried for cover whenever the mournful rise and fall of the air-raid siren sounded. One night, when we were fire-bombed, I'd been stopped from fighting off the bombers. The cornfields opposite our house were in flames, you could even see the blaze through the thick blackout curtains. We'd taken shelter under the heavy kitchen table. I was indignant. I grabbed my wooden spinning top and, yelling: 'Me bomb Hitler back,' rushed to the window. I was about to hurl the top at the German planes, straight through the blackout curtains, when I was grabbed from behind. Dad pulled me back under cover and held me down. The old table was our air-raid shelter that night; the proper one (the corrugated iron *Anderson* in the garden) had flooded. The *Anderson,* sunk partly into the earth of the back garden, had benches and a few damp comics to 'keep the bairns quiet' until the *All Clear* siren sounded its unbroken, pure and hopeful note. The garden shelter was prone to flood, so we gave it up and sat out the raids under the sturdy table, often with my sister Dorothy doing her school homework.

Later, we gave up the table for the coal store, which was indoors and off the back kitchen; father put the coal outside, made the coal-store tidy and gave it a coat of whitewash. We sat in whatever shelter we had and listened to the throb of engines overhead and the crump of distant explosions. We grabbed each other whenever there came an ear-splitting blast from something close. Our gas masks were always at hand, in a cardboard box that rested inside a canvas bag suspended on a shoulder strap. The grown-ups had scary masks of black rubber, with one window for both eyes and a snout with a round green filter on the end. I had a child's version that was dark red, had two round eyepieces, and a soft flap for a nose that moved to show I

11

still breathed – they said it was a special *Mickey Mouse* mask and was good to wear.

The incendiaries were unloaded onto us in 'bread-baskets' of seventy-two bombs at a time, each one designed to smash through roof tiles and burst into flame. After the fire-bomb raids, local kids searched among the blackened corn for bomb cases; these were about twelve inches long and had fins on the end that made awful whistles as they fell. The Germans reckoned we'd be in terror and be demoralised by the screaming noise. Some burnt-out bomb cases would still warble a bit if spun around on a length of old rope. Small though I was, I managed to hide a couple of those 'spinners' in the cupboard by the fireplace where I kept the few toys I owned. Sometimes a mother would have a fright when she found an unexploded incendiary in her child's treasure box.

We get off the bus on Hartlepool headland to step into the long, curved sweep of draughty Northgate. My four-year-old legs skip along mossy cobbles up Frederick Street, followed by a woman of forty-three who shows the first signs of motherly stoutness. We reach a house that has paint flaking off the door. Mam's sister, Aunt Alice lets us in. The house is dark and smells of cabbage and old clothes. I'd rather be at home. In a room downstairs, an old woman lays under blankets on an iron-framed bed. Her face is smaller than Mam's; it's brown and covered in deep wrinkles, there's not one bit of her skin that's smooth. She stretches out a skinny arm and points to Mam's shopping bag.

In a thin voice: 'Have you owt nice in your bag today, missus?'

'We'll see, in a minute,' Mam says. 'Have you lost your tongue, our Harry? Say hello to your grandma.'

Dad. Charles William Nicholson.
Newly volunteered.
Royal Field Artillery 1914

Mam. Dorothy Anne Nicholson (nee Horsley)
1920. Showing her best side.

My sister and brother, Dorothy and Kenneth. 1931

2

Eccentric

This child is eccentric, scrawls the form master on my school report. I've puzzled over that tag ever since, but I like eccentrics, they are interesting, there are not enough of them about.

In the glow of a gas mantle, the doctor, with the courtesy of the time, delivered me *beneath the sheets* on June 7th, 1938. It happened in our house halfway down the terraces of Lily Street (the side that never felt the sun) on the headland of 'Old' Hartlepool, in County Durham. Our living room, without grace of hall or porch, opened directly onto the cobbled street. The back of that single downstairs room, with its odour of home-made, woollen rag mats, yeasty dough rising by the fire, and acrid pipe tobacco, let out into a built-on kitchen with its brown pot sink overhung by a wheezing hand pump that fed the house with well-water.

The lavatory huddled in the corner of a mossy yard, a chilly, whitewashed brick building (with a candle for light enough to illuminate the big black spider that lurked in the shadows). The chamber was just big enough for the necessary. Anyone who used these places will remember how whitewash would smear their clothes as they squeezed around to pull the chain.

Coal gas, from the town's coke and gas works, lit the house by means of fragile mantles that popped and hissed on either side of the fireplace. The mantles would be ignited by a taper lit from the fire in the cast iron Yorkshire Range – a fire that crackled and spat small explosions. Explosions of sandy, salted seacoal gathered from the shore at low tide: coal washed down the coast from colliery waste tipped into the sea at Blackhall a few miles to the north, sorted and graded by a current known as the Longshore Drift; coal that leaked from the cargoes of foundered southbound coasters, and from the bunkers of steamships lost to storm and mines, bombs, and torpedoes. We were never short of something to burn.

We had no electricity, nowhere to plug in the television set, but that didn't matter – we had not heard of such. It would be over ten years before the *lunatic's lantern* came to our town and eighteen years before we owned one.

'Aunt Meggy' (actually my father's aunt, Margaret Harbron – nee Evans) lived next door in an identical house, but her downstairs room did service as a shop. The store had a small counter behind which that plump, dignified lady spent her day seated by her fire of seacoal. She sold her goods from shelves packed with groceries: boiled sweets, dried peas and haricot beans, sugar in blue bags, blocks of lard, cooked ham, loose tea, and Garibaldi biscuits. Potatoes, carrots, and swedes slumbered in sacks on the floor. On fine days she would sell through the sash window directly into the street. This was a house rented by the Salvation Army side of our family. I was in awe at the smartness of my half-cousins, resplendent in their black and red uniforms, and by the shiny trumpets they carried about.

Even though we moved from Lily Street when I was about 12 months old, we were frequent visitors for years afterwards. Across the street, on the sunlit side, lived Jimmy Deathers. He was an irrepressible, wild and mischievous urchin. On visits to the old street, I would slip away with the Deathers lad to hunt for crabs in rock pools at low-water. Lily Street, and its partner, Mary Street, were condemned and demolished under a slum clearance order in the 1950s.

In 1939 we moved to 55 Warren Road, a council house on West View estate, built across ancient, stabilised sand dunes. The network of roads and crescents of semi-detached, three up, two down, houses was begun in 1938 to house families cleared out of the 'slums' by an enthusiastic socialist-minded council bent on clearing away the unsanitary conditions of the Headland. They demolished the most ancient district, 'The Croft', home of my mother's family of fisher-folk since the 16th century. Its jumbled network of yards and ginnels beat as the ancient heart of the town. If it had survived today it would be a listed and carefully protected part of our heritage. Alas, today it is a municipal garden with rose beds and benches; the quaint passageways of the fisher-folk are entombed many feet below.

Our furniture travelled to the new house on handcarts, pushed by strong uncles who coughed a bit and spat into the gutter because of their time in Flanders. They took great care of the handsome Welsh organ and an acoustic hand-wound gramophone with Queen Anne legs.

When modernity came, the Welsh organ languished in my bedroom and the gramophone was cranked only on special days. We had shellac records with a picture of Nipper, a Jack Russell terrier, cocking his ear to a speaker horn; the label said: *His Master's Voice*. We had *Abide With Me* and *Rescue The Perishing*. The polished, pious voices and

19

their precise enunciation, intrigued me as I made the hymns swell and fade by opening and closing the gramophone doors. Billy Williams cheered us up in dark times, belting out *When Father Papered the Parlour*. I favoured Gid Tanner and The Skillet Lickers with *Hand Me Down My Walking Cane* – this latter, I've just discovered, is Blue Grass. Mam would get weepy when the Hartlepool singer Chick Henderson crooned Cole Porter's *Begin the Beguine;* she'd tell me once again how the lovely, haunting voice of Chick was snuffed out in Portsmouth beneath one of Goering's air raids.

The old hand-wound gramophone made a brief comeback when my teenage sister, Dorothy, began to go to dances. On Saturdays, she would come home with the latest music, on records that required modern delicate needles, needles that I was forbidden to touch. The Ink Spots filled the house with ballads – such as *I Don't Want To Set The World On Fire*. Even the Ink Spots could not hold off the march of the wireless set. The new machine was electric, with a dial that lit up in its polished Palladian plywood front. Dad controlled the knobs with his blunt ship-builder's fingers – he tuned with artilleryman's concentration through the ether for Luxembourg. He had a wire outside to get the Long Wave – it climbed up the wall with the roses. By squeezing round the back of the cabinet I could squint through the grill and watch the valves come to life; the glow seemed to increase as they strained for voices from Athlone, Paris, Dortmund and Hilversum, and marching music, and strange, thin warbles that sounded like ghosts of the drowned in exotic seas. On shortwave, the voices were always foreign; and at the far ends of the dial, Morse code tweeted and squawked like a tree filled with birds. The valves stood about in little groups, with dust-felted overcoat shoulders – like Dad and his mates might have done when there was no work, and grass grew in the shipyards.

These notes are being typed into an Apple iMac computer that boasts gigabytes of memory, yet my father went to war on a horse and my mother's mother could not read nor write. It occurs to me that change has come with the blast of an accelerating whirlwind, and I can only wonder whither it heads.

Just how far back can memory probe? I recall lying on my back, in a pram or cot, but certainly in the 'front kitchen' of the house in Warren Road. A large face peers down at me and says, 'Hello, you little bugger,' or something of the sort. I have a feeling the face belonged to Uncle Henry, the fireman, and our family tenor. Henry sang *Bless This House* and *I'll Walk Beside You* (he would sing this at my wedding) at family events; it would bring a lump to the throats of strong men and make the women wet-eyed.

1941. Again in Warren Road, I'm under the front kitchen window looking across at my father's chair, in the corner by the cupboards and fireplace. Kenneth, my sick brother, is in Dad's chair making funny faces at me and I'm frightened. I don't understand that he is ill with bone disease of the shoulder from an injury, and he will die soon when he is fifteen. He is well-wrapped-up this day and snug in a heavy dressing gown. Kenneth had been on the beach and was hit by a heavy building stone dropped onto him by a lad above on the new Hartlepool promenade (Father had helped to build this same seawall during the big depression of the 30's when the work was rationed out among those on the dole). In the days before miracle medicines, he died slowly of bone gangrene.

1943. At five year old, I'm sent to the infants' school in Miers Avenue on West View council estate. The little school is a group of prefabricated huts. The first day is

21

enlivened by the struggles and howls of those children who don't want to be there, and the horror when one of them 'fills his pants.' Later, jealousy comes when others began to run to school in bare feet and I'm not allowed to be so daring. Truth is, they are shoeless because of poverty; *my shoes are at the menders* is the standard excuse for bare feet. After school, they might run home newly fitted with discarded 'sandshoes' (plimsolls) from the school cupboard.

A memory floats up of a dreary journey in a pushchair, being wheeled by our neighbour, Eva Jones, about three miles from West View estate to the shops on the Headland. I'm left anxious and miserable, strapped into this pushchair outside the Co-op, whilst 'Aunt' Eva is inside hunting for bargains. She is a good sort really. Later, as I grow, my growing is encouraged by the rich 'fatty cakes' she feeds to me at her back door towards which I'm drawn by the heavenly smells of her baking. Eva's brother has been killed at the evacuation of Dunkirk, but the man she will marry, (the tall Coldstream guardsman, Arthur Ashley), manages to find a boat and gets home. Arthur's kidneys fail in the early 1950s and Eva spends many years as a widow. She's forever full of bawdy cheer and brings merriment and blushes to my parents with her ripe language and cheeky stories about her nights in the 'Brus Arms' where she does stints as a barmaid. Her outrageous, great-hearted behaviour makes her well-loved. Often, she would be in our house to 'borrow a cup of sugar' and would hover for a while to tell us stories that brought tears of mirth to my, usually quiet, father.

Eva's father, Mr Jones, is old, small and sinewy. His knotted arms fascinate me with their blue lacing of faded tattoos; he is a grizzled veteran of the Boer War. His wife is bedridden; on the windowsill next to her bed she grows seedlings for the vegetable garden. Mr Jones keeps racing pigeons and he shows me how best to send the cock birds to a race. Now, after 70 years, I try to see him again. It is 1946 and I am eight:

'Now then! What does the young'un know today?'

Mr Jones sits at the end of a white-wood table in his back kitchen. He sups tea out of a white-enamelled tin mug with a blue rim and leafs through the Northern Daily Mail. His daughter Eva has called me from the back garden, 'Harry! Climb over the fence and get a fatty cake while they're hot from the oven.'

Mr Jones keeps rabbits in hutches, in lines around the back garden. They are mostly Flemish Giants, big meaty animals, good for putting on the Sunday table with suet pudding boiled in muslin, then smothered in steaming sage and onion gravy. We also have rabbits. My dad keeps Blue Beverens, another large breed from Flanders – they kept us well fed when Britain was surrounded by U-boats that tried to starve us out. Their kind should one day be honoured for their sacrifice. Mr Jones' Flemish stud buck is a yard long and strong enough to kick down the hutch wall to get at the doe in the next compartment. Mr Jones is also clever at hunting for crabs on the rocks at low tide. He's made a long, thin iron rod, hooked at the end, that he pokes into the deep cracks and crannies around the rock pool edges. He drags out big edible crabs and brings them home to keep alive in the family's enamelled iron bath. Until all the crabs are sold nobody can have a soak. People from up and down the street call in to inspect them and take one home to boil. I peep into the bath. Six crabs scuttle about, claws tied up so they don't fight each other. I don't like to imagine how it feels for those crabs when they're tossed into boiling water.

Eva shouts through a cloud of Wild Woodbine cigarette smoke. 'Hey, Dad, do you remember when you caught that big conger eel and kept it in the bath?'

'Aye, I do. That Tommy Heron down the street bought her and when he'd done the gutting he found a shiny gold ring in the belly, the jammy devil!'

'And he sold it to Ikey Bloom at the pawnshop for a lot of money. You weren't best pleased.'

'Aye, by rights I should have had my share, but the miserable beggar gave us nowt.'

'And you've not spoken to him from that day to this.'

'He'll get no more out of me – he can sling his hook.'

I listen to all this while I chew contentedly on the fatty cake, and roll the greasy pastry around my tongue.

'Right, lad', he nips his Woodbine and drains his tea, 'I'm going to see to the birds now – if you want to watch.'

Mr Jones' passion is his shed full of racing pigeons. The house roof is spattered and streaked with droppings, and the women on either side rush out to take in the washing when they hear him rattling the tin of pigeon corn and calling, 'Howway, howway' as the birds collect along the roof ridge after a race. He then hurries to get them into the loft and recorded on the pigeon clock as soon as he can, but sometimes they just sit in a row and stare down at him. If they dawdle like that his shouts can shift from a coaxing soft call to angry yells of, 'Howway, ya buggers!'

The pigeon loft is painted in green and white stripes to help the birds find it. We go in. Wings flap, dust and feathers float about. They're locked in this morning because he must prepare his best bird to send on the railway for a big race.

'Sit down there and I'll show you a secret, but make sure you never let on to anyone about it.' His gnarled hands reach into a pen where there's a red-chequered cock with its hen bird who's sitting on a pair of white eggs. He gently

24

lifts the cock bird out of the cage and holds it in front of me. 'Now, young'un, look at this feller. Feel those flight muscles in his chest. See that bonny 'eye sign' – he's got Belgian blood. I sent away for him. He cost a good few bob and there's nowt to match him in this town.'

He gives the bird to me. I take hold with two hands, gently, but firmly so that he feels safe. Specks of dust dance in the shafts of light that come through the ventilation slats. In the sunbeams, his feathers flash with patches of gold and red and bronze in between white chequer marks that gleam like mother-of-pearl. I tremble with admiration and his head turns and he fixes me with a steady ruby gaze. Pupils intense black and the iris flecked with gold, the 'eye sign' of the top Belgian racers. I have a lump in my throat, from a mysterious new emotion. Mr Jones looks down at me, a twinkle in his faded blue eyes.

'Now you howld him properly for a minute. He can beat them all in today's race, but just to make sure … Watch this.'

He reaches into the next pen and takes out a blue cock and puts him in with the red cock's wife. The blue cock straightaway starts strutting up and down, cooing, chest all pouting and swelled up.

'Now, lad, howld the red'un up so he can see what's happening; keep tight howld on him mind.'

His hen's in the top cage so I have to stretch up on tiptoe, but today I feel taller and older. I know I won't drop this bird, even though he starts to struggle at the sight of his mate being displayed to by that blue cock. But he struggles harder. His smooth, strong wings are almost free. Then a panicked thought: What if his wings get loose and one gets broken, what if he can never fly again? I call out in what I think is a manly voice. 'Mr Jones, I can feel his heart pounding and he's fighting to escape!'

'That's just how I want him! Right, let's get him into the basket and off to the railway station with the others. He'll not mess about on the way home. After what he's seen, yon will go like Billio.'

(Billio might refer to Stephenson's steam-engine, 'Puffing Billy', or to Garibaldi's Genoese General Biglio, who would encourage his troops with, 'Follow me! Fight like Biglio!' No doubt the chequered cock flew fast and brave.)

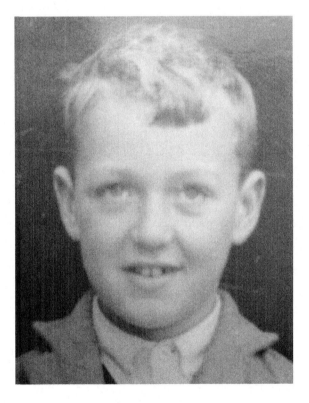

The author at 8 years;
soon after the red chequer incident.

3

Unidentified Flying Objects

1947 West View Housing Estate, Hartlepool:
Great excitement. Hundreds trek with festive air, sun hats, picnic baskets, and barking dogs, to the 'One Arch Tunnel'. The tunnel beneath the *London and North-Eastern Railway* embankment leads to the sea.

Our beach, the North Sands, is declared free of land mines (though within the year a boy will die when a vagrant sea mine drifts ashore). It's been a grim, hard war, but now it's over and folk can once again cavort and caper on beaches and along two miles of pristine sand dunes carpeted in waves of blue-green marram grass that sway in the breeze. This sweep of shore, the colour of pale gold when the sand is dry, has been closed for eight years. It was held to be a choice spot for a German invasion and therefore mined, and blockaded by barbed wire, concrete tank traps, and pillboxes with angled sniping holes. The tunnel is less than a mile from home and wonderful it is to sprint through, yelling off our urchin heads at the echoes. We kick off our shoes and run through silken sand. Not all the barbed wire is gone – one day my bare foot rips open, and I trail home drips of blood.

The empty dunes have become rich in wildlife, have frocked themselves in flowers: cranesbill, burnet rose and cowslip, and they float with sky-blue and copper-coloured butterflies; so beautiful, I experience a yearning ache I don't understand. In this summer heat, the harder, older dunes drone with black and scarlet burnet moths that circle yellow drifts of bird's foot trefoil. I covet these lovely insects and cannot resist the urge to collect, study, name, and label. Dad makes me a proper box to hold the precious specimens; the lid bears the legend: *Ministry of Food*. I don't realise that this is the start of a lifetime's fascination with wild things and wild places.

I feel summer will last forever. Deep in the dunes, shelducks nest in abandoned rabbit burrows. I lay flat – reach deep into the burrows and take out lost golf balls which the ducks bring home and try to hatch in a nest of down alongside their dozen olive eggs. People at the golf club pay good money for the best balls.

Alas, paradise will be murdered. The worthies on the council, and in the town planning office, deem the lovely sand valleys perfect for the entombment of Hartlepool's refuse. Flocks of raucous scavenging gulls rise up through the fumes of decay as bulldozers smooth down the cap of soil to gradually bury the corpse. Whilst this dumping proceeds, sand extraction is licensed and many hills of summer gold are hauled away in lorries – huge American veterans of the North Africa campaign. A mile of dunes is transformed from what could, fifty years later, be rated an SSI, a Site of Special Scientific Interest, into a rampart of fire ashes, sauce bottles, and dead cats. As the North Sea keeps up its relentless work to restore the headland to the island it was in the days of Beowulf, other shorelines are able to share in Hartlepool's exhumed rubbish as it floats south on the Longshore Drift. Almost seventy years later, on stiffer limbs, I'll ascend such dunes as survive. I'll watch for shelduck, listen yet to the throb of larks, the whispered poems of the marram, and ponder what it is to be old.

Further up the coast, just below Crimdon Dene, at the far end of an undulating golf course, is a picturesque wooded dell we know as Pyitt's Wood. A stream runs through this sheltered hollow and into the sea. From the gurgling water, I bring home infant Atlantic eels and red-bellied sticklebacks to join the colony of frogs and newts in the little brick and cement garden pond Dad has built me among his leeks and cabbages. At Pyitt's Wood, I spy on furtive 'bird-limers'. They know the branches that song birds prefer and paint them with a sticky paste made from boiled mistletoe or the bark of the wayfaring tree, and catch linnet and goldfinch for sale as cage birds. These are rough men I dare not challenge. The meaning of Pyitt is a mystery (but decades later I'll discover it's the old, local name for the magpie – *the pied one*). The dank wood reeks of wild garlic as innocent feet crush the spring ramsons. I wriggle through the impenetrable mass of gnarled, ancient hawthorn. Each year the magpies sweep in with twigs to repair their domed nests. They croak and clack while they weave new twigs into storm-worn roofs. A friend, Peter Hicks, rears one of the chicks as a pet. He lets it fly away when it is grown. I rescue a carrion crow that has been shot, and a baby tawny owl which I'd found cruelly strung up in a tree. My birds live for a while in our shed along with the rabbits. But I struggle to cope with their ever open beaks and so free them in quiet woodland as soon as they can fend for themselves. I imagine their wild spirits in the sky, and I'm happy.

I don't like Mondays. The house is grim. When I come home the back kitchen is choked with steam from the copper clothes boiler. Mother glistens from her efforts at the poss-tub. She pounds rhythmically with a mighty wooden poss-stick, up and down, up and down, in a tub of hot, foaming soapy water and clothes. As other clothes boil in the gas-fired copper, her strong arms turn away at the mangle to wring steaming water from bed sheets. She is red-faced. Strands of hair cling to her proud, flame-damaged features. She's determined to finish the wash before cooking food for my sister Dorothy and me – and for Dad, in time for him cycling home from work. Dad abandoned his trade as a riveter when the shipyards closed in the 1930s and is now a warehouseman at the Co-op grocery headquarters in Baltic Street. Mam's already done her work on the school dinners; she is a canteen supervisor. We aren't a rich household, so her meagre wage is needed. In the evenings she might sew: make dresses to order, or do alterations, for extra money.

I shrink from the chaos of wash day. I take out my dog, a brave-hearted Border Collie and Spaniel cross I call Peter. He's black and tan, and hairy – with a flag for a tail. We escape from the house. I carry a sack and long knife to gather sowthistle, dandelion, groundsel, and coltsfoot. The plants grow in rank abundance on the now derelict corn fields that used to burn in wartime when we were fire-bombed. But the plenty will not last; factories seem to sprout from the ground. A little stream, the Howbeck, where I'd fished, is culverted as the fields of my childhood are stripped for light industry. The lush weeds, the 'green meat', are fodder for our rabbits, Dad's and mine – Blue Beverens, Flemish Giants, and Dutch. If it's bad weather I'll sit with the rabbits in the cabin and maybe muck them out. To sit quietly in a shed, breathe the scent of sweet hay, and watch rabbits as they munch on green-stuff, is to know a special sort of peace. Even so, it's best to be careful of the black and white Dutch buck who marks his territory; his hutch is at face level and he can spin round fast and spray me with hot, stinking pee.

There's pain in this world, but I try not to be squeamish. Dad shows me how to kill a rabbit and prepare it for the oven; the U boats are no more, but we are still hungry. The war had been punctuated each weekend by a rabbit hanging up, dripping blood from its nose into the kitchen sink. One day I fish off the pier and hook a blenny in the eye ... it screams when I take out the hook. I give up fishing for a few years.

With my saved sixpences I've lately bought some white mice; they are fat, pink-eyed, and inhabit a wooden crate with a built-in nest box for privacy. They churn out babies in a pungent nest of chewed-up newspaper. But the babies are not white, they are all sorts of colours and patterns. One day I catch sight of the real father, a wild mouse. I watch him squeeze his skinny, rubber-boned body through the mesh of the chicken wire. His mongrel babies also come and go through the mesh just as they please. Everything gets out of hand; we will soon be overrun. I cannot think what to do, so I release them into the garden. They move into the compost heap. I sometimes see them dart about Dad's onions – they seem happy enough.

One day, Mam takes me to a fair at Seaburn, a seaside resort further up the Durham coast. The bus throbs and lurches its way through the Durham coalfield. The seats are upholstered with a red cloth that itches my bare legs. We stop at pit villages: Blackhall Colliery, Horden, Easington. Miners and their families get on. The bus fills with pipe smoke, a strong sort that makes your eyes water. Mam fiddles with a catch and opens a little window. Then through Sunderland and across the ship-filled River Wear. It's supposed to be a treat, but it's a fateful trip and one which skews the course of my life. Later, she'll blame the dirty bus seats for the scalp disease.

This ringworm is an aggressive sort which attacks scalp and eyebrows. At Newcastle, my head is shaved and the scalp irradiated with ultra-violet light. It's deemed to be such a rare species that I become an object of instruction for trainee doctors. I'm to be isolated from other children until the ringworm is vanquished. I must wear a skullcap to cover a plastering of foul-smelling ointment. I shrink from meeting people, I feel unclean. It will be nine months before I'm allowed back to Throston Road Primary School.

It's a difficult time for a nine-year-old. I'll have gaps in my learning. But my parents scrape together enough money to buy a second-hand set of Arthur Mee's *Children's Encyclopaedia*. I adore these handsome and heavy, blue volumes. My uncluttered mind feasts on all ten of them. I imbibe the names and routes of great rivers. I copy the maps of continents and colour-in mountain ranges and deserts. I'm immersed in exotic flora and fauna: coco-de-mer, emu, dodo, great auk, platypus, echidna, okapi, quagga. My mind sails across oceans and calls at tiny islands. Then there's Piltdown Man and his ascent from the ape. Everything enthrals. I absorb a child's portion of Socrates, learn of Diogenes and his barrel, and meet the Buddha. When I return to school I score nil out of a hundred in an arithmetic test but amaze the geography master when I can locate the Stanovoi Mountains on his map of Siberia. It seems to me that knowledge of our home planet, and the life that dwells on it, should be revered.

(In 1953, the skull of Piltdown Man will be exposed as a hoax, a cobbled together fraud of orang-utan and modern human – but I get over it.)

Twelve months later, with a crop of new hair, I pass the first half of the entrance exam for Henry Smith's Grammar School but fail part two. No Latin for me. The same thing happens when I try for the Technical College. I'm doomed to the rough-house of Galley's Field and then to the din of the factory floor.

Galley's Field Secondary Modern School is stern and tall, with passageways clad in brown and cream glazed brick. The school is divided into halves; boys and girls rarely catch sight of each other unless they stand on the shoulders of a comrade and peer over the top of the playground wall. What goes on in the 'Girls' is a mystery except that we hear they are taught French. Our request to learn French is turned down. We are told that we might have French once we get the hang of English.

A famous 'old boy' of the school is Reg Smythe. Reg became the newspaper cartoonist who created the *Daily Mirror* character *Andy Capp*. Andy is a working-class figure who never actually works. His hobbies are pigeon racing, darts, snooker, and betting on horses. Few realise that the scenes and dialogue are drawn from Reg Smythe's memories of Hartlepool.

A spur to passing the entrance for the Grammar School is the initiation to Galley's Field. We spend our final year at primary school in a state of anxiety, the passing of each day at Throston Primary brings our martyrdom on 'The Pole' one day closer. On the awful day, quaking with fright, we are ushered by monitors from the safety of our classroom, into the walled playground at playtime. From out of our huddled groups we are pulled, one by one, by the mob and led to the place of torture. The pole is an iron pillar; its only function is to support the bike-shed roof. For some reason, a bolt has been fitted through its eight-inch diameter, about four feet off the ground. The victim is wrapped around the pole so that the bolt presses into his body between the shoulder blades, at the same time his feet are lifted off the ground as two lads pull at his legs from behind and two others heave likewise on his arms. Spread-eagled thus, and wrapped around the pole with the bolt bruising into flesh, we are pummelled about the body by various cross-eyed bullies and snot-hung cowards. So we are initiated. It is to be is the last time the ancient ritual is enacted; several fear-induced truants are questioned by the headmaster, and mothers make protests, so the practice is banned.

A couple of years before the Pole torture, in 1947, in the winter of the great snow when hedges and fences will vanish, something strange crosses our sky.

'Goal!' Rueben Wright shouts as the lop-sided, leaking football skips through the last of the snowmelt and crashes into the garden gate. The metal sneck clatters as the wood of the gate takes the shock and a bit more green paint falls off. Five of us are playing street football; each of us has a gate to defend. We usually play until some resident of Brus Crescent tires of the noise and chases us into the winter dark. The ball is kicked into play and we begin again: tackling, shoving, catching hold of sleeves and dribbling with our booted, slack-socked and scab-kneed, bare legs.

Rueben is knocked onto his back. From his prone position in the middle of the road, he points to the sky. 'What's that?' Hovering above the railway embankment is a blue disc trailed by a stubby yellow tail. We stand transfixed. It seems about half the size of a full moon and is moving towards the north, above the line of the railway.

'It's a rocket! Let's run to the tunnel and get onto the sands – there must be a shipwreck.' We run – but, after fifty yards, slow and stop. 'That's never a rocket. It's not coming down.'

In a huddle we watch the 'rocket' fly north up the coast at the same height and at the same leisurely speed. It gets smaller and smaller until we see it no more. We've no words for the object (it will be six years before *UFO* is coined) but we know it for something strange. Next day, the local newspaper, *The Northern Daily Mail*, has a brief report about an unusual light moving northwards along the coast at Hartlepool. A similar light had been seen flying parallel to the coast as far north as Blyth in Northumberland, about 90 miles away. The newspaper approached the RAF and was told none of their aircraft had been in the area at the time.

More UFOs: In 1956/7 the Suez Canal was blocked for six months when the Egyptian dictator, Gabel Nasser, scuttled ships in the waterway to impede the British, French and Israeli joint invasion of the Canal Zone. I was by this time a radio officer in the Merchant Navy and was inconvenienced by the lengthened sea journey from India to New Orleans and Liverpool. We were now routed around the Cape of Good Hope. I sailed at this time with Thos and Jno. Brocklebank Steam Navigation Company, out of Liverpool. During its 5,000 mile detour around The Cape from Calcutta to the Gulf of Mexico, a ship of our fleet had an encounter with a UFO.

The intriguing story soon spread around our twenty-four ships. The nearest I came to its source was when I met (over a few beers in the Missions to Seamen hostelry in Calcutta) a friend of the third mate of the ship in question. I've forgotten the name of the vessel, but it would have begun with Ma, like all Brocklebank ships: Malakand, Marwarri, Mahronda etc. She was in the empty South Atlantic heading for New Orleans via Good Hope, on a lonely long-distance route. In the early hours after midnight a bell-shaped flying craft, adorned with lights, appeared alongside a few hundred yards away. It hovered above the sea and kept pace with the ship. The mate on watch, the British helmsman and an Indian lookout (*puree-wallah*) were witnesses. The captain was roused from his bunk; he appeared on the wing of the bridge in pyjamas, stared at the object, then instructed the mate to call the strange craft on the Aldis lamp. So they signalled 'what ship?' – whereupon one of the 'flying bell's' lights blinked a few times as though in acknowledgement before it rose into the air and sped away.

All Brocklebank ships were official weather recording vessels and transmitted daily observations (OBS messages) to Portishead Radio, a signals station near Bristol. The message structure, apart from coded wind directions and barometer readings, included a section for unusual phenomena. The contact with the flying craft was inserted into that day's OBS message to Portishead. About two weeks later the steamer docked in New Orleans. A reporter from the local radio station had somehow picked up the story and boarded her to persuade the third mate to go on local radio that evening to 'tell the folks about the UFO sighting.' Shortly afterwards, two plain-clothes officials came aboard and spoke to the captain. It was made clear that if he wished for a 'trouble-free turnaround' on the American coast he should not allow the radio interview to take place. The third mate was instructed by the captain to remain aboard and have nothing further to do with journalists.

A bit more: About 1965 I was conversing with Bill Boagey about UFOs. Bill was an old friend from West Hartlepool who had been mentioned in dispatches for his exploits as a motorcycle despatch rider in the First World War. Bill said that he and his fellows were used to seeing white 'jet trails' over the trenches in France, 'just the same marks in the stratosphere as modern jets leave behind them,' and this at a time when manned flight was restricted to balloons and low level, piston-engined, biplanes. When asked by the men what these trails in the sky might be, the officers responded: 'Just atmospheric phenomena – keep your eye on the Hun!'

While Bill is in my mind I might tell about how he came to be 'mentioned in dispatches'. He was delivering orders to another British position on the battlefield; this was an isolated farm. Lance Corporal Boagey of the Royal Army Ordnance Corps rode his motorcycle into the farm courtyard as usual, but to his surprise saw that it had changed hands, it was full of Germans sitting around against the walls eating their lunch. Revving up his machine, Bill did a roaring circuit around the yard, shot past the ranks of startled troops in sausage mid-bite, and before anyone could grab a Mauser, zoomed out by the same gate.

The author at 14 with Peter the mongrel.

4

Cheat

After the Great War, Bill Boagey returned to his job as a plater in the shipyards of William Gray; he spent his leisure hours immersed in local history. It was through our shared interest in genealogy that we came to meet in the 1960s; in fact, we discovered our families were joined in 1861 when Mary Boagey, daughter of a fisherman, wed the joiner William Nicholson, my great-grandfather. Bill was self-taught in Latin and an argosy of local knowledge. Should something of archaeological interest turn up on Hartlepool Headland (the site of the Anglian monastery founded in 640 AD by Hieu, under the guidance of Aidan of Lindisfarne), researchers from Durham University would consult Bill Boagey before opening the ground.

Together with my lovely wife, Beryl, we made a complete transcription of the parish registers of the Norman church of St. Hilda. Those great grey walls, supported by flying buttresses, and soaring roof, were dedicated to Hild, the second Abbess of Hartlepool. The registers were so rich in material from my mother's family (Horsley) and the Boageys that we decided we might as well copy them from the first page in 1566, through to 1837 when birth, marriage and death records went into national records. Beryl keyed them on an antiquated mechanical *Underwood* typewriter. She used carbons so that we produced four bound and indexed copies – including one for the *Society of Genealogists*. After three fascinating years deciphering scripts that evolved from crabbed, but ornate Tudor hands, through Jacobean, into sweeping eighteenth-century flourishes, the task was complete in 1968.

Scattered among three hundred years of sparse detail of forgotten lives were curious tragedies and notable happenings:

6 January 1577. Baptised: George Horsley child of Lancelot Horsley. (Lancelot is my earliest known ancestor.)

9 December 1596. Christofer Harte, John Harte ye elder, John Harte ye younger, and Thomas Todd were all of them drowned out of one boat.

13 May 1597. Friday before with Sunday in the afternoon William Raughton, Christofer Chester the younger and Willyam Mathewe, servant to William Wilkinson, did go furthe of the haven in a small coble to meete a Scottishe shipp that was laden with cargo and were cast out of their coble and were lost.

13 Febuarii 1599. Sic memoratus tertio Februarii in navem Londinensis introibat ubi cum magistici socio. (A King's ship from London enters the harbour?)

9 Feb. 1643. George Willabye, souldier slain with a muskat and buried. (From 1644 to 1645 nine soldiers, including Scots, were buried. For several years the Scots garrisoned Hartlepool in favour of Oliver Cromwell's Parliamentary forces.)

1697. Memorandum that James Snowdon and William Harreson, collectors for the Royal Aid sess, cheated most abominabbily the town of Hartinpoole, gathering duty the value of ytt where it was not due.

10 Feb. 1716. Buried, Nicholas Ward, unfortunately smoor'd to
death in sinking for a draw well in his father's backside.
7 June 1727. Buried, Mary Farthing, a stranger who by the
Coroner's inquest was found to be murder'd by William Stephenson,
merchant in Northallerton, to whom she was pregnant. She was
thrown over the rock at Maiden Bower.
21 Feb 1776. Buried, Thomas Bates, alias Tom Again Tide.

Perhaps Bill Boagey knew my father who was a ship
riveter in the yards and also in the Great War. Dad was on
horseback, a driver with the Royal Field Artillery, at Ypres
and at the Somme, and later in the confusion of the
Balkan stalemate in the mountains along the Greek
frontier. It was so hot in the malarial marsh of their camp
in Salonika that they 'fried eggs on top of the rocks.' As he
saw me onto the train at West Hartlepool station, to join
my first ship, he warned me of the Bay of Biscay and
recalled his own sea voyage to Salonika on a troopship.
The horses vomited through the Biscay crossing and he
had to clean up the mess. He urged me: 'Never be a
volunteer; never play cards on railway trains, there might
be cardsharps aboard; never go with women who want
your money.' (Since then I've never played cards on
railway trains.) These scraps were all he offered of his
experiences. I discovered years later that he was shipped
out wounded from the Battle of the Somme with damaged
knees and wrists, and a head wound. I imagine a shell
landing close to the ammunition tender he drove,
throwing the whole rig, horses and men, into the air. After
bouts of malaria in Salonika, he was discharged in the
Summer of 1918 and ordered back to the shipyards.

Father, with four friends, 'Took the King's Shilling' one
week before War was declared, thinking, along with most
others, that it would be over by Christmas and an
adventure not to be missed – he was away four years. The

volunteer friends came back without physical harm except for haemorrhoids from wet saddles. Young Tommy Hudson didn't go – he was one of the friends – his mother pleaded with him to stay at home; he was her only child. When the German squadron of heavy-cruisers, the *Blucher*, the *Moltke* and the *Seydlitz*, steamed through morning mist to Hartlepool, flying British flags, stood off shore and bombarded the town, Tommy was cycling home from work and was killed in the street. His workplace in the shipyards was hit and a German shell passed through his bedroom without exploding. My father became almost a substitute son to the Hudsons, and so I became a grandson. With eyes like blue forget-me-nots, the old lady regularly gave me whiskery kisses. Tommy's parents lived into a devoted old age; blind Charlie Hudson to 99 and Mrs Hudson to 103.

During the Great War my mother, Dorothy Ann Horsley, worked as a tailoress. She became engaged to John Broom. He was a stoker in the bowels of the battlecruiser *HMS Queen Mary*. Three years old, and named after George V's consort, Mary of Teck, that warship suffered in the Battle of Jutland. The *Queen Mary* took a German shell from the *Seydlitz*, and then one from the *Derfflinger* which detonated her magazine. She exploded, broke in two, and was lost. Eighteen sailors were lifted from the sea, but over twelve-hundred perished. The first my mother knew of the death of her fiance was when a man cycled along Bedford Street, her home, calling out to the houses: 'Queen Mary lost with all hands.' Mam soon parted with John's letters. His grief-stricken mother demanded that she hand over the letters so she might have something of her son 'to keep by her.'

Another father might have been,
But Johnny Broom the stoker,

In blazing anthracite and steam,
Died in Jutland's firestorm.
Died a young girl's dream.

After the Great War, Dorothy Anne met a returning soldier and they married. Charles William Nicholson was a sought-after bachelor with a restrained and gentle character, together with good looks. Mam would sometimes say, in reference to her damaged features, 'It was the marriage of beauty and the beast' (I would cringe when she said that). Even so, there was a life-long love between these two good people. They went on to have five children, of whom just my sister, Dorothy, and I, survived illness and mishap.

The day looms when the stout Victorian doors and red brick walls of Galley's Field school will release fifteen-year-old boys into the world of work. Career officers speak. Visits are arranged to industries reckoned likely to give us jobs. There are four main choices for the likes of us not of the Grammar School: the shipyards; the Expanded Metal Factory; the steelworks; or the coalmines. On the guided visit to the metal factory, we are marshalled in an apprehensive throng to be blasted by an appalling din. Amid the stench of hot oil, monstrous machines rip lozenge shaped holes in sheets of steel. But I want to roam the World. I've been reading of adventures in lands of solitude, wild rivers and mountain forests inhabited by elk and wolves. My woolly young mind daydreams of such a life in a sunlit, hazy future – in the meantime I must dodge the infernal industries which swallow up lads like me.

There is a farm beyond Elwick village where I earn a few shillings doing odd jobs, mucking out the cow byre and potato picking. I'm always happy there, I especially like searching for clutches of eggs that the hens hide in the barns. A disused red brick windmill towers up in its fields (it still stands in 2017, a listed building, restored as a dwelling). The route to Benknowle Farm is five miles by pushbike, uphill. The farmer is short, ruddy-faced, gruff but kindly. He says, 'Well, you seem to be a useful sort of lad. I'll set you on.' I settle for a life on the land, with tractors and pigs, the grass-breath of cattle and the friendly reek of steaming manure. A few days before the farm job starts, I bump into a schoolmate who intends to join the Merchant Navy as a steward. Training is just six weeks and then he is off to sea. My heart pounds. The Sea! Of course! I'll become a ship's steward and go to sea – see the world! At last, I'm fired up. Mam's response is: 'How can you be a ship's steward when you can't even fold your own clothes?' Dad says he doesn't mind: 'As long as you end up with a trade, you won't go hungry.' I cycle up to Benknowle and tell the patient farmer of my new plan. He says, 'Aye, well. Good luck to thee.'

But sister Dorothy is now married to a ship's engineer. Arnold Green is due home on leave from Elder Dempster's run to West Africa. Arnold is asked to 'Have a word with our Harry.' Dorothy doesn't think much of my future – as she puts it: 'Emptying piss pots and wiping up sick.' Arnold intends to sit the exam for his Chief Engineer's Ticket at South Shields Merchant Navy College. He urges I visit the college with him to ask if I could take the entrance exam for the Radio Officer course. He tells me, 'A Sparks job is much better than work as a '*pot wallah*'. I'm taken aback – my school results have been so poor. I'm too callow and woolly-minded to think through the implications of a technical education, but I respect Arnold and so agree to his plan.

All comes at a rush. I stand in line with a lot of boys and men outside the Marine College in Ocean Road, South Shields. We queue for the entrance exam for the eighteen-month course leading to the Post Master General's certificate for marine radio officers. I bite my nails. I know nothing. Nearby, a clever lad from Grammar School holds forth about wireless matters; his father is a radio amateur and he works with him in his radio shack – he talks of valves and circuits – I don't understand a word. My heart sinks. It sinks again when I see the paper. The exam is a set of questions, such as: What is the unit of electrical current: an ohm; an amp; or a volt? Tick the correct box, etc. After writing my name, I stare at the paper. We were not taught this at my school. What do the words mean? I freeze. On my left is the lad from his dad's wireless shack; he's ticking the boxes with confidence. My eyes reach out. I furtively note where he put his ticks and do the same. Like this, I pass. I'm a cheat, but my urge to survive buries all sense of shame.

At marine college, I will wake up and flourish. The half-hour of deceit leads into and beyond the merchant navy, through the early days of commercial television broadcasting, and climaxes with operational responsibility for the largest TV drama studio in Europe. The lad whose paper I copied, twice fails his seagoing exams and gives up. He joins the army.

However, I'm yet only 15 years old and the college will not enrol students under 16. I must wait a year. I'm sad the adventure is delayed. But a pause might be good – too much has been happening of late. Father takes me to his old boss in the Co-op grocery warehouse to ask for a job. The manager says, 'Billy, he's your son and that's good enough for me.' I become an errand boy at the little Angus Street Co-op, opposite the West End Cinema in West Hartlepool.

For eighteen shillings per week I deliver grocery orders. I ride a heavy grocery bike, with a huge basket on the front. When not making up orders and cycling about the streets with them, I weigh sugar and flour into different-sized paper bags and am proud of the neat job I make of folding in the tops. In 1953, sugar comes in two-hundredweight jute sacks (one-tenth of a ton) – it is barely within my strength to drag them from the storeroom. Butter and lard arrives in blocks and must be cut up, weighed and wrapped in greaseproof paper, in half and quarter-pound portions; I make up tiny, two-ounce packets of butter for pensioners of meagre means.

The old people are kind to me, and some tip me a couple of coppers (pennies) or a three-penny bit, or occasionally, even a silver tanner (sixpence). Old ladies invite me inside their simple terraced homes to ply me with tea and scones, and conversation. One stout lady, with a bit of a moustache, always gives me *Camp* – bottled coffee essence with chicory; it's black and strong and takes some getting down. Each house has its own mix of smells: cabbage and kippers; baking bread and cakes; cats and smoky coal fires; furniture polish and clip mats. Staffordshire pottery spaniels stand on the mantelpiece alongside sepia pictures of boyish soldiers of thirty-five years earlier. The soldiers look smart in their new uniforms and gaze into the camera before they go off to be machine-gunned on the barbed-wire of No Man's Land, in the 'Great War For Civilisation.' But I know nothing of that war except that Dad has medals in his special, private drawer, medals that he says he'll never wear, heavy round medals with bright ribbons that I'm allowed to look at on Sundays. I'm sad when the old ladies dab their eyes and tell me about the men in the sepia pictures.

The storeroom at the rear of the shop has a recess for storing potatoes and a wooden structure with shelves for holding bread and cakes. After a few days, if the cakes are unsold and will soon be stale, we are allowed to eat them during tea break. I devour more expensive cream cakes than I'd ever dreamt to see and manage to sneak a few home for my parents. I've watched how the manager slices meat on the dangerous hand-wound machine that hisses like a snake when it slices through a flitch of bacon. I've seen him, at closing time, slip a parcel of rashers into his satchel; he spotted me watching, and looked a bit flustered. But he's a kind man and never gets angry when I drop a jar of jam.

The manager, and the foreman (who fought the Japanese in Burma), expect me to do the dirtiest of jobs. In October a terrible stink manifests from the dark void of the potato store. Overnight, hundredweights of spuds have become soft and black. We've been shipped part of a blighted harvest. A stream of white puss-like fluid creeps out of the store – the stink makes me gag. It takes me a stomach-heaving hour to shovel out the mess, and an hour to wash out the store with eye-watering disinfectant. It's far worse than the time I discovered a side of bacon infected by a wriggling ball of blowfly maggots. The foreman cut them out with a knife and had me wash the flitch with vinegar until it smelt sweet again, ready to be sliced up and sold.

One day the front wheel of my bike hits the kerb as I wobble up from the dairy loaded with two crates of milk. I fall off. Forty-eight smashed pint bottles make a mess in the road. A milky river rushes down the gutter and into the drain. Another day, the manager gives me a shilling and hands me the shop cat in a sack; I must take her on the bike to *The Destructor*. The cat is supposed to catch mice, but she has begun to scratch at, and rip open, cornflake packets. I peddle slowly towards The Destructor to pay the workman the shilling for her 'putting down'. She is shut in a box and gassed. Through a glass screen, I see her struggle for breath and then 'go to sleep'. I feel sick.

After a year at Angus Street, I'm transferred to a mobile shop for two months – I'm now sixteen. It has a crew of three; the plump driver/manager, the foreman – a beanpole in a white coat – and me, on duty among the vegetables at the rear. It's a converted bus. My working space is the passage along its length, between the shelves of groceries; in this cramped space I cling on as we lurch along winding country lanes and up potholed farm tracks. I find security by squeezing into the stern, amongst the sacks of potatoes and carrots.

We stop at a certain isolated cottage where the manager always insists on carrying the lady's box of groceries into the house. The foreman winks at me. The manager takes a long time over the delivery; he returns relaxed but flushed. When the manager goes on holiday, the foreman carries in the lady's groceries and takes just as long. I have a hazy idea of what might be going on, but while I wait I listen to the skylarks in the fields, or I prepare for Merchant Navy College by going over the Morse code in my head. I read and translate into dot and dash code the words on the cardboard boxes – words like *Cherry Blossom Boot Polish,* and *Frey Bentos Corned Beef – dit dit dah dit, dit dah dit, dit.* We move off again. With rattling tins of peas and beans and stewing steak on all sides, I sound the Morse in my head: *dah dit dah dah,* practising and practising so as not to appear too stupid when I start college in a few weeks' time.

Dad has sent away for the big textbook essential for my course: *Telecommunications Principles by RN Renton.* I have it open on my knee in the swaying mobile shop. It's full of circuit diagrams and something called trigonometry – cosines and tangents. I don't know how to begin. But it starts with the Morse code – I keep checking until I've learned it by heart. I note there is also the Greek alphabet, which must be just as important, so I chant the twenty-four letters over and over. They imprint on the snow desert of my mind: alpha beta gamma delta epsilon zeta eta theta iota kappa lambda mu nu xi omicron pi rho sigma tau upsilon phi chi psi omega.

After Monday to Friday, and Saturday morning, on the mobile shop, the weekend arrives, and with it the rest of life: hanging about the streets with friends; the latest music; combing hair; squeezing pimples by the mirror. Though there is a flicker of interest we make no sustained effort with girls, except for Saturday nights when it's the 'thing' to be seen at the Queen's Rink showing off our dance talent. We try out steps we pick up at a class where a painted, scented matron steers embarrassed lads about the floor in the waltz, quickstep, tango, foxtrot and, if her mood is suited, the black-bottom. At the Queen's Rink, there is jitterbug and jive! In 1955, Rockabilly arrives with Carl Perkins' *Blue Suede Shoes* and we escape the tyranny of the foxtrot. Peter Hicks buys a pair of brown suede shoes and dyes them blue – they turn folks' heads. We grow our hair like Tony Curtis, into the DA (Duck's Arse) style and go in for extremely narrow ties. The teenager is invented, and we are the first. These are the days of the Teddy Boys (the new Edwardians) who wear thick crepe-soled shoes (known as *brothel creepers*), tight trousers and draped jackets with velvet collars. Some of them roam around in a gang, looking for a fight – we keep out of their way.

5

Sea-coal And Morse

As I grew, I sometimes helped Dad gather coal off the North Sands, a golden, two-mile shore, backed by dunes of silky sand. Seacoal sustained the working families of Hartlepool through bad times. In the Great Depression of 1929, and through the Thirties, the shipyards closed and Dad, like hundreds of others, was 'out of work'.

Mam and Dad married in 1924, but five years later they were 'living on the Dole'. They had rooms in a house on the Headland, in sight of the sea. Dad would part the curtains early to see if there was blackness on the beach; if coal had washed up he would be out with his rake and sacks. He had big biceps and thick forearm muscles from his years hammering rivets into the sides of ships. He'd also been an amateur wrestler in the Cumberland style.

When I was small I was much impressed by Dad's stamina; he would cycle the six miles to Blackhall Rocks, wheel his bike down a rough track to the cove beneath yellow cliffs of magnesium limestone, close to where the colliery dumped waste onto the shore, and where seacoal was plentiful and deep.

Dad probably admired the great natural arch that guarded the double sea-cave that some scholars reason was the dwelling place of Grendel's mother in the Saga of Beowulf. He would load up his heavy *Raleigh* bike with three, or even four, bags of dripping coal, haul them up a rough track to the cliff top, one by one, and then wheel them home in a single load to Hartlepool. He eased his legs by laying his body across the bags so as to freewheel down the hills. I often helped him rake the coal into heaps, until the time came when his face looked granite grey and he seemed too weary to carry on. Then I gathered most of the coal for the house, but rarely braved the Blackhall Rocks run – I didn't have a man's muscle to heave a loaded bike up Blackhall's ferocious incline from the shore.

At fifteen, my strength comes. In 1953, Durham County is still dotted with coal mines. The collieries on the coast dump rock spoil, and rejected slaggy coal, by conveyor belt and aerial bucket straight onto the inter-tidal zone. Tides wash back and forth. They suck the waste into deep water, only for storms to fling it back onto the beach – all the while the light coal is separated from the heavy rubble of grey rock. Wave action worries at the coal. It becomes sorted and sifted by size, shape, and mass, so that the ebb tide drops graded layers of coal along the strand. A strong current runs offshore. The Longshore Drift sweeps the seacoal farther south, slicks it onto the North Sands, or traps it feet thick amid the rock pools off Hartlepool Headland.

This February night I'm on the shore at turn of tide. My pitch this time is close to the looming towers and settlement tanks of the Palliser Works. The factory, with its corrugated roofs and settling tanks coated white with dust, extracts magnesium from the sea. It was Britain's only source of that kiln brick and metal hardener, and stood as a prime target in the recent war. The works are long and narrow, which is why the Germans did little damage – instead, the bombs fell among the houses where we live. They sprinkled us with phosphorus incendiaries so that the fires would guide the heavy bombers. Dad was one of the local men formed into volunteer squads of fire-watchers; armed with stirrup pumps they would tackle the incendiaries. When fire bombs ignited fields of wheat opposite our house, it was too much; Dad went out in the morning to discover acres of glowing ash.

I scan the run of the sea for tell-tale signs of coal. It's a bonny ebb tonight. There's a moon that lays the shore pale and flat, and a north-east wind that bites, likely from Siberia, straight off the North Sea. It gets through my knitted balaclava. I flash the bicycle lamp at a curled wave, wipe a drip off my nose, and nod. The breakers are black. They hiss and growl with coal.

Peter, my black and tan mongrel, is messing about in the soft sand at the foot of the dunes. He's found a dead gull. He's rolling on it now. His long coat will stink and I'll have to bath him. My shout stops him and he slinks, with guilty eyes, back down the beach. I lean against the bike and wait; rake, jute sacks, and shovel ready. Coughs and spits and points of light reveal three other gatherers who know the signs. They wheel their bikes into position close to me. I have to hold my place. Only if the rough men come with their lorry, will I move.

My fingers are numb; I put them in my mouth, four at a time, and suck on them till the pain goes. I recall the night I found big coal in the dark but had to scrape off an inch of snow to get at it. Tonight the coal will come in rounded by the action of sand and water. It might be as small as match heads and spread so thin on the sand that it's useless to gather. But not tonight. After yesterday's storm, it could be the size of walnuts and lay six inches deep. I listen to the gravelly rattle of coal as the waves crash and swill up the beach. Tonight it will be the best. A wave recedes and I run forward with the rake, plunge it into the coal, and pull. Roundies! Beautiful round black coals like black damsons. I'll sell them for half-a-crown a bag! This cast will be fifty yards long, and there'll be others. More bike lamps and torches are coming down the beach. Get a move on …

I rake and heap the roundies into three piles, watch them drain, then shovel them into hessian sacks. Three bulging sacks, tied at the neck, is all I can manage. I've fifty yards of soft sand to negotiate before the hard surface of the Palliser Works track. I drag the bags over the sand, one by one, to the track and load up. Three hundredweight is enough for my old, but tough and heavy, CWS bike. Two bags beneath the crossbar and one on top. I'm sweating now – that nithering wind is welcome. I lay my chest across the loaded bike, breathe in the reek of wet jute, and push. She moves and gathers momentum. I've a mile to go. The trick is not to get into a speed wobble and spill the bags – they are strained and dripping – they could burst. This lot is worth seven shillings and sixpence. Peter trots ahead as we enter the tunnel under the railway embankment. He gives his usual deep bark – and barks again at the echoes.

I'll get the coal home straight away and go back for another load. Tomorrow, once Mam and Dad have their share, I'll call on my regular customers. They love roundies – they burn so bright. But they are rare. In calm weather, the seacoal is small stuff the size of barley grain. I struggle to get a shilling a bag for that, if it sells at all. Mam will use it, though. She rams the fine stuff into an old cornflake box and lays it on the fire so that it bakes and the tars bind the fines into a solid brick that burns nice and slow. My best seacoal is a third of the price of commercial coal from the pit, and I'm making money. Soon I'll have enough for a lightweight racing bike.

I'm a keen cyclist. But my racing bike is an old *Dawes* handed down from my sister. It's heavy and the three-speed *Sturmey-Archer* hub gears are sniffed at in the 1950s cycling clubs – the cogs and chains of *Campagnolo Derailleur* are now the thing. In Rogers' cycle shop there hangs a glorious royal-blue frame, a lightweight *Hill's Special* racer made from *Reynolds' 531* tubing. My heart yearns for it. The cost of that frame, plus wheels, racing tyres, handlebars, cranks, chain, and saddle is £32 (six times Dad's weekly wage) – I buy it with the money I earn from seacoal, odd jobs, and the hoarded half-crowns Uncle Tom gives me (he married Mam's sister, Amelia – but she died young). Gears are so expensive I settle for a fixed wheel, much cheaper and folk see it as the choice of a tough guy. The new bike represents over seventy seacoal expeditions.

I ride every weekend, in all weathers, on long trips with the West Hartlepool Club or with a small group of hardy lads in search of feats of endurance. I'm a strong cyclist, grit my teeth and don't fade out. I delight in hill climb challenges. Along with a friend, Peter Hicks, I ride continuously on fixed-wheel with a stripped down bike – one brake and no mudguards. We streak past others on their expensive multi-geared machines. We set out to defeat the most gruelling hills we can find, to conquer them on fixed wheels. When I'm grey I'll motor up Sutton Bank's 1:3 gradient and my car passengers will roll their eyes as I recount that conquest yet again.

One day a dozen of us, strapped into the pedals and tightly bunched, are tearing along the main road to Thirsk. On either side, hedges of hawthorn enclose pastures filled with dairy cows; ahead looms the escarpment of the

Cleveland Hills, blue and purple in the September haze. There's a yell as someone clips the wheel of the rider in front. The centre of the mob collapses in a mash of legs and frames. The rear rides into the chaos on fixed wheels and are flung down – I'm among them and land on my face. There's blood aplenty, bits of road grit in the flesh, and I've lost some skin. I scramble out of the chaos, pull the bike free, then limp to the grass verge. I grimace with pain, and with the thought that tomorrow is my first day at Marine College ...

With plasters on my forehead and chin, and a strip along my nose, I begin the weekday train journeys from West Hartlepool to South Shields with a khaki, army-surplus haversack of books. Crammed within is a flask of tea, and a pastry pie of corned beef and potato laced with pungent sage, prepared by an anxious and loving mother.

I've developed a shy courtship with a tall girl who is a clippie on the buses. On lucky days she takes fares and punches out tickets on my bus from Winterbottom Avenue to the railway station at West Hartlepool, and so I ride free. The train chugs up the Durham Coast route, through the colliery villages of Blackhall and Horden, through Ryhope and Seaham Harbour, then Sunderland, Low Shields, High Shields and Tyne Dock. I can see our house from the high embankment as we swing around West View estate. From that bedroom window, I sometimes watch the record-breaking *Mallard*, in blue livery, steam her way north along that line.

I share a carriage compartment with four other lads on the same course. One, rather wizened but highly intelligent fellow, spends the journey whistling his way through classical music – until we tell him to 'put a sock in it'. A big, raw-boned lad is an amateur boxer who lately was attacked in the street by a couple of young thugs; he left them sprawled on the concrete. Another regales us with accounts of his courting adventures. The fourth, a fragile blond lad with a rolled curl for a quiff, snuggles into a corner, says little, but is all ears.

The return trip has one hazard. Tyne Dock station is crowded with women and girls going home after a shift at Wright's biscuit factory. A raucous flock of them seeks us out every day and makes for our carriage. Even the classical whistler goes quiet. The biscuit women tease us mercilessly and think it huge fun to see us blush. We have no peace until they get off at Sunderland.

The first months at college are a struggle; I have a poor grasp of algebra and am abysmal at mathematics generally. I know I must work hard – in the second term we will tackle trigonometry, followed by the mysteries of *infinitesimal and continuous change – The Calculus,* essential for a grasp of alternating current theory. Without AC theory there can be no mastery of tuned circuits and radio communication. A couple of men take an interest and help me to come to terms with *The Calculus*; then its beauty becomes clear and I'm fascinated. My mind wakes from the dream bubble of childhood and I forge ahead.

In Ocean Road, close to South Shields Marine College, is a large snooker hall where many lunchtimes are spent. It's a seedy, smoky, cavernous place with plenty of tables for the merchant navy students to sprawl across as they take awkward shots in between mouthfuls of packed lunch. I become good on the tables … well, had not my father once been the captain of a billiard team? Otherwise, part of that hour might be spent eating a luscious, hot meat pie from Hart's bakery up a back street behind the college. I sometimes stand above the entrance to the Tyne, watch merchant ships steam in and out of the river and wonder about my own journeys when I qualify. In fine weather, it's good to lounge and dream on a bench amid the mossy foundation stones of Arbeia (fort of the Arabs), the Roman fort of 120 AD that guarded the maritime supply route to Hadrian's Wall.

Mature men make up half my class; some are retraining after military signals jobs; there are a coal miner and a plumber. I get close to men who sailed during the war on 'Special' radio certificates (truncated versions of what we seek). 'Specials' had been allowed in wartime. They'd been rushed through to a lower degree of competence. Because of U-boats, mines, and bombers, trained wireless operators were in short supply. (Britain had lost 27% of its merchant seamen, over 30,000 men, including 1400 radio officers).

By 1954, with the war over for nine years; the 'Specials' are no longer allowed to be in charge of a ship's wireless station, with the exception of trawlers. Men are upgrading their 'tickets'. I've come to see one of the 'Specials' as exceptionally bright – a fellow from the little Baltic state of Estonia, one of the precious flotsam who washed up in Britain as the Nazis advanced. We get on well. Despite his sharp mind he struggles to send clean Morse – his hands tremble. He accounts for this – and his stammer – as due to three misfortunes. His ship was alongside in Sunderland Dock when a German bomb went down the funnel and exploded. He emerged from the wreckage unscathed, though somewhat shaken. After that, he was seconded to shore-side military work. One day he was sent into the field to cut through high voltage cables. He had been assured that the power was off. However, the cables were still live. The current welded the jaws of his cutters together and he was severely electrocuted. But, again he survived. Later, a large transmitter valve exploded in his face. Luckily he wore spectacles, but I note how his cheeks are pitted as though attacked by worms.

The tutors are former merchant navy radio officers who had been at sea during the war, except for the senior tutor who'd been wireless operator in a Sunderland Flying Boat on anti-submarine patrol. The flying boat took a hit and fell out of the sky. The crew bailed out. The wireless man's leg smashed as he hit the sea. Today this stocky little man walks with a decided limp. He has a stern manner and I'm in awe of him. He keeps a straight face when a student throws a lit jumping cracker down the stairwell just as he ascends. It begins its staccato chain of small explosions in the crown of his brown trilby hat. By the time he reaches the classroom we are like monks in profound silence, at our desks, wrestling with the characteristics of the beam tetrode, or the effect of nightfall on the reflection of signals off the Kennelly-Heaviside Layer.

The tutors are admirable men who have seen and lived through much; convoys, torpedoes, lifeboats. They must have devoured books and expanded their knowledge on the long weeks at sea. One, after hearing me mutter a curse as we struggle with a problem he had set on the blackboard, to do with *'the square root of minus one'*, pauses the class to give a dissertation on the Anglo-Saxon origin and ancient meaning of the expletives he'd overheard me employ.

They prepare us for the practical side of the exam. The inspector from the Postmaster General's Office is known to sprinkle faults among the college transmitters and receivers which we must locate and repair by a process of deduction. Generations of students had built up a folklore of examiner's tricks and this becomes the front line of our strategy before we resort to logic. First, press home all the thermionic valves – some of them will have been loosened. Next, check that all of them glow – he will have put in some duds. Then inspect the relays and remove the tiny bits of paper he's slipped between the contacts.

There's no need to overtax the brain until that's all done. This resourcefulness will make us all the better to survive the peculiar mixture of wireless rooms we'll encounter on rusting tramp steamers far from port.

After fifteen months we can attempt the exam. Although *'Radio Theory and Practice'* is tough, I get through. On the day of the Morse exam, I'm nervous. I'm alone with the examiner. He sits opposite, across the heavy mahogany bench, and keys out confident and elegant Morse at twenty words per minute. I read it through headphones and dash it down on paper. I catch most of it, but not all. Then it's my turn to send. He listens to my keying through headphones – I cannot hear my own signals, I'm not allowed phones for the sending test, I must judge it by the feel of the Morse key.

The examiner is void of expression as he watches me rest my left elbow on the wooden bench and cup the hand over the ear to contrive a passable transducer. I make sure to demonstrate the correct grasp of the key, and then begin. I make the opening signal: *dit, dit, dit, dah,* three times. The heavy brass, *Post Office Pattern* Morse Key sends a satisfactory booming reverberation through the bench, up the left arm bones, and into my ear. I fight to calm my right hand. Trembling seventeen-year old fingers spray out too many wobbly dots and dashes. My *dits* are too long, and my *dahs* are too short. I fail Morse – but pass Theory and Maintenance.

We are permitted one re-sit of the Morse exam. If we fail the re-sit we must do another year at college. I'm advised by an old hand to go to the chemist in Ocean Road and tell him the problem. The pharmacist understands immediately – he's used to students appearing at his counter. 'Something to calm the nerves, young man?'

He drops two blue capsules into my hand. 'Swallow these twenty minutes before the exam. That'll be two shillings.'

They explode in my stomach like a double whisky and I feel great. Relaxed by Benzedrine, I sail through the Morse test. I'm certificated.

Aboard the trooper *Dunera*, my first ship.

Dunera at Southampton.
Richard Parsons/Michael Cranfield collection

6

To Sea

On a chill December morning in 1955, a 2nd class, Postmaster General's certificate of Competence in Radiotelegraphy and the Operation of Marine Radio Stations thuds onto the doormat. It states my name is Harry Nicholson, height 5ft 8.5 inches, blue eyes, light-brown hair and fresh complexion, and that I've no special peculiarities. I'm thrilled and my parents are proud. I enrol with The Marconi Company (which rents out operators and wireless gear to merchant shipping companies) and within two days am instructed to join the troopship *Dunera* as fourth radio officer. The vessel is berthed at Southampton, three-hundred miles south, via London. I don't feel anxious, though I face a fog of the unknown. As yet, I don't know what I don't know . . .

Dad waves me off from the platform at West Hartlepool railway station. In dark overcoat, flat cap, and carefully polished boots, he raises his right hand and holds it motionless above his head. I wave back as he diminishes to become a vague image, not knowing he has only two years and five days left.

The local diesel train drops me at Darlington station, the site of the world's first passenger line. I board the

Edinburgh to London express, drawn by a monstrous steam engine that voids gouts of steam with wuffs and huffs as she pulls away. Outside the swaying lavatory, I lower a window and peer out at houses and trees that slip past. The locomotive gathers speed. The air becomes blue and sparks scurry along the embankment. Lumps of soot sweep into the carriage, so I heave on a leather strap to pull the window shut. I amble back to my seat next to an angular soldier and opposite a stout man who reads the *Times* and smokes a pipe. It's 230 miles to London – I'll have one of the boiled egg sandwiches Mam has packed.

I'd been to London once before. In August 1945, Dad feared for my mother's mind; she was still tortured by grief over the death of my brother Kenneth back in 1941. Dad put us both on the train to London to stay with his younger brother Jack and his boisterous family downriver in Woolwich. London seemed awash with purple buddleia in flower along the tops of broken walls. Wild sown, it made a brave show amid the rubble of slates and shattered bricks on the bomb sites. An entire street of houses would be levelled where a *doodlebug,* a flying bomb, had landed

Mam loved to explore old churches, castles, and museums: we gazed at the tombs of Nelson and Wellington, alongside other mighty ones in the crypt of St Paul's; we peered through the iron railings of Buckingham Palace in the hope of seeing the Queen. The Queen didn't appear, but we watched the changing of the guard; I saw one black horse drop a pile of steaming dung. We saw the Crown Jewels and Traitors' Gate at the Tower of London; climbed the great steps to the Natural History Museum to gaze at the vast blue whale in the great entrance hall and where, in a side room, I drooled over cabinets of exotic butterflies.

I was seven and gripped my mam's hand tight in Trafalgar Square on the day Japan surrendered (Germany had surrendered four months earlier – on May 7th). The new Prime Minister, Clement Attlee, had told the people to 'Go out and enjoy yourselves', so they did. Thousands of revellers crammed Trafalgar Square; we were squeezed, jostled and shoved among swaying throngs, parting only to let lines of dancers pass through, doing the Conga. Then great circles would form to dance the Hokey Cokey, joyfully singing: *'You put your right hand in. You put your right hand out. You do the Hokey Cokey and you wave it all about ...'* Yankee sailors and girls in uniform threw each other about the square, dancing the Jitterbug. Soldiers and sailors, wearing each other's caps, perched on the shoulders and heads of the giant stone lions that guarded the base of Nelson's column. Others jumped in and out of the fountains, uniforms plastered to their skin, hair in disarray. Some American G.I.s, exhaling beer fumes, clustered around Mam and gave her kisses.

With that festive memory in my head and a bloated cheap suitcase rubbing my shins, I navigate across London from the draughty and smoke-filled Kings Cross Station to Victoria Station. I take the Tube, the underground electric railway. People sit in rows opposite each other and try not to catch each other's eye. But something is amiss at Victoria. There's a blockage on the direct route to Southampton – I must travel via Brighton.

I pay five shillings extra (the equivalent of two bags of best seacoal) to travel by the electric powered *Brighton Belle*. She's a lovely old luxury train with umber and cream Pullman coaches that have vases of fragrant flowers and curtains at the windows. Tea is served as we roll through Surrey into Sussex, through cuttings, and tunnels under the North and South Downs.

The adventure leads onwards to sprawling Southampton Docks. Huge sheds and the lavender-grey hull of a Union

Castle liner, fresh in from Capetown, tower above my taxi. The three red funnels, with black tops, of the Blue Riband holder, the 81,000 ton Cunarder, *RMS Queen Mary*, rise above all else. When I see her, my own vessel seems puny.

I sign on the trooper on 9th January 1956. *HMT Dunera* is a white ship with one buff funnel. She's 12,000 tons, built in 1937, owned and operated by The British India Company, but on permanent charter to the Government for the transport of the Military. She can ship a thousand troops to and from the British bases overseas. They are numerous at this time: Gibraltar; Malta; Cyprus; Aden; Ceylon; Singapore; Hong Kong; Japan; and smaller stations around the world.

I've no inkling of a dark episode in the wartime past of my first ship. People of Germanic origin, still in Britain, were considered a security threat after the fall of France. Many Jews, mainly scientists, academics, and artists had fled to Britain from Nazi Austria and Germany at the outbreak of the war. Under the orders of Winston Churchill, over two thousand of those refugees were shipped to Australia from Liverpool on the military transport ship in July 1940. While passing through the Irish Sea, *Dunera* was struck by a torpedo that failed to detonate; a second torpedo passed underneath the vessel, which was miraculously lifted out of its path by a huge wave. The refugees were badly treated on the fifty-seven-day voyage, in appalling conditions, for which the Army commanding officer was later court-martialed. In contrast, the merchant navy crew treated the prisoners with kindness. Churchill realised his error, and declared it: 'A deplorable and regrettable mistake'. He stopped further deportations, and in 1942 they were released. A thousand joined the Australian Armed Forces; a thousand returned to Britain to work as interpreters or in intelligence. After the war, many remained in Australia. Their arrival is now seen as the greatest injection of talent to enter Australia on a single vessel. *Dunera* survived to take part in the capture of Madagascar in 1942, the Sicily landings in 1943, and the invasion of southern France by the US 7th Army.

I'm seventeen and a half, and junior radio officer in a complement of four, and overawed by everything. I recognise nothing in my new workplace apart from the Morse key; the equipment is not what I'd trained on. The two senior men seem grumpy and stern. The 'Chief' is a squat man, close to retirement, who tries to be kind in a gruff sort of way; the 'Second' is about fifty, superior and aloof. The young 'third sparks' is an extrovert, a confident and irreverent Clydesider; this being his second trip to sea he now has disrespect for the seniors – when they are out of earshot. It's apparent that he will be 'showing me the ropes' – all sorts of 'ropes'.

The next day a complete lifeboat drill is arranged; the boats will be launched into the harbour. I'm told that, as an officer, I'm in charge of one of two lifeboats that have wireless cabins in their bows. We will take the boats around the harbour, from where I'll make contact with the ship's wireless room and properly test the lifeboat transmitter and receiver. The crews line the decks on stand-by for the 'abandon ship' order. I stand at the head of the crew, shrinking into my uniform. I fight off waves of anxiety and cobble together an air of confidence, but my palms are moist and my throat closes. This is only my second day on a working ship, so what on earth do they expect of me? But, as the only officer in the boat crew, I'm technically 'in command'. Am I supposed to organise the launch? What do I do? I've not been told. The crew is entirely Indian Lascar sailors, some with years of experience at sea and a couple with medal ribbons. Most are from West Bengal and few speak English. Fortunately, we have one British deck officer cadet, about my age but with a couple of voyages to his credit and the benefit of lots of boat training at navigation school. Also, he speaks some Lascar. This young chap understands my predicament and, with quiet discretion, takes over. He organises the launch of the lifeboat from its davits and has the rope ladders run over the bulwarks. He indicates how to use these ladders and we descend in pairs, down the sides of the ladders. There are about twenty Lascars, plus the cadet and me, swaying around and trying not to crash into the oil-slicked hull of this huge ship.

Once in the boat, I face the cadet, 'Look after things for me this time and I'll see you all right for a few beers.' (I don't know that cadets are forbidden a supply of alcohol and must rely on friends.) He grins and immediately sets about giving orders to the crew. A serang (an Indian bosun) starts the engine. We chug our way into open water trailed by a cloud of blue diesel fumes. I dive into the tiny wireless cabin to be confronted by equipment I've never seen before. I switch on the transmitter and receiver and begin frantic calculations about what to do next. The cadet pops his head through the door, with a stout woven wire in his hand saying, 'Hey, Sparks. I've got the mast up and the aerial rigged, what shall I do with this end of it?' I think quickly: 'It must be the earth wire; chuck it into the sea – that's the best earth.' Then follows a pointless circling around the harbour as I hammer away at the Morse key, pouring Morse code straight into Southampton Water, via the 'earth wire', whilst feverishly tuning and adjusting the 'quench' control to get some reply from the squealing TRF (Tuned Radio Frequency) receiver. This 'Straight' receiver is a simple design but needs skilled hands. I haven't much idea what I'm doing; although I know the theory, I've never handled a TRF before. I fail to locate the ship on the receiver dial; only warbles and squeals fill my headphones. We eventually notice that the other boats are making their way back. As I climb over the bulwarks, dejected and demoralised, my new uniform daubed with oil and rust, the chief sparks greets me with, 'I didn't get anything from your boat, Fourth!'

The entire business is unfair. I'm humiliated. The two senior radio officers will be having a huge laugh at my expense. They should at least have demonstrated the equipment and offered a morsel of advice before the exercise began. After all, I've been aboard my first ship less than twenty-four hours. I feel aggrieved and don't warm to either of them after that day. I'm overawed by their authority but still think them pompous, cold, and disinterested in the well-being of their young charges. Will things get worse? The Glaswegian 'third sparks' takes me around the Southampton pubs that night and 'puts me right' on a few points.

As we roll across the Bay of Biscay laden with troops, I make rapid progress in the wireless room. I'm soon competent enough to be left in sole charge of the station and survive my own watch keeping. By Gibraltar, I've grown in confidence and recovered the dignity I'd lost after the lifeboat humiliation. I take down verbatim a long broadcast every night at about 2 am; it goes on for about forty minutes. It's a newspaper sent out in Morse for ships at sea. The military officers expect it on their breakfast tables in the morning, so I transcribe the Morse then type the result onto Gestetner stencil sheets. The templates go to the Purser to be printed up into newspapers. It has world news, sport, and stock market prices. This is tedious work but, although I've never used a typewriter, within a few days I'm making a decent job of it. I try harder until accuracy increases enough to type directly (with two fingers) at twenty words per minute, straight onto those

Gestetner Duplicator sheets, ready to be mimeographed. I'm proud of this; even the chief seems pleased, in his gruff and grumpy way. I do miss occasional words in news reports, but I can intuit what is missing and insert what I imagine it should say – nobody is the wiser. The stocks and shares market reports are a pain, they are so boring. I can lose concentration and miss a few. Some military officers notice and a complaint is made, so I now look at yesterday's figure and insert it after altering it a penny or two. No more complaints.

I eat with the other junior officers in a panelled saloon that has palm trees in pots. The senior officers are at tables with admirals, colonels and squadron leaders. We have white tablecloths. In this rough sea through Biscay, the Indian stewards raise the fiddles (wooden barriers) around the table and pour water from jugs onto the cloths to prevent the crockery from sliding to the deck. I remember Dad's recall of his own voyage through the Bay, how his horses were sick, how he had to clean up their vomit. He would be amazed to see me seated at a table as grand as this. I bring to mind Mam's advice as I stare at all the silver cutlery: 'There'll be lots of knives and forks and spoons. Before you start, wait until you see what the others pick up first, and copy them.' The menu is mounted in a silver holder; some of it is in French. Poisson is soup – I know that from reading the labels of HP sauce bottles at home. 'Always move your soup spoon away from you,' Mam said. Today, I'll begin with soup. An officer orders prawn cocktail; it looks amazing – I'll try it some other time. For main course, there is something called Curry Hindustan. I've never heard of curry, so I order Chicken Maryland.

We are running to Kure in Japan (the Commonwealth base that serviced the recently finished Korean War). On route, we will call at the British bases at Cyprus, Aden,

Ceylon, Singapore and Hong Kong. Shortly after we enter the Mediterranean we make an unexpected visit to Algiers in the French colony of Algeria. This will be my first experience of foreign parts, so I'm excited at the prospect. However, we are to be in Algiers for just a few hours, and the chief gives Third and me strict orders not to go ashore; instead, we are to service the lifeboat batteries and otherwise make ourselves useful. I'm starting to realise Third's hot-headed irreverence. But I'm easily led. After a quick check of the battery system, he says, 'Bugger this for a game of soldiers. Come on. We won't be missed.' We slope off ashore; long, navy-blue bridge coats hiding our uniforms.

At the dock gate, French soldiers stand guard inside a sandbagged redoubt, with machine guns mounted. There is rebellion in the colony and France is fighting a bitter war with the independence guerrillas. Under the circumstances, we are surprised to see a straggle of British servicemen also heading ashore. But there's no obvious sign of danger. As soon as we leave the dock a shifty looking man appears and offers to buy my bridge coat. Then a car draws up and two alluring French women, and a swarthy chap in the driving seat, try to persuade us to go with them to some place or other. The third sparks, after he chaffs them a bit in Clydeside Scots, says we don't have time and hurries me off to town whilst I ply questions as to what the women intended.

We climb the hill, take in the spicy scents of Berber and Arab cooking, and dive into a maze of overcrowded narrow streets, jabbering foreign tongues, minarets and Moorish arches, kohl-eyed women … and some kohl-eyed men. Gendarmes are on patrol. We try icy French beer in gloomy bars and try more at tables in shaded yards out of the fierce sun. We don't realise that this ancient huddle under the walls of the Kasbah is a base for resistance to

French rule. All motion freezes at the sonorous blare of a ship's whistle. The *Dunera* prepares to sail! We leg it back to the dock at top speed.

We rush through the gates and along the jetty. It's obvious that the pilot is aboard and the ship about to cast off. The rails are lined with troops and crew all grinning, it seems, directly at us. I cringe with embarrassment. Third shouts a pained, 'Bloody hell!' We reach the foot of the gangway just as loud cheering erupts from the troops. We are in trouble. But the cheers are not for us – they are for a Royal Navy matelot who weaves through the gates, beneath the machine guns. He carries his inebriated comrade across one shoulder. We slink up the gangway, relieved not to be the ultimate cause of delay. But there, at the top, glares a pair of piggy eyes set in the grim bulldog face of the chief radio officer. He's beside himself with fury. We are now banned from all shore leave until Singapore. So Cyprus, Port Said, Aden, and Colombo are not to know our feet this trip. Even so, we got to the Kasbah!

7

East

Cold hands grip the rail as the troop carrier heaves in a gale. The gale sprang from the Gulf of Lyons and has chased our tail since Cape Bon. I'm bemused; in Arthur Mee's *Children's Encyclopaedia* I'd read about the fabulous Mediterranean, nursery of Greek and Phoenician myth, yet I see no sign of Cyprus, the Island of Copper, Adonis and Aphrodite. Cyprus wears a black mask of rain as we toss about at anchor off the port of Limassol, unloading green-faced soldiers into launches.

Formerly part of the Ottoman Empire, Cyprus was annexed by Britain after the defeat of Turkey in the Great War. But the soldiers we put ashore face EOKA, a savage guerrilla group of Greek Cypriots who want unity with Greece. Against EOKA is the Turkish Cypriot TMT; these two attack each other with ferocity. EOKA targets anyone of British origin, soldiers and civilians. EOKA shoots men in the back who are out shopping, plants bombs in cinemas and attacks anyone who disagrees with their cause, even other Greeks. It's a mess. Almost four hundred British servicemen will die, among them an army surgeon attending to Greek villagers. I will come to understand all this in later years.

Meanwhile, my adolescent naivety, by degrees, fades away as I grow to fill my job. We must keep radio watch even though anchored. This vessel is on charter to the British Ministry of Defence; it's fitted out solely for the transportation of military personnel – we carry no other cargo. The Third and I must work our eight hours per day, seven days a week. The only break in the regime occurs when we are tied up in port, when radio transmissions are forbidden.

After one night in the anchorage, we plough through grey seas for the Suez Canal. *Dunera* arrives in Egypt in the midst of a rare snowfall. So much for the Mediterranean. But, even though the minarets and flat roofs are snow covered today, Port Said is the gateway to the Tropics and the exotic East. The architect of the Suez Canal, the Frenchman, Ferdinand Marie, Vicomte De Lesseps, stands in green oxidised bronze at the port entrance (by year's end Egyptians will rope him up and haul him off his plinth).

Aided by tugs, *Dunera* noses up to mooring buoys to wait and be assigned a place in the next canal convoy. We don't realise that the Suez route will close in nine months, when the British, French, and Israeli armies attack Egypt after Gamal Abdul Nasser seizes the waterway from the Anglo-French Canal Company. Nasser has the enthusiastic support of the USSR whose tanks will soon roll into Hungary to crush the anti-communist uprising.

Immediately we moor, a flotilla of bumboats sweep in and sling accurate ropes to make fast to our bulwarks with grappling irons. We are surrounded by little wooden craft crammed with leather goods, carvings, trinkets, and their vendors who beseech our custom. 'Mr Chief, we take any money,' they shout. 'Good business. Me work for honest Jock MacGregor. Special price for you! Leather belt – white camel leather! Leather pouffe, genuine Rolex watch, dirty picture with English schoolteacher, famous donkey of Alexandria. Anything you want, we have. Cheap!'

Money and goods rise and fall, up and down the hull, suspended in straw baskets on lines. Yells of protest come from the odd soldier, then feigned declarations of outrage from the bumboats, then pleadings, pass to and fro. The vendors can shriek like a wounded owl if you offer a lower price. There's barter, banter, laughter, the impugning of parentage and integrity; and the haggling goes on.

A tall and well-built Egyptian trader known as 'Jock Ferguson' is permitted to board. This Egyptian has privileges denied to other traders. Jock Ferguson claims he is the son of a Scotsman, yet he looks decidedly not Celtic, with eyes the colour of black ink and a complexion close to that of a well-worn saddle. He's known to countless British seamen and can speak with a Glasgow, Liverpool, or a Cockney accent depending on the ship's port of registry. He deals in all manner of exotic souvenirs and goods: Turkish carpets; plum-coloured fezzes; 'rare' postage stamps; decorated boxes; lewd postcards; pith helmets. He can supply Spanish fly (made from the dried and powdered remains of certain blister beetles of the meloid family) for encouraging erections. The crew are mostly virile young men, so Jock has no takers for his potion. Just as well, really – it's toxic. The Marquis de Sade experimented with it, and the Roman poet and philosopher, Lucretius, is rumoured to have died from an overdose.

Jock is jealous of his privileges; there are other bumboat men who claim to be Jock Ferguson, and woe betide a fraud if he corners him. I find there have been 'genuine' Jock Fergusons in Port Said since about 1890; the 1911 version claimed he was, 'frae Pitlochry' – perhaps it is a lineage. One competitor, a Jock MacGregor, who adjusts from Scots to Cockney depending on his customer, says he's born in Sauchiehall Street, Glasgow.

Jock Ferguson is famous among the navies of the world. Jock can supply most things and is keen to buy whatever he might turn to profit, particularly ship's stores, or 'scrap'. He's a charming rogue who brings flowers for any ladies aboard. He's: 'Honest trader – not robbing bastard of a bumboat man.' Even so, we lock up all stores and equipment. These watermen have a light-fingered disposition, so one cannot be too careful in Port Said. At the southern end of the Canal, at the entrance to the Red Sea, Jock Ferguson has an 'opposite number', another Egyptian, one who glories in the name 'George Robey', also known as 'The Prince of the Red Sea'. The real George Robey was a British music hall performer. Perhaps Jock Ferguson was similar.

In November of 1956, after the humiliation of Nasser's army and the successful invasion of the canal, President Eisenhower will threaten to wreck the British economy; the USA will refuse to allow the IMF to give emergency loans to Britain unless it abandons the invasion. He insists Britain, France, and Israel withdraw. Jock Ferguson is pro-British and collaborates with the invaders. In the care of the British Army, Jock Ferguson will flee to Cyprus with his family. He has no future under the triumphant Nasser. But, by 1960, Jock Ferguson is back in Port Said, cheating and charming customers.

About twenty vessels enter the canal, southbound in convoy. Astern of *Dunera* is an ancient steamer that belches acrid black smoke and soots from a tall, narrow 'Woodbine' funnel. She has raked masts and flies a flag that depicts a cedar tree. She's the *Astarte* from Lebanon. *Astarte* is followed by a dozen assorted cargo ships, Greeks, Finns, Swedes, Danes and British. At the rear of the convoy, for safety, is a line of oil tankers bound for the Persian Gulf. We are in third place behind a Royal Navy destroyer and a P&O liner laden with emigrants for Australia. We creep through at a sedate eight knots, so that the convoy's bow waves do not damage the sandy canal banks. As we go south, beneath our keels creatures from the Red Sea drift north on the slight current, some to colonise the Mediterranean.

Troops line the rails of our lower decks. They set up a shout. They yell obscenities at an Egyptian farmer on the west bank of the canal. The farmer wields a big stick and beats a tethered donkey. The donkey hangs a mute head as though in weary resignation. The farmer looks up at the great white ship sliding past and the hundreds of soldiers that swear down at him. He stops beating the donkey.

Two-thirds of the way through, we enter the Great Bitter Lake – an ancient salt valley inundated when the canal was cut in the 1860s. Our convoy anchors in these still, blue waters, beneath a blazing sun, to allow the north-bound convoy to pass through.

A British cargo ship, belonging to Alfred Holt & Co. – an elegant 'Blue Funnel' boat registered at Liverpool, steams by our stationary vessel. To my mind, they are the most beautiful fleet of ships and are sublime examples of sensitive naval architecture. I shade my eyes against the dazzling glare off the water. The name on her flared bow might read as *Cyclops*. A guttural Merseyside shout comes from her deck, addressed to us: 'Any Geordies aboard?' (A Geordie is a native of Newcastle on Tyne, in Northern England). There's a handful of replies from our troops: 'Aye! Aye!' A roared response comes across the rippled glass of the convoy's wake: 'Then – hang the bastards!'

After fifteen long hours and 120 miles we are free of the canal, and in 10 more hours free of the Gulf of Suez. Desert horizons fall away on either side. I glance at our chart and note the gynaecological disposition of the twin northern gulfs. It is as though we will be expelled down the western fallopian tube into the arid uterus of the Red Sea.

I'm deeply impressed by the Red Sea. For three and a half days we glide through motionless heat along a highway of liquid, shimmering brass. In anticipation of the furnace, we've been ordered to change from navy-blue serge uniform jackets and long trousers, into white shorts and shirt. I'm told to fit the white, tropical cover to my cap – a cap I avoid wearing whenever possible. (We'll stay in tropical kit until the East China Sea.) Our cabins have no cooling, apart from a nozzle that blows a weak stream of air from somewhere in the engine room. There are electric fans, I have one whirring now in my narrow, single-berth cabin. At the end of each watch, I need a shower and a dry shirt. The only break in the mirror surface of the sea, apart from our bow wave, are sudden shoals of flying fish that break surface and leap six feet to glide on modified fins, flashing like arrows for fifty yards. The western sky is transformed by a sublime display of colour as the sun sinks into the endless deserts of the Sudan. The climax comes with a brief green flash across the horizon immediately the sun has set. Radio watch here is painful. The region has continuous electrical activity in the atmosphere and the static on the watch frequency of 500 kilocycles makes a perpetual roar in my headphones. It brings on weary headaches.

A string of barren islands of rock, ranged across the narrows, marks the southern end of the Red Sea. We pass between them and through straits of Bab el Mandeb – The Gates of Weeping – so called because this was a major crossing place for chained Africans, destined for the slave markets of Arabia. Bab el Mandeb is guarded by the sheltered harbour of Aden at the entrance to the Arabian Sea. In 1839, the British East India Company landed Royal Marines here to occupy the territory and stop attacks by pirates against British shipping en route to India. In 1956 it is still garrisoned by Britain as a Crown Colony and refuelling port. (In 1990, Aden will merge with Yemen.)

We creep into Aden harbour beneath shimmering cliffs of bare rock and glide through a motley collection of cargo ships and tankers. They are mainly British, with a sprinkling of Swedes, Finns, and Greeks. I note a few warships, destroyers and frigates. We moor to buoys alongside a small island, a former leper colony.

The heat of Aden is extreme and I wonder how it's possible for anyone to exist here; the still air is arid, without a hint of breeze to dry the sweat. Even so, there is a British garrison, and a thriving township of Arabs and Somalis solely given over to buying and selling. It is a sort of 'free port' – without tax. Everything you ever wanted is here, at the cheapest prices on the planet. The ship charges fifteen shillings for a bottle of gin from its 'duty-free' bonded stores, but the ship chandlers in Aden can supply the same gin for just six shillings and three pence. I watch the bumboats come and go between moored tramp steamers. Their crews are buying gin by the crate, and perhaps a camera and a watch to resell illegally in India at good profit. It is smuggling, so they will need to take care.

Some of our soldiers climb into launches and disembark. I look out for the National Serviceman I'd become friendly with. He hails from my home town. We enjoyed a chat on the lower deck until the chief radio officer noticed and told me not to spend time with the troops. He gives me no reason. I'm growing to dislike that man. I now visit the troops' quarters only when I deliver the rare telegram. There is always a sentry on duty at the entrance. He straightens at the sight of my uniform, with its epaulettes that carry a bit of skinny, wiggly gold braid (supposed to represent electricity, I assume) and gives me a smart salute. I resort to a smile and a nod; I'm Merchant Navy, and only seventeen, for goodness sake.

The track from Aden to the island of Ceylon takes us straight across the Arabian Sea. Only the Maldive Islands intervene: a thin chain of coral atolls that grow as a crown on the tips of submerged mountains. For three days we trailed a white wake across the glass of the Red Sea; now we have six days of the Arabian Sea with bows dipping and rising through marching ramparts. As we head into the dry winds of the North-East Monsoon, the blue-green ridges and troughs seem to go on forever. *Dunera's* sides give out a wavering groan, and passageway doors rattle and bang, as her bows climb and ride over a twelve foot swell that stretches horizon to horizon without relief. The wind is near-gale force and on our port bow. With our high profile, the helmsman cannot relax. I note the way the foredeck heaves and snakes as though alive. The saloon deck is polished timber – it doubles as a dance floor. The planks make 'pop-pop' noises that run across the deck in quick succession. I mention it to one of the mates. 'It's fine,' he says, 'Be grateful she's riveted throughout. Riveted ships flex in this sort of sea. It's a good sign. Welded ships can crack and break in two.'

On this crossing, I'm keeping extra watches. Third is having a few days in hospital with dysentery. The hospital is deep in the troops' quarters. I pass by an area of stacked bunks where soldiers pass the time. They play cards on the beds, or recline on them to read novels, or write letters home. Third is in bed looking pasty-faced but cheerful enough. The Scot approves of the flat tin of twenty-five Marcovitch 'Black and White' cigarettes I've brought him;

it has a picture of a London dandy, in white scarf and top hat, on the lid.

'How come you've got the trots? What does the quack say?' I ask.

He lights a Marcovitch, curses the catering department, and rubs his belly. 'The quack reckons it's because of the wee bananas we picked up in Egypt. The black bit at the far end is loaded wi' nasties. It's where the flower grew. I've been eating the end. Nobody said to cut the bugger off!'

Singapore is the first port I'm allowed ashore after the episode at Algiers. It's only eleven years since the Japanese occupation ended, but you'd hardly know. The island bustles with life and trade. In the anchorage, launches come and go like buses. I venture ashore with the third sparks again. After a few icy beers he has the idea to have a tattoo done. Inside a friendly Chinese tattoo parlour we inspect the book of art. I come off lightly with a small and, I think, refined image on my forearm of an eagle carrying a snake. My friend has had more Tiger beer than me and comes away with a dagger the length of his forearm; it's decorated with thistles and the banner: *I love Scotland*. Fortunately, he hails from Greenock, on the Clyde. The short sleeves of our tropical shirts don't hide the tattoos. When the chief sees them, he blurts out, 'You pair of daft sods!'

The island is hot and moist; soon our shirts are clinging to our skin. We pass a man in the street who looks like an Indian; he gives me a scowl of dislike that will stay in memory for years. That evening we explore the '*New World*' and the '*Happy World*'. These fairgrounds specialise in entertainments for the Chinese, who make up the bulk of Singapore's people. They are vivid places filled with the savoury vapours of chophouses, and noisy with open-air

Chinese operas that blare out from raised stages. There are dragon dancers acting out dramas, gongs and lutes, and high-pitched, incomprehensible singing. We drift into one of the 'taxi halls'. Entrance is free, but we buy taxi dance tickets at a kiosk – one Straits Dollar each (one shilling and threepence). Smoking joss sticks yield up the perfumes of sandalwood and jasmine – perhaps as an offering to the gods, or perhaps to mask smells from the nearby monsoon drain. We relax with more Tiger beer and eye up the assortment of Chinese girls seated at tables about the dance hall. Any ticket holder can approach a girl, give her the ticket, and she will dance with him. No fondling allowed. I choose a sweet, delicate creature and we glide around the floor until the music ends. Then I give her another ticket and when the music starts we waltz off again. We sit at a table. I buy drinks and try conversation. She'll claim her commission on the tickets and drinks at the end of her shift. It's a happy interlude. She is intelligent and decent. It's her living.

Forty-five years later, by air, I'll arrive in an independent Singapore with my wife, for a few days as guests of a Chinese friend. I'd been one of Sieu Li's Buddhist meditation teachers in Sheffield when she was at University studying for a higher degree. She and her father are amused when I tell them of those 'Worlds' and what we did there; so the father takes me to one of them. I recognise the noble entrance. It still stands but is now shabby with peeling paint. Inside, the operas and dancing halls are no more. All has degenerated into a series of dusty scrapyards and workshops. I'm saddened to look upon the change. The Singapore Government does not favour entertainment of that sort going on in their smart, modern, but rather prim country. It's thought-provoking to discover that my guide (head of the family) had worked in the 'Happy World'. He pointed to where he'd toiled as a bakery lad at the time of my visit. We might have passed in those crowded, roistering lanes. I might have eaten his confections. It was hardly fifty steps from where I taxi-danced with the Chinese girl.

The new Singapore is an organised and sober place. All is modern. Even where we used to anchor is now dry land; reclaimed and fashioned from Singapore's waste. People fly kites on mown grass while the new ground settles before it is built over. Shipping is now anchored miles out to sea, but they are vast ships that could swallow *Dunera*.

After Singapore, the trooper crosses the South China Sea to the Crown Colony of Hong Kong. We have mild seas; it's too early in the year for typhoons. *Dunera* noses toward the anchorage in Victoria Harbour, through flocks of small craft that seem indifferent to the great white ship that creeps through. Hundreds of little fishing sampans loiter around us. They have covered areas where families conduct their lives. The fishy smoke of cooking fires drifts from arched shelters. Elderly women squat in the sterns, mending nets. Children jump from the sampans into the still waters of the harbour to swim like water-babies, then clamber back on board. Three-masted Chinese junks drift past under battened lug sails; Hong Kong has five thousand of this ancient design. Old steam ferries pour out columns of black smoke as they ply between the peninsula of Kowloon, on the mainland, and the island of Hong Kong. On either side, the huts of slum dwellers cram the steep hills. The main town is handsome with covered jetties, tile-roofed warehouses, and stately colonial buildings. We moor alongside a floating barge that acts as a pontoon. Here we discharge garrison troops before heading, almost empty of passengers, for Japan. The third sparks and I catch a water-taxi to shore and wander the crowded streets. Tin Lok Lane (The Lane of Heavenly Happiness) is the centre of the coffin making trade – lots of sand-papering and hammering – but there's food and haircuts too.

The route to Japan leads through straits that separate mainland China from the island of Formosa/Taiwan. The mainland has been overrun by Chairman Mao's insurgent communist army. Seven years earlier the Kou Min Tang army, under General Chiang Kai-shek, evacuated the Nationalist government and took refuge on the large island of Formosa, to become the Republic of China. The Taiwanese hold some small islands close to the mainland, Quemoy and Matsu. There are regular artillery exchanges between Communists and Nationalists. The little islands are pounded and their garrisons burrow ever deeper into tunnels. Both sides are jumpy. Vessels that use the straits might be fired on. In Singapore and Hong Kong I'd noticed tropical trading ships with the Union Jack painted large on the sides of the hull, in the hope they would not be targets in the Straits of Formosa (once known as *The Black Ditch*). We pass through in the dark. The straits are a hundred miles wide. As we cut through a rippled sea under a star-crusted sky, there's a hint of muffled gunfire away to port. *Dunera* cruises at half speed through flotillas of tiny sampans that fish in the darkness. A few oil lamps twinkle on flimsy hulls. This is a shipping lane. I wonder how many families wait for those who are run down by urgent steamers that hurry through the night.

8

'Geisha'

Kure is a port on the Inland Sea of Japan, a sea bejewelled with islands. It lies at the southern end of Honshu, the main island of the archipelago. Kure was Imperial Japan's main naval base and had been heavily, but conventionally bombed by the American air force. I know that Japan had been atom-bombed eleven years before my visit, but I'm ignorant of the details. I'm ignorant of the fact that Hiroshima, a mere forty miles to the west of here, is where '*Little Boy*' was dropped from the Boeing B-29 Superfortress '*Enola Gay*'. In that first nuclear attack, 66,000 died instantly. Over the next three months, a further 70,000 people succumbed.

We ease into Kure and prepare to berth alongside a jetty that carries cranes and railway lines. I peer over the side as we tie up. I'm fascinated by the rows of portholes along the side of the jetty. The long structure is built over a line of scuttled ships; all superstructure has been levelled and replaced by concrete. Perhaps they had been aircraft carriers. I gaze up into the faces of Japanese dock workers, who return impassive stares; perhaps they had been soldiers.

Kure is now the main British Commonwealth base in Japan for operations in the Korean War, a conflict brought to armistice three years ago. The town is off-limits to American forces. Instead, there are Australians, New Zealanders, Canadians and British in evidence, most awaiting shipment home. *Dunera* has been a regular visitor, but the base is due to close; this is to be her last assignment to Japan.

The third radio officer was here on a previous trip; he insists I visit the ship's clinic for 'essentials' before we go ashore. The surgeon expresses no surprise to find me at his desk. I breathe in the pleasant vapour of antiseptic while I consider what to say. I've had no dealings with him before now, but he seems friendly enough. He's a tall, lean man, with chiselled, film-star features that I suppose would have some ladies weak at the knees. I rest my gaze on the heavy braid on his uniform cuffs: two wide bands of gold separated by a handsome strip of blood-red velvet; more eye-catching than the captain's four gold rings, I reckon.

'You'll be after your shore-side supplies, young fellow?' He gives me a knowing smile. 'I note you're only seventeen, but I suppose I shouldn't let you loose without protectors.' He tosses a handful of paper packets onto the desk. 'Be sure to use them.'

I pick one up. In bold print, the packet declares: *Moa.* Beneath the title is depicted a bird that resembles an ostrich. I recognise the species as one of a genus of extinct flightless birds formerly abundant in New Zealand, but hunted to extinction when the Maoris came ashore – I'd read about all this, years ago, in my Arthur Mee's *Children's Encyclopaedia.*

He goes on: 'If you forget to use a sheath, be sure to apply one of these kits.' He drops three little boxes beside the Moa packets. 'Seafarers fondly refer to those as *Dreadnaughts.* Read the instructions before you venture ashore.' I catch the hint of a twinkle in his eyes.

I speedily scoop up the supplies in the hope that such activity will take his gaze away from the blush that heats my cheeks. But he's not finished with me yet.

'You'll find the pretend geisha of Kure mysteriously attractive. Don't be tempted by ladies of the street. Relax only in those bath-houses restricted to officers; they are government licensed, inspected, and should display FFI certificates. My official caution is not to visit those places at all.' He pauses. 'But I'll be ignoring my own advice.'

'FFI, sir?'

'Free from infection, Sparks. Good day to you.'

A hundred yards beyond the red bricks of the dock gate a gaggle of girls in kimonos bears down. They hold hands and laugh as they form a circle of siege around Third and me. There's no aggression – just giggling, and invitations to go home with them. These girls are much more affable than the Japanese dockers. I suppose we are their means of livelihood; a livelihood that declines now that the Commonwealth battalions are going home. Surgeon told us to keep well clear of street women, so we duck beneath the linked arms and break free of the ambush.

Third knows where he's going. 'Come on, Harry. Up the main drag, across the railway line, then second left.' He has in mind a special place he enjoyed on his previous trip.

After a walk through unfamiliar cooking odours, perhaps rice and fried fish, we stop at a sprawling bungalow structure, built of stout timbers, with storm shutters at the windows. It's set in a tended garden where little monkish statues peep out at us from elegant shrubs. We pass beneath a plum tree that's in pink flower. A mature lady sits cross-legged at the entrance. She stokes a large pot of glowing charcoal. The *mamasan* rises, puts her palms together and makes a little bow, then leads us inside. I have a twinge of anxiety.

Within, all is delicate. The room smells of cedar. Thin smoke trails rise from three sticks of incense mounted in a little blue pot of rice grains. The walls are formed from sliding wooden frames. They carry translucent paper panels that fill the building with a soft light. She seats us on cushions, then claps her hands. A girl appears, bearing two small glasses of beer on a rattan tray. A half-a-dozen others follow her, all in kimonos with tall combs and fans in their piled-up hair. They line up along the wall and make little bows.

My tall, Scottish friend swigs his beer, gets off his cushion and walks across to an angular, rakish-looking woman. They leave the room. I take a sip of beer – all eyes are on me. A more rounded girl, not much older than me, gives a lovely smile. I smile back, and straightaway she advances, takes my hand and leads me to another room.

It's a large room decorated with pictures of black and white, red-crowned cranes, in pairs, some flying and some dancing. There's a bed without legs on the floor. The pillows are cylindrical. She strips and indicates I should follow suit. Once naked, she looks me up and down. I feel a degree of confidence – I'm tanned, muscled and, though slender, about a dozen hairs have recently sprouted on my chest. She nods with approval, then examines me with cool fingers. I suppose she's checking that I'm FFI. She smiles, chatters a bit in Japanese and seems to have little English. Adolescent fumbles in the chilly back lanes of Hartlepool have not prepared me for this. I'm sober and I'm nervous.

Beneath the bed covers, she soon realises I have no experience. She gives a delighted laugh and calls out, 'Ah! You cherry boy!' A sliding frame opens in the wall and a little flock of girls rushes in. They nod, giggle and smile, then, after a bit of chatter and a quick round of applause, file out of the room and close up the wall. I'm alone again with this pretty, round-faced girl, who has kept her hair tied up. With tender humour, she shows me what to do and, before long, all is well with the world.

Third Sparks is also happy. He persuades the *mamasan* to let us call again tomorrow morning and take the girls out shopping.

Next morning our two ladies of yesterday are waiting, together with two others who have joined the outing. Shopping is cheap here; I buy a translucent china tea service with images of a geisha's face in the bottom. It costs £1 (almost an eighth of my week's pay), but it's for my mother. The girls are not demanding; we buy them the few small things that take their attention. It's a delight to sit with them in a teashop, eat aromatic cake, drink green tea, and attempt conversation. Their eyes dance with fun. These people (at least the women) are so gracious; how can they be the same stock that worked to death our captured soldiers on the Burma railway?

Next day the ship fills with a New Zealand battalion – many of them look like Maoris, swarthy, broad of face, and large of limb. I wonder if they've been using their Moa protectives. We'll ship the twelve hundred to Hong Kong, where they'll change vessels and steam home to Auckland.

Before we sail tomorrow, three of us venture ashore to try one of the bath-houses. The best establishments are reserved for NCOs and officers; the common soldier is kept out, he will have his own places of relaxation. One senior officer of *Dunera* has his second home in one of these bars cum bath-houses: He has a romantic attachment to the *mamasan*, and she to him. He's issued an open invitation to junior officers to repair to that place, whereupon a fuss will be made of his shipmates.

The building is similar to yesterday's pleasure house, but its gardens are more refined. A graceful bridge straddles a pool where handsome carp drift like stately spirits of greenish-gold. There's a circular patch of raked gravel on which stand ceramic pots that hold ancient pine trees in contorted miniature. It's like walking through a painting.

The bar is crowded with Australians, but we find a table. One Australian, a big sergeant, is louder than the others. His friends try to calm him, but he seems intent on drinking himself to oblivion. They whisper that he's had a telegram to say his father has died.

The senior lady, the *mamasan* is weepy and clings to our ship's officer. *Dunera* has been a regular visitor. *Mamasan* and our officer host are like husband and wife. But *Dunera* has embarked her last contingent of the military and will not return to Japan. Our officer is sad but expansive. He intends to 'push the boat out'. Our food and drink, and 'whatever else we desire,' are on him tonight. The three of us settle in for a memorable evening. Girls of the premises, in gracious kimonos, soon invite themselves to our table.

There's a girl serving at the bar who puzzles me. She is sour-faced and unfriendly. A lady at our table explains that it's because the girl's family had all died in the atomic detonation above Hiroshima.

The Australian has become louder. His embarrassed friends make apologies. A woman comes, speaks to him gently, and shepherds him away like a lamb. Another woman appears by my own elbow, smiles and tugs at my sleeve. So I follow her into the garden, to sway a little in the sweet night air, and gaze at the stars. I'm a bit muzzy-headed, but meekly assume that, like the Australian, others have deemed it time I was led away.

The bath-house is a separate building in the garden. I follow the woman upstairs. Half-way up, on a landing, two old women sit wrapped in heavy kimonos; they keep warm at a bowl of glowing charcoal. They stop me and ask for 'cigarette'. I open a flat tin box of fifty 'State Express 555'. I always go ashore with a couple of tins; they are cheap from the ship's bonded store and make a useful trade. They help themselves to a few, then take the whole tin from my hands and wave me on. I'm in no condition to make a fuss, so I follow my lady guide up the next staircase, into the bathing room.

This is the first time I've had a proper look at her. Her eyes are a little narrower than those of the girls in the bar, and she's not as pretty. Her expression is calm, almost serious, perhaps a little sad. She is slender, hair in a tight bun, and could be twice my age. I assume she is the official bath attendant and so strip when she indicates. While she inspects me to ensure all is FFI, three young girls enter lugging buckets of hot water. I grab a small towel and make an attempt at decency. They pour water into the enamelled iron bath. It becomes a relay of steaming buckets of bath water, up and down the stairs, until the bath is deep. The room by now is clouded by steam and I struggle to see, but the woman wants me to step into the bath. I dip a toe, and yell out, 'It's scalding! Cold water! Bring cold water!'

The girls arrive with buckets of cold until I judge it safe. Through the steam, their expressions tell that I've tried their patience. However, the bath water is now perfect and I sink down to soak, but the bath-woman climbs into the other end and proceeds to rub me all over with soap and loofah. My head is clearing fast. The steam thins so that I can see her soberly for the first time. Yes, she is not a girl, she's a proper woman, about thirty-five. But she seems kindly, so I decide to go along with whatever is customary.

As we lay in the bath, my hairy English legs alongside smooth Japanese, I muse on how different this is to life in Hartlepool – that gritty old town on the other side of the world. What would my cycling pals think of this? The matter of what my parents might think, I thrust firmly out of consciousness. It's only three years since I was gathering seacoal on the nithering North Sands, but it feels an age has slipped by.

Today, a soak in a hot bath, with an exotic lady, stirs the senses. When the bath grows cool, she towels me down as though to burnish the skin, until I tingle; I feel aglow – like the old women's charcoal fire.

No passageways run through this building. There's a series of rooms, all interlinked, in the manner of a Tudor mansion. I follow her through two little rooms and glance at people already in bed. They don't seem to mind us flitting through. My bedroom is next. The bed is on the floor, a hard mattress and hard cylindrical pillows. I'm wearing just a bathrobe, and begin to wonder where my clothes have got to – I saw the bucket girls in the bath place take them away. After all the excitement, I need to lie down. The woman slips off her bathrobe, gets beneath the covers, and snuggles alongside me. She has few words of English and doesn't giggle like the young girls, but we commune well enough by smiles and touches. The bath lady produces a little, domed tin and opens it. She picks out two slender, brownish, hand-rolled cigarettes, lights them both and passes me one. The flavour is unusual but strangely relaxing. She does this at intervals throughout the night.

Occasionally, people flit across the room, en route to another. After midnight a squealing girl rushes through, with the Australian sergeant in pursuit. He is roaring like a bull. Two women run after him. We two, shoulder to shoulder, puff on strange cigarettes in silence and stay alert until the fuss dies down.

Daylight filters through the paper-panelled walls. The lady is sound asleep at my side. Third Sparks, in a bathrobe, sticks his head into the room and in a stage whisper says, 'Come on! It's time we were off!'

I roll out of bed and don the bathrobe. 'Where's my gear? I've no shoes. They took my clothes away!'

'All downstairs, along with mine, being polished, sponged and steam-ironed. Come on. Our taxi awaits.'

The lady stirs. Opens her narrow oriental eyes. She gives the hint of a smile. I put my palms together – like I'd seen them do – make a little bow, and whisper, 'Thank you.'

Ready for the second trip.
Dunera at Southampton as the fog disperses.

9

Second Trip

It's early April 1956. *Dunera* returns to Southampton, where I 'sign off'. There's delay going through Customs; they've had a tip-off that our ship has drugs on board – the culprits are a group of Chinese in the engine-room crew. So, I miss my train – the fast express – miss my connection and am stranded on Darlington station for the night, in my native County Durham, among a mass of Geordie soldiers trying to reach home on a two-day pass. I'm tired, cold and hungry. There's a tea stall preparing to shut up shop for the day; the owner sells me a pork pie.

Darlington is where steam railways began. I munch the cold pie in front of Stephenson's *Locomotion*. She looks grand considering the noticeboard says she began life in 1825. Famous as the first engine to haul passenger coaches, she stands on a plinth on one of the platforms. The boiler is encased in wood. Complex arms and cranks sprout from the engine so that she looks like a fat grasshopper with excess legs. Next to *Locomotion* is the *Derwent* engine of 1845.

There's a chill in the night air so I settle down for a rough night on the waiting room floor lost in a sea of snoring khaki, and breathing a cocktail of odours.

Ten days is my earned leave allowance for three months 'deep sea' service. It doesn't seem much after working seven days a week, apart from Sundays in port, but my parents are pleased to see me. Dad gives a noncommittal grunt when he sees the tattoo on my arm. Mam doesn't mind, she's overjoyed that I'm safe; every time our local coast was wild with gales she would worry, even though *Dunera* was probably gliding through glassy tropical waters, escorted by flying fish.

Peter, my mongrel dog, goes into ecstasies. His hairy flag of a tail drums against the furniture and his eyes gleam. Mam says, 'He's been a proper devil since you left. Getting up to mischief. Staying out all night when he sniffs a bitch on heat. All the dogs around here will soon look like him. A lady in Miers Avenue tied her old bitch to the table leg but he got in. She's had just one pup, mind; being a bit past it. But her owner is pleased.'

'I'm sorry about all that, Mam. He'll be missing the woods and his runs across the dunes. I'll take him along the North Sands and tire him out. It'll be good to smell wet dog again.'

Peter's soft brown eyes gaze up as I speak. I'm sad to have betrayed his trust. I fondle his hairy ears and wish he could understand.

My parents are living easier. Instead of tired, handed-down chairs, there's a new settee and two armchairs in the front kitchen. I'm impressed. To help my costs at Marine College, Dad went without. He gave up his five-bob a week on football pools competitions and signed up for overtime in the shipyards. It's natural to send them the major part of my wages now that I'm earning as much as

Dad does in the yards on the River Tees. My employer, the Marconi Company, sends them £5 a week from my wage of £7-10 shillings. In our town, it's usual for sons and daughters to do this. When youngsters start work they put their wages into the common pot, until they marry and leave home. But Mam puts some of the money away and acts as my savings bank when I run short.

Dad appreciates the big box of duty-free cigarettes. Mam is astonished when she sees what I've brought her from Japan – the pink kimono, and the tea service with a geisha's face in the bottom of each cup. When I clear the old house, twenty-five years later, I'll discover both treasures in mint condition.

The leave days fly by all too soon. But it's good to be eating Mam's cooking again. She makes sure I am 'built up' with 'boiled in a muslin bag' steaming suet pudding stuffed with sage and onion, corned beef and potato pie, and *panackelty* – that great dish of Durham County: bacon, carrot, swede, and parsnip casseroled in luscious gravy beneath a layer of sliced potato, baked until the top is crisp.

My friends make a fuss at first – after all, I've voyaged twenty-thousand miles and have a touch of the sailor's rolling gait. After a few enquiries as to 'How was it?' their main preoccupation submerges my tales: we gather at the home of a lad with access to a record player, and enough spare cash to buy the latest hits. In January, when I sailed, Bill Haley was top of the charts with *Rock Around The Clock*, and here in mid-April he's climbing again, with *See You Later Alligator*. At the vast Queen's Rink Ballroom we throw ourselves around and risk dislocating girls' wrists with our efforts at Jive, and Rock and Roll. From a distance, we must look like a mob of crazed Zulus. Between wild gyrations in the centre of the floor, we hold the girl as close as we dare and cruise clockwise around the perimeter, doing a slow waltz to the *thump de thump* of the local band, and a hired Geordie crooner who carries off a decent rendition of Jimmy Parkinson's *The Great Pretender*. The evening closes with Fats Waller's, *My Very Good Friend the Milkman*. Some of us might even walk a girl home.

I venture out with my pals for one tough cycling run of sixty miles but struggle to keep up with even the slowest of them. I'm crestfallen. I've lost my hard condition. It's not because of homely plates of *panackelty*, but is the fruit of sedentary life at sea where work is just a hundred yards and two ladders away. Hardly any muscle is needed to turn a few knobs and tap out Morse on a brass telegraph key.

On my return to Southampton, the night-time docks are shrouded in swirling fog so white, so dense, that I'm fearful of falling into the harbour. It's close to midnight and there's not a soul to ask the way in this gloom. I creep alongside the wharf sheds until I locate *Dunera's* white hull. I lug my suitcase up the gangway, nod to the Indian watchman, and grope around until I locate my cabin door – second on the right down the starboard alleyway. I switch on the light. A face with glare-puckered eyes rises from my pillow. Someone's in my bed! He must be a drunk. And I'm travel weary.

'What the bloody hell! Get out of my bunk! What are you playing at?'

He rubs his eyes. 'Sorry, mate. I'm fourth radio officer. I was told this is my cabin. I've just signed-on *Dilwara* today.'

'Come off it! This isn't *Dilwara;* you're on *Dunera,* and you're in my berth.'

He's now well awake and sits upright in the bunk. He sniffs. 'You'd best walk a bit further down the quay. You'll find *Dunera* tied up just astern of us. *Dilwara* is her sister ship, so they're identical.'

The penny drops. I cobble together an apology and beat an embarrassed retreat.

After more groping through fog I discover *Dunera* and locate my old cabin. The light is on. There's a willowy young chap in my bunk reading a novel. I stay calm this time; there'll be a sensible explanation. The pale-faced fellow is the new junior. Fresh from college, this will be his first trip. He's not an outgoing character; seems a bit diffident, but he tells me the news. The Scotsman who 'showed me the ropes' in foreign parts, has signed on a tanker and I now have his job. I'm to be third sparks and will inhabit the slightly larger cabin just next door. Scotty was a likeable rogue and I learnt much when led astray by him. Perhaps we'll meet again in some 'watering hole' in a distant port. But I don't give it much thought. Life rushes on.

Next day I watch 800 British military personnel ascend the gangways. We embark a mixture of engineers, riflemen, dragoons, and fusiliers with kitbags on shoulders, together with knots of airforce and navy people. Destined for Singapore and Hong Kong, the ranks are appointed to bunks in the ship's huge lower deck dormitories and their officers to more salubrious accommodation on the upper decks. Once the bustle has settled down we cast off.

It's a bright, breezy day in the Solent. We cause some confusion when we slip through a yacht race off the Isle of White. Our decks are crowded with passengers excited to see the gleaming white pinnacles of the Needles coming up fine on our port bow. Surf boils around the base of the sea stacks and the great whale-back of Tennyson Down rises above. The 140-foot granite cross that is the memorial to the poet, Alfred Lord Tennyson, towers at the highest point of the great chalk hill where he walked. The watchers are soon distracted.

On the starboard side, the world's largest vessel is powering her way to Southampton from New York. The Cunarder's three, black-topped, red funnels dwarf our puny, buff smokestack. Eighty-thousand tons slicing through the Solent raises a bow wave that rocks our 12,000 tons. We give a blast from our whistle in salute. *The Queen Mary's* reply is a bray from her horn as sonorous as any from the great pipe of a cathedral organ. I'm filled with wonder. Like us, she was a trooper during the last war. Painted grey, she came to be known as *The Grey Ghost* as she zigzagged the oceans with her cargo of 5,000 troops. Hitler offered a prize of $250,000 to any U-boat commander who could sink her, but her massive engines and 32 knots (twice our speed) kept her from harm. She had shipped a total 800,000 troops, a figure which caused Churchill to declare that *Grey Ghost* had shortened the war by a whole year.

The start of this second voyage is easier; I've developed a competence in my job, and a familiarity with ship life, such that I'm free of the humiliations that marked my first trip. Though I fail to get close to the new junior – he's not an outgoing sort and seems wary of me – I soon make friends with one of the new engine room junior officers. Alan is a bold Londoner, good looking and confident. He's on his first trip, and at twenty-one has just finished his engineering apprenticeship at some firm in the capital.

We've managed to go ashore in Port Said where he does not appear as taken aback I am, by the gagging smell of bad drains and the chaos of this town at the entrance to the Suez Canal. Though I'm still only seventeen I have a taste for chilled lager in warm weather. In the bar where we land the local men eye us with cold glances as they suck on the communal hookah and blow smoke in our direction. Perhaps, unlike us, they can see the future and will watch British paratroops descend on the town in six months' time to route Colonel Nasser's Egyptian army.

One indifferent beer in Port Said is enough. We grow nauseous at the filth of the town and at the number of flies that perambulate around the rims of our beer glasses, taking sips of froth. Each time we take a drink, we must brush them off and wipe away their footprints and whatever else they have deposited.

It's mid-April and the Red Sea is a hotter oven than when I came through in January. People can be short-tempered with the heat and sweat of the place. Since Southampton, the senior deck apprentice: a tall, raw-boned, ginger-headed lad, a couple of years older, has been baiting me. I need to put an end to it, so I challenge him to a fight. We are to meet that night on the boat deck and have it out with fists. We keep the duel a secret, except for the other deck apprentices and my engineer friend. Alan will be in my corner as my 'second'. In between watches, he prepares me for the encounter; shows me how to keep up a guard against punches and how to feint and then strike hard. I absorb as much as I can, but I'm anxious.

I make efforts to be steady, but perhaps my voice has a tremble. 'Alan, I won't last long. He's over six-foot. He's agile and lean, with muscle and a long reach. I'm just five-foot-ten, and don't have his clout.'

'Then don't hang about, Harry. Get stuck in straight away and hit him hard. Go for the nose. Make him bleed. He's a bully and likely a coward. You've plenty of fire and grit, so use it!'

Alan makes sure we arrive early so he can put me at ease and give more advice. The hour comes, and we are alone on the boat-deck. Half an hour later we are still alone.

Alan breaks the tension. 'That's it. He won't show. It's your day. Let's crack open a few cold ales.'

Next day, at breakfast in the saloon, the senior apprentice will not meet my eye. The baiting ceases.

We slip ashore at Aden, along with hundreds of our service people. We poke around the market; buy a Swiss wristwatch, a Felca with luminous hands, to replace my cheap Ingersoll, and a couple of bottles of Gordon's Gin at five shillings apiece. All is amazingly cheap; Aden is a tax-free port. Next call is The Rock Hotel and its famous air-conditioned bar. Alan and I lounge in armchairs beneath a ceiling vent that drops a column of chilled air straight onto our perspiring brows. While the sweat evaporates, we sip splendid lager from glasses beaded with condensation, Tuborg imported from Denmark, and pretend to be colonial gentlemen. The waiters are in white uniform, with brass buttons, topped out by a fez of cherry-red felt.

Contented after such luxury, we stroll back behind a pair of lanky sailors off an American warship. Slightly in front of them is a pair of short and stocky British soldiers. The American sailors are elegant in crisp white jackets and long white trousers. Sarcastic comments about the 'Limey guys' baggy khaki shorts' float back to us on the warm evening air. The baiting continues for fifty yards along a street of Arab stalls.

Alan grabs my arm and slows our pace. We freeze. The little soldiers glance at each other. On a hidden signal they spin around together and, with workmanlike fists, fell the sailors in seconds, then smartly turn about to march away.

Two beanpole figures, clad in white uniforms, are crumpled in the red Aden dust holding their bellies. For a few moments, the shop Arabs look on without comment, then continue trading. We cautiously go forward to lend the sailors a hand. But the two friends scramble to their feet, check for blood, and find none. They dust off their uniforms, refit their caps and, comradely arms around shoulders, head for a bar.

The sun drops behind the great double rock of Aden and a breeze arrives. Amid the dust swirls, traders are lighting oil lamps. Moths flutter in from the prickly desert scrub. Nightfall is rapid at this latitude of 12.8 North. It's time we hired a bum-boat and got back to our ship.

After the narrow Gulf of Aden, the Arabian Sea opens wide before us. It's the time of monsoon transition when the dry North-Eastern fails and gives way to the wet South-West Monsoon. The winds and the sea are uncertain how to behave, but I'm comfortable in five-foot swells. I've been deep-sea for five months, felt queasy sometimes, but have yet to be sea-sick.

Between watches, I read up on photography and turn my little cabin into a dark room. This trip, I've brought a Kodak Box Brownie camera and, like a miser, take a few snaps (film is expensive). I develop the *120* film (60mm wide) in pint beer glasses filled with branded chemicals. The book asks for distilled water, but ship's tap water (who knows where that's from) will have to do. I rig a string across the cabin from which to hang the prints while they dry. It all goes well enough, except that the first attempts turn streaky and yellow because I forgot to wash off the fixer solution. Otherwise, I entertain myself by reading adventure novels: H Rider Haggard's *Alan Quatermain; King Solomon's Mines;* and *She.* Between the Haggards, I explore the westerns of Zane Grey. I become lost in these stories, so much so that the continual twin-screw vibration and *thud, thud* beat of *Dunera's* twin five-cylinder Doxford-type opposed piston oil engines fade from consciousness.

10

Vat69

From the deck, I often gaze at tropical night skies and wonder at the immensity of it all. There are constellations to puzzle over: Ursa Major and Cassiopeia on either side of, and rotating around, the Pole Star. I learn how to locate the obvious, like the three bright stars of Orion strung out in a straight line; and the planets, how they wander through the fixed stars. If I'm puzzled, an off-duty navigation officer is always a good man to ask about such things. Sometimes, there are showers of meteors out of the north-eastern quarter, and just as rare, the winking light of the first jet airliner, the De Havilland Comet.

As I prepared to join my first ship, Arnold Green, my mentor, sister's husband, and ship's engineer, cautioned me: 'You'll see wonders, Harry. So much wonder that it might come to seem commonplace. Don't ever be a cynic. Fill yourself with memories for life.' His words stay with me. I hear them again as the mysterious Sumatran coastline, low on the horizon, slips past. They come when dolphins dance in our bow wave, and when a black fish the size of a bed, the manta ray, with 'wings' outstretched, leaps from an emerald sea, and flops back with a booming thwack. 'It's only dislodging parasites,' says the cynic. But, sixty years later the manta will still boom in my mind.

On my watch, in the Straits of Malacca, our main transmitter fails. From the readings on the meters of the *Marconi Oceanspan,* I deduce which stage has the problem. With the front open and the side removed I literally *use my nose* to locate the fault. A rolled wax-paper capacitor has gone short circuit, I can see a dribble of molten wax on the side of the cylindrical can. The value is 1.0 microfarad. A nearby resistor has been destroyed by the short circuit. It's so blackened I can barely read its colour code: brown, black, red – that's 1k.ohm. I can fix this fault.

I'm going through the spares cupboard when the chief walks in. 'What are you doing, Third?'

'The Oceanspan has a fault, sir. I know what's wrong, so I'm sorting out the right spares. You can see where the problem is by the state of that capacitor.'

He peers into the transmitter and sniffs. 'Yes, there's a leaky coupling can, and a smell of burnt shellac.'

'Shall I heat up the soldering iron?' I have it in my hand.

'No leave things as they are. We'll be in port in thirty-six hours. Marconi shore-side maintenance will put it right. Head office says to use them whenever we can. I'll write out a cable to Marconi Singapore. Meanwhile, use the emergency transmitter.'

'But there's not enough power in it to reach Portishead, if we need to.'

'Don't argue, Third. Just do as I say.'

As soon as we moor in Singapore harbour a quiet Chinese chap climbs aboard. He's dressed in khaki shorts and shirt. He opens his bag of tools, gets to work, and has the Oceanspan operational within the hour. I feel aggrieved – I could have done that. I've been denied my first chance to exercise my maintenance skills. All the training I had at marine college seems wasted.

Hong Kong is *Dunera's* terminus on this trip. Once again the harbour is alive with the comings and goings of crowded sampans propelled by clattering engines, and the stately junks that glide through late evening with sun-sewn rubies in threadbare, battened sails. Chinese children bob, happily naked, around their floating homes. These youngsters seem to glow with health – ashore, similar urchins will be compressed into the maze of high-rise tenements hurriedly built to house the masses of refugees that fled from mainland Communist China. Hong Kong has burgeoned and suffers from the highest population density in the world.

Our visit is without event. But among the military we embark is the commander of the crown colony's naval base, his wife, and sixteen-year-old daughter. The daughter, Diane, and I become firm friends and innocent sweethearts. After we sail for Singapore, she often peeps through the porthole of my cabin to see if I'm off watch and to persuade me to stroll the boat-deck beneath a sky awash with stars. Diane is blossoming. Together, we look over the side at the ghostly blue lights of phosphorescence that illuminate the tracks of passing ships, and the flaring sheets that rush past us as the phytoplankton respond to the wash of our hull. I tell her what Arnold had urged, and how we should remember all this. In this way, our return voyage is all delight until we anchor in Singapore harbour where the captain decides the *Dunera* shall host a grand ball.

Freshly showered, Alan, my Londoner friend, walks into my cabin, black hair lightly pomaded with Brylcreem, and in his dress uniform. He carries a bottle of Scotch whisky and two glasses, but today I'm stuffed-up and miserable with a bad head-cold.

'Harry, fancy a few braces before we head for the dance? Diane and Mary will be there.' His eyes twinkle. He's seeing a lot of the dark-haired Mary.

'Sorry, I'm not fit for prancing about. I'm on watch at 0400 to take the ship's newspaper. Rugby Radio is a seven-thousand miles hop and takes some finding; I'd best get a few hours kip. Anyway, I've an empty stomach – I couldn't face dinner with this cold.'

'Just take a nip or two to help the snuffles, then I'll leave you in peace, and head for the bar.'

He's a good friend, so I acquiesce. The nips of VAT69 have an ameliorating effect on my cold. The whisky gets to work on my brain and between us we soon take down the level of the bottle. I'm invigorated and cheerfully don the cummerbund and monkey jacket handed down to me by brother-in-law.

To ward off rain, the deck is tented by awnings. A military band plays waltzes and foxtrots. Fairy lights drape the hulls of the lifeboats and loop between pipes and ventilators. Powerful spotlights dazzle the eyes. The lights attract Singapore moths – big moths with the eyes of owls on their four-inch wingspan. Some flutter to the deck and are in danger of a squelched death beneath a waltzing heel. I flit through the dancers and rescue a few moths, cupping them between my hands. On the starboard side, away from the lights, I release them into the night, and go back for more. It occurs to me that some dancers will think me a clown, but some of these helpless creatures are *Saturniids* – gorgeous silk moths – with downy wings of sumptuous yellow and tan. They flaunt long and delicate swallow-tails. They flop around helplessly, so I pick them up expertly with the wings closed and the thorax between finger and thumb. I can do nothing for the *Sphingidae*, the hawk moths that dash like darts among the lights; confused they collide and bang their heads until they fall to the deck and buzz away to find shadows beneath some table.

I manage to have a dance with Diane. She reckons I'm an eccentric, but says she likes me all the more. As we float around the deck I try to explain that I've been passionate about Lepidoptera since I was in short trousers. I'd send off my pocket money to mail-order live cocoons of exotic moths. With one of Uncle Tom's half-crowns I could even buy a pair of the papery cocoons of the *Tree of Heaven* silk-moth. I'd suspend them by cotton thread from twigs and, to mimic a rain-forest climate, would spray them each day with warm water from an old perfume bottle. After a few weeks they twitched as the moths struggled to emerge. My parents would invite the neighbours into my sparse bedroom to watch the downy creatures slowly unfold soft packets of crumpled wings, then stretch and stiffen them into glory. Gnarled, old Mr Jones, who was tattooed, kept racing pigeons, and had been a soldier in the Boer War, offered: 'Well, I'll go to Shields! In all my time I've never seen owt like this!'

After escorting the sweet and lightly perfumed Diane back to her parent's table, I rejoin my shipmates to discover it's my turn to buy a round of cold beers for the two junior engineers at my table. There's no sign of Alan, but I'm told he's taken Mary up to the boat deck. There's a crush at the bar, and I have a problem. Each time a space appears, our huge first mate moves into it and blocks me. I notice he is not trying to order, but merely dominates the bar and loudly holds forth among the army officers. He's a vast man – tall, with shoulders and rear end like those of the famous Durham Ox exhibited at Darlington in 1799. I conclude he is playing with me. So, being of light frame, I duck below his elbow and surface at the bar counter right in front of his capacious middle. He gives a grunt of protest as I emerge to catch the barman's eye and order three chilled Tiger beers.

Back on the dance floor the cocktail of my head cold, empty stomach, and shots of VAT69, is all too much, and I keel over. I surface again as I'm carried to my cabin, in the arms of shipmates. They strip off my monkey jacket and cummerbund, then stretch me on the bunk and switch off the lights.

After five hours of unconsciousness, I awake with a start. It's 0400 – I must search the dial for the main British telegraph station, Rugby Radio, before the Press transmission at 0448. I fill my washbasin and dunk my head. The tepid water clears my fog and helps bring the mind to attention. I use a comb, then head for the wireless-room. The alternators come to life with the usual rising whine and run up to speed. When the receiver dials are fully aglow, my fingers click switches to short-wave. The right hand spins the tuning knob, then slows to fine tune as I listen intently through the headphones. I'm wide-awake now and soon find Rugby's GBR call-sign on the 4mc/s band. At this hour in Singapore, the path of the signal is entirely through the night shadow. This frequency is perfect for long distance hops that bounce multiple times off the ninety-mile high Kennelly-Heaviside ionised layer (for a daylight path I would have selected 12mc/s). Rugby is clear: GTZZ de GBR, endlessly repeated to help ships with a press subscription to tune-in. The transmission of the newspaper will be sent at twenty words per minute and will fill six foolscap pages with world news, horse racing results, and stock market valuations.

I load the upright Underwood typewriter with a fresh roll of wax-coated Gestetner paper and type the headings for tomorrow's breakfast-table newspaper. I've not had ten-fingered typing lessons, even so I'll type at a steady twenty words per minute with two fingers, straight from the signal – it saves a laborious transcription, and I'm pretty good at it. British shore station operators key lovely Morse, but the Press I'm about to take down comes from a punched tape machine – it's devoid of human character, but it's crisp and clear nonetheless.

Because of the headphones, I don't realise someone stands behind me until I sense a presence. It's the chief radio officer – my boss. My heart shrinks so it feels like a walnut. He's dressed in a vest and baggy khaki shorts. My eyes rest briefly on a curiosity that marks the old man's plump chest – he has a third nipple. He scowls and gives a grunt.

'I see you're all set up, Third! Can you cope? After your performance tonight, I'd not expected you to make your watch. So I got out of bed to take it.'

'I'm fine, sir. Rugby is coming in nicely, and I'm ready to go.'

'I can see that. Now listen: You're to report to the captain after breakfast, to explain yourself. Make sure you're in fresh laundered whites. Wear your cap, then remove it when you're in his presence. I'll leave you to it, then.'

He mutters to himself, then pads out of the wireless room in bedroom slippers. I put the headphones back on and, with a tremble in my fingers, retune to GKA – now that the receiver has warmed up, Rugby Radio has drifted along the dial to become a faint warble.

Next morning, cap tucked beneath arm, I stand before the captain's polished mahogany desk with its inset of blue leather. While he writes on foolscap with a fountain pen I gaze around the spacious day-room with its bookshelves, couch, and gleaming brass portholes. I note the four bands of gold braid on his epaulettes and the handsome head of grey hair set on stout shoulders. He lays a sheet of blotting paper on the writing and regards me with stern eyes.

'I hear you were inebriated at my ship's ball. Furthermore, my chief officer informs me you were pushing him around in the bar.'

I'm flabbergasted. How could I push around the mate's massive body? 'No, sir. I merely ducked beneath his elbow to get to the bar counter.'

'You had no business to be in the bar, young man. You are seventeen and therefore below the legal age for consuming alcohol. I've instructed the Purser: From today you are denied access to alcohol on this ship. Now you can go.'

I replace my cap, then walk out, shamefaced. So, that's it; no cold beers; I'll have to make up perspiration loss with iced lime juice. No matter – I like lime juice.

The chief makes no comment but instead orders me to service the lifeboat batteries. I suppose it's a mild enough punishment to have to clamber in and out of the lifeboats, lugging battery logbook, distilled water, and hydrometer. But, today, everyone is wilting in the heat of Singapore's anchorage; they'll all be haunting the shade except for me.

Word spreads fast. As I go about my work, I'm astonished at the goodwill from my shipmates. Old hands nod to me and give knowing winks. On the poop deck, I pass the open cabin door of our four helmsmen. There is a low call in soft Hebridean tones: 'Hey, Sparks. In here.'

The quartermasters are seated around a table beneath a whirring electric fan. They are men from the Outer Hebrides, from Lewis, Uist, and Barra. They've lined faces and grizzled hair. They look old enough to be my father. There's a card game in progress and tumblers of whisky on the table.

'Shut the door, laddie. We've heard you've had your tap stopped. Sit ye down and share a wee nip wi' us.'

Not wishing to offend these noble seafarers, who probably survived wreck, torpedoes, and mines throughout The Great War, let alone World War Two, I accept a small one. I take careful sips while they make it plain that *to have your tap stopped* is a badge of distinction among long-service seamen. They relate how their own taps were on occasion stopped when serving two-year stretches on the Indian Coast in tropical tramp steamers. They're impressed that I've joined an exclusive band at such a tender age.

I stay for an hour, listening to tales of the sweating Indian Coast; tales of days when ships had raked masts, clipper sterns, and were coal-fired, with fire-boxes stoked by muscular men stripped to the waist. They insist that I call again whenever I'm parched.

Two days later, *Dunera* casts off from the jetty to a Gurkha military band playing *Will Ye No Come Back Again?* on massed bagpipes. The voyage to Southampton via the Suez Canal will take three weeks. Diane remains a staunch friend and we promise to write after we part. Her mother sends me imperious glowers, but her father favours me with a twinkle-eyed grin. I live from day to day, do my watches, and try to avoid situations that bring trouble.

Dunera docks in Southampton to a background of world tension. It looks like the Egyptian dictator, General Nasser, an ally of the USSR, will seize and nationalise the Franco-British owned Suez Canal inside the month. He'll close the Straits of Tiran, and deny Canal access to Israeli shipping. Britain will need her troopships on standby if there is to be a response. I might be destined for a war.

On July 3rd, 1956, I stand before the desk of the manager of the Marconi Company office in Southampton.

The chief is explaining how my lapse in behaviour in Singapore fell short of the vessel's standards and that I should be replaced. The Marconi manager sighs and wearily declares I'll be transferred immediately to another vessel. I make a protest – I'm owed ten days leave and my parents are expecting me home – but the chief angrily tells me to: 'Shut up, boy!' (Boy? I'm livid. I turned eighteen last month!)

The manager seems a quiet and decent sort, and I search his features hopefully. He strokes his chin. 'There's the *Orsova*, an Orient liner in Tilbury Docks on the Thames, short of a junior R/O. She's 28,000 tons and only two years old. She's loading for Australia with emigrants. It would be a fresh start for you.' He looks me up and down, meets my eyes intently, then sighs. 'But perhaps, in your case, she's not the most suitable berth.'

I'm left wondering if he thinks my Hartlepool breeding is unfit for such a posh vessel. (Only later will I hear gossip that the chief R/O on that Orient boat is notorious for his interest in his more toothsome juniors. The Marconi Company could not keep them on the ship – they would clamour for release as soon as they docked from Australia. Was it because my unformed youthfulness put me at risk? Or did the Marconi manager intuit I'd be the sort to respond with fists?)

He seems lost in thought. He opens a file, flips through the pages, stabs one with a forefinger, then comes to a decision. 'You'll take the train to Cardiff today. We'll book you into 'The Missions to Seamen' for your bed tonight. Report to the Cardiff shipping office tomorrow to sign on.'

'Sign on what?'

'She's general cargo. You'll sign coasting articles. You'll stay with her about three weeks while she loads for deep sea. After that, we'll find you another berth. Collect your rail travel warrant from the office next door. Have a good trip.'

(In November 1967, Dunera was sold to Revalorizacion de Materiales SA, and scrapped at Bilbao, in northern Spain)

The James Nourse tramp *MV Hughli* at Liverpool.1949.
Norman Hesketh/Malcolm Cranfield collection.

11

Tramp

I've sent off a telegram – a brief one to my parents to say my leave is cancelled. They have no telephone, nor do any in our neighbourhood. Telegrams once brought a sense of dread. But that aspect of war has faded and folk no longer shudder when the telegram boy peddles down the lane on his bicycle.

Tonight's lodgings are comfortable, a single room at *The Flying Angel* – the Cardiff Seaman's Mission. It's my first night in any sort of hotel. I decide to take it steady while I work through this new experience. There's wholesome steak and kidney pie for evening meal. I polish it off, then fill up with apple pie and custard. Lovely food, and almost as good as Mam would set before her menfolk. I've bought a copy of *The Daily Telegraph*, a big newspaper recommended by brother-in-law Arnold as the best paper for engineers. With my technical background, I fancy I'm somewhere between technician and engineer, even though Arnold says real engineers have letters after their names.

I settle with a pint of Welsh bitter at an alcove table in the bar. I wrinkle my nose. The ale smells suspiciously sour. The thin scum of froth, as excuse for a head, deserves the contempt of a North-Easterner. Cameron's Brewery in West Hartlepool makes a more robust beer, with hops that bite the tongue, and a head that rises up, climbs over the rim of the glass and foams onto the table.

There's boisterous banter and laughter by the beer pumps from a crowd of white seamen. They are crew off some ship and seem intent on drinking the place dry. They look like a rough crowd. I primly avoid all contact by burying myself in *The Daily Telegraph* – I'm determined to keep out of trouble.

I buy a bottle of Newcastle Brown Ale to take away the taste of South Wales beer. Newcastle Brown is decent stuff and deserves its unofficial title: U-boat Fuel, or Lunatic's Broth. Afterwards comes intermittent slumber in a soft bed. I stir at unusual sounds outside the window: the songs of homeward-bound pals after a 'night on the beer', the occasional bicycle bell, the gravelly honk from the horn of an Austin Ruby car – otherwise there's silence in the small hours. Strange to be without the constant throb of a ship's engine resounding in the bulkheads.

After breakfast, I dial for a taxi to bear me and my gear to the Cardiff shipping office to sign aboard the new ship. I lug my bags outside and wait on the pavement for the taxi. The rough crowd from last night is also on the pavement, with their motley array of bags. Their taxi pulls into the gutter. They load up and drive off.

My taxi is next in line – but my bags have vanished! The rough crowd has taken them. I jump into the taxi and shout, 'Follow that cab!'

We pursue it into Cardiff dockland, past coal wharves and warehouses. We lose them once when a long coal train trundles through and we must halt at a level-crossing. But my driver does an intuitive three-point turn over more railway lines, dodges between some sheds, and spots our quarry in the distance. It's pulling away from a filthy old ship.

Her white superstructure is yellowed and chipped. The plates of her black hull carry vertical streaks of rust. She sports a buff funnel, with black top and a red Neptune's crown just below. She has a list and leans against the dock like an old whore at a bar.

I run up the gangway to discover a pile of bags stacked on the empty deck. I rummage among them until I retrieve my own.

There are footfalls on the rust-flaked steel plates. 'Now then! What are you up to?'

It's a huge man. He reminds me of the mate of the *Dunera*. A sense of grievance and injustice hits me. 'You clowns went off with my gear back at the Mission. I've had to chase you all the way through Cardiff bloody docks.' My protest becomes louder. 'I don't suppose you buggers will pay the extra taxi fare!'

He says nothing, but steps forward with menace. I grab my bags and scurry down the gangway.

We weave our way to Cardiff Shipping Office, where I put my signature to ship's articles for a berth on the motor vessel *Hughli*, presently in Cardiff. We return through the cobbled streets of Cardiff's famous Tiger Bay area – me watching the taxi meter – and onto the docks. We dodge more coal trains and wind our way between sheds and cranes until we draw up alongside the *MV Hughli*. Horror fills me when I realise it's the same noxious tramp on which I'd recently had that altercation.

The big man is on deck again. He glowers down at me as I creep up the gangway. He looks even bigger than before. 'You again! What the bloody hell do you want this time?'

'I'm your new radio officer,' I mutter.

'And I'm first mate,' he growls. 'I can see we're in for an interesting trip!'

I shrink back, but catch a twinkle in the man's blue eyes and note how his lips fight back a touch of mirth.

The motor vessel *Hughli* (named after that branch of the Ganges estuary on which Calcutta is rooted, and into which that city pours its effluent) has been in foreign waters for two years. She has come home to Britain for a maintenance service and to change crew. She's a 6,589-ton cargo vessel of the James Nourse Line. The crew numbers about sixty, of whom thirteen are Europeans (including two Polish engineers and a Maltese donkeyman); the remainder are Indian Lascars, except for a sprinkling of Chinese in the engine-room. From the aft accommodation waft the vapours of spiced fish and simmering ghee.

There's just one radio officer, and that's me. Now that I've six months of sea experience I'm officially empowered to be in sole charge of a wireless station. My watch keeping will be eight hours per day, comprised of four two-hour stretches with two-hour breaks, and then ten hours off. But I'll be called upon to operate the D/F (direction finding equipment) whenever the bridge officer needs the bearing of some radio beacon. Should I be off watch my absence from the wireless room is covered by the Auto-Alarm, a device that detects a simple, incoming distress signal, and rings a loud bell in my cabin. The bell is situated just a few inches from the position of my ear when I'm in my bunk. I've a large cabin but it's chilly. This ship is designed for the tropics, so the door opens directly onto the deck, to catch whatever cool breeze might pass by.

The *Hughli* was built in 1943 and is registered at London. Her 3-cylinder Doxford engine drives her at a plodding eleven knots. Two masts support winch-driven derricks for loading cargo in ports without access to shore cranes. The seven-stranded phosphor-bronze wire of my radio aerial is strung between those masts. She has four hatches on her steel deck that open into capacious cargo holds that carry bales of cotton, chests of tea, railway lines, manganese ore – or whatever else the shipping agents arrange. She'll take cargo from any harbour, river, or creek, to anywhere else. She is an opportunist warm-water tramp. On her last voyage, she spent two years away from home and, from what I hear, for much of that time she tramped between the Caribbean and the Pacific via South Africa.

I glean much of this by listening to the conversation that ranges around the long table in the ship's saloon where we officers eat. The saloon has none of the luxury panelling of my last ship. This vessel is a hurried wartime construction. The bulkheads are steel, with rivet heads dotting the numerous, chipped layers of white lead paint. We all sit together, the ship's master/captain, the chief engineer, and the rest of us. Among our thirteen officers there's none of the prim formality of the great saloon of the troopship *Dunera*, with its many tables arranged by strict hierarchy of rank. The crew of *Hughli* are not much inhibited by the captain at the head of the table, though he does tend to dominate the talk. He's a grizzled Scot who's been at sea about forty years. I join them for dinner, a bit flustered by the recent taxi adventure. The saloon has the mouth-watering aroma of Asian spiced food.

An Indian steward, in starched white jacket, ushers me to the table. 'Marconi Sahib sit here,' he says, with a Bengali lilt.

There's a place for me, two chairs from Captain Stuart. Beneath bushy brows, he fixes me with sea-faded eyes.

'I'm your new radio man, sir,' I venture.

'Oh, yes? And what would your name be?'

'Harry Nicholson.'

He nods at my accent and wrinkles his eyes. 'Harry Nicholson, eh? That sounds like a collier out of the Tyne.'

There's a round of laughter. 'So, Harry Nicholson, what part of Geordie-land are ye from?'

'Hartlepool, sir.' I know what's coming …

'Ah! That's where they hung the monkey, isn't it?' Another round of laughs. 'Why hang a poor wee mite of a monkey?'

I consider the usual riposte: 'Have you lost your father?' but think better of it. I'll try a more considered approach. 'Hartlepool's townfolk were a simple sort in those days. During the war with Napoleon, a French ship was wrecked in Tees Bay. The only survivor came ashore at Hartlepool, clinging to a raft. It was the ship's pet monkey wearing a little uniform. Local fishermen captured the creature and took it to the mayor. He questioned it, got only a jabbering reply, and decided it was a French spy. He ordered execution. The monkey was hung from the mast of a coble on the shore. But it's only a legend. Mind you, I've heard that a local pub once displayed a stuffed monkey on the bar counter. It had rope burns around its neck.'

There's silence, so I turn my attention to the chicken curry before it gets cold.

Bill Coleman, the first mate (who I confronted over my lost bag), gives me a nudge. He speaks a cultured, but still thick-tongued, Merseyside. 'That's a good story, Sparks. You're well informed. I'd not heard the full explanation before today.'

Captain Stuart stops sucking on a chicken bone. 'I've always said the Geordies are daft as rags.'

The chief engineer speaks for the first time. Like the mate, he's also from Birkenhead. 'Some would have it that Geordies are Scotsmen with their brains bashed out.' There are a few cautious snorts.

'Better than Yorkshiremen,' I respond. 'They're said to be like Scotsmen bereft of generosity.' There's a howl of laughter, but Captain Stuart's face has a Fifer's glower. I worry I've gone too far. I should keep my mouth shut.

The captain stops chewing to wipe his mouth with a napkin. It leaves a yellow curry stain on the freshly-laundered linen. 'You can poke the Scots as much as you want. It's nae bother tae me. I'm no Scot. I'm a Pict!' He gives the rest of us a glare. 'The Scots are invaders from Ulster. I descend from the original inhabitants of Caledonia. I'm pure Pict! We've been in Scotland forever. Nobody knows where we came from.'

I fail to keep quiet. 'I've read somewhere that some scholars think the Picts might be one of the Lost Tribes of Israel.'

The cutlery around the table falls silent. Captain Stuart's eyes bulge. He takes a long swig from his glass of water.

Stefan, the engineer across from me, breaks the hush. He is the younger of the two Poles; a man with gentle eyes. 'Harry. Tomorrow we sail. Tonight we go ashore for visit pub. You come along?'

Eleven of us head up Bute Street through the district of dockland Cardiff's Tiger Bay. It's the most multi-ethnic place I've been to. Tiger Bay is populated by the descendants of sailors from the world over: Norwegians, Somalis, Yemenis, Spaniards, Italians, Caribbeans, West Africans, Irish. Some say forty-five nationalities have settled here.

We begin at a pub called the *Cape Horn*, move on to the *Quebec*, then the *Salutation*, before settling down for the evening in the warm, clammy heart of the *Custom House* with its gap-toothed professional ladies. I've just about had a surfeit of brewer Brains' best Welsh ale by now, and keep drifting off in between long contemplations of the huge, multi-coloured mirror behind the bar. My new shipmates seem to be having a drinking competition. After a good deal of urging, I contribute with an attempt to swallow a pint of Black and Tan in one go. After that encounter with the mixture of Guinness and beer, I want no more.

I'm a bit unsteady on my feet as we head along Bute Street, and back to the docks. But I now have friends who guide with affable good humour. We halt at a 'hot pie and chips' shop that keeps late hours; it seems the beer has given the crew a ravenous hunger. I want none, so they stand me outside in the dark while they order their suppers.

The mate says, 'You wait there, Sparks. Don't move. See that terrace across the road? That's where Shirley Bassey was born. She's not there now. She moved up the road to Splott.' He dives into the brightly-lit shop. I lean with my back against the steamy window and try not to breathe in too much of the savoury beef and onion vapours. So, the coloured singer Shirley Bassey was born just there, I muse. She's all the rage this year. She's the singer of *Stormy Weather*. Why has she gone to Splott? And what is Splott? I lose interest and close my eyes. Everything's gone to Splott.

At breakfast the next day, the table is empty except for Captain Stuart and the wizened chief engineer. The ship's master is in a foul mood.

'Were you out with them last night, Sparks? I see you're still on your feet. Where did you get to? What did you eat ashore?'

'Why, sir? Where is everyone?

'They're away in hospital enjoying the stomach pump. They've got food poisoning. Didn't you hear the commotion last night when the ambulance came?'

'No, sir. I didn't hear a thing.'

'I'll ask you again. What did you consume?'

'I had nothing, just some rubbish Brains' beer. But the others filled up with meat pie and mushy peas in Bute Street. That place opposite Shirley Bassey's.'

'The feckless buggers! That'll be where they got poisoned. I'll need to tell the authorities. Meanwhile, we've missed our sailing. We'll try again tomorrow if those bloody clowns are discharged as fit.'

'What are our next ports, sir?' I butter a piece of toast and cover it with marmalade.

'Antwerp, then Rotterdam and London, then deep sea to Cape Town. Then, who knows where?'

'I'll be leaving you in London.'

'Leaving us London, Sparks? How so?'

'I'm not coming deep sea. I signed coasting articles only.'

'Really, Sparks? Did you not read them? You signed deep sea papers. You're articled for two years with this grand vessel.'

The Nourse tramp *MV Hughli* berthed at Liverpool 1949.
Norman Hesketh/Malcolm Cranfield collection.

12

Shanghaied

'I've been Shanghaied. I've been tricked!' I stamp up to my cabin to change out of uniform. In my shore suit, I rush down the gangway. An empty taxi is pulling away from an oil tanker. I flag it down and get in.

At the Shipping Office, I demand to see the articles I'd signed. They are indeed two-year, deep sea articles. I should have read them, but I'd been assured by Southampton Marconi Office that I'd be on coasting articles only – which meant I could sign off at any British port. An hour later I'm in the Cardiff Marconi Office, frustrated and angry. The manager finishes his phone call to the Southampton Office. I notice he bites his nails.

'I'm sorry to tell you there's nothing we can do.'

I raise my voice: 'Then I'll walk off the ship! I will not be Shanghaied!'

'The Marconi Company does not Shanghai its employees. Mr Nicholson, listen to me. If you desert a vessel, you break your articles. Break your articles and your Seaman's Record and Discharge book will be confiscated.

That will be the end of your seagoing career and, since you are now eighteen, you'll be immediately called up to do your two years National Service with the military.'

'I don't care! I'd rather do my two years in the Army than serve two years on that tramp. I'm telling you straight – I'll walk off that ship and you can rip up my certificates!'

He sighs. Drums his fingers on the desk. 'Please keep calm. Don't be rash. Stay with the *Hughli* for the time being. We'll find a replacement for you before she goes deep-sea.'

I know when to stay calm. I've rehearsed all this in my mind. I keep my tones low and measured: 'Fair enough. London is her last port. If no replacement turns up in London, by the day prior to sailing deep-sea, I walk off – then the Marconi Company will come up with another operator in pretty short order. No ship is allowed to sail without a radio officer, and that's the law. Any other officer, even the master, can be absent, but not the sparks. *Hughli* will have to stay in dock until the new man arrives.'

We'll be casting off soon. In the wireless room, I'm reading equipment manuals, investigating motor-alternators in the generator cupboard, checking the electrolyte in banks of lead-acid batteries and putting them on charge, running the transmitter into a dummy aerial, fiddling with the receivers, trying to become familiar with strange equipment. Usually there is a couple of hours handover by the outgoing operator, but I've not had that advantage and must rapidly become familiar. The mate has just informed me that a new calibration of the radio direction finder is overdue and will happen in the Bristol Channel, once we have cleared land.

He pokes his head through the chart room hatch. 'Have you ever done a D/F calibration, Sparks?'

'I haven't. But I'll see what the manual says about it.'

'Oh, it's easy enough, but you need to be on your toes. We stand off the channel light vessel and make a turning circle; that way we get to calibrate both sides of the ship. Lightship puts out a radio beacon. The bridge takes a visual bearing of her every five degrees of arc, and you take a radio bearing at the same time, and note it down. You plot the difference between the two bearings on graph paper, and that's the calibration done. The graph makes a sort of double correction curve – one for each side of the ship.'

'Thanks. And how soon is that after we leave Cardiff?'

'Just a couple of hours. Best sharpen a pencil or two.' He closes the hatch.

I try to remember the times I did dummy radio bearings at South Shields Marine College. We used the Bellini-Tosi system of fixed, crossed loops that fed a goniometer. This ship has the same system, so I switch it on and rotate the tuning knob for nearby beacons. There they are, each on a different frequency. A specific call sign in Morse Code is followed by an extended dash. I try a few, rotating the goniometer so that the long note drops to almost zero. That's the null point. Flick the 180-degree ambiguity switch, and read the bearing off the dial. Correct the reading from that angle's point on the calibration chart, and there's your bearing.

Shouted orders penetrate the wireless room. Ropes are lifted from bollards and splash into the dock to be hauled in by winches fore and aft. The engine turns over at a leisurely pace. From the porthole I see we have a tug at our side, giving us a nudge. Another tug has a hawser fast to our bow and tows *Hughli* towards the lock gates. It's high tide, so the gates are open. *Hughli* squeezes through the lock, squeals as she scrapes her hull against massive fenders of woven manila, and slips into Cardiff Bay. The bridge telegraph rings the engine room for half-ahead. The *thump-thump* of our Doxford diesel engine grows more rapid, hawsers splash into the water, and the tugs set us free. I turn my attention back to the radio gear.

'Coffee time, Marconi Sahib.' Mingel, the elderly, soft-eyed Goanese steward, who looks after me and a few other officers, has crept silently in with a cup of coffee and two digestive biscuits on a silver-plated tray. He's a Christian. Moslems have issues with pork and Hindus with beef, so Goanese Christians are favoured for the catering department. Moslems tend to be engine room firemen and Hindus find work as deck sailors.

Mingel is a canny old chap, he sports a medal ribbon on his white tunic. I wonder which ocean in WW2 earned him that. We are expected to refer to a steward from the Indian sub-continent as *Boy* irrespective of his age – seems daft to me, but I suppose it's a hangover from the days of the British Raj. I remind myself that Goa is an ancient Portuguese colony on the Indian coast south of Bombay. I've heard tell that India bides its time until the day it seizes Goa, which the Portuguese have occupied since 1510.

I sit back in my chair, headphones around my neck, and take a pull of coffee. As usual, it's made with cloying condensed milk, and so sweet that I swear my gums retreat in horror.

'Sparks!' The broad face of the first mate is at the hatch. 'As per your request, the crew's private aerials are lowered, and the derricks all stowed ship-shape. Bristol Channel lightship's dead ahead. We'll be making our turning circle in a few minutes. Are you ready?'

'Yes. I'm tuned in.' I'd been doing nothing else for the last hour but find null points in her signal, and prepare. And, hoorah! I remembered to send the obligatory message to Portishead Radio that we had departed Cardiff for Antwerp. I'm dry mouthed. Such a change from being one of four, with a chief to tell me what to do.

The mate lights a Gold Flake, takes a drag and exhales a stream of aromatic smoke into the wireless room. 'Right, then. Every five degrees we'll ring a bell like this.' A rusty rasp comes from a bell screwed to the bulkhead above the D/F. He goes on: 'The same instant, the bridge takes a visual bearing, and you'll do the same with the D/F.' He vanishes from the hatch. I hear him give orders to the Indian sailor on the wheel. The helmsman is a dignified *serang*, an Indian rank, equivalent to bosun.

The *Hughli* heels slightly as she steers to starboard.

The apprentice's face, with its wisps of adolescent fuzz, appears at the hatch. 'Standby, Sparks.'

The bell croaks and I take a bearing. It croaks again and I take another. I've hardly noted it down when it rasps again. The lightship is so close that the signal is violent in my headphones. I turn it down – so far that I lose it. Buzz again, take a bearing. For pity's sake, why do they go so fast? The ship should go round slower. Buzz again, take a bearing – I might have missed the one before that. The gaps in my bearings become frequent. I shout through the hatch, 'Slower! This is all too fast for a decent job.'

There's another rasp from the bell and a voice, 'Skipper told us not to mess about. He doesn't want to waste time on this. Anyway, that last bearing completed the circuit.'

'It's no good. There's too many gaps. We'll have to go round again.'

The mate comes to the hatch. 'Go round again? Do you want us all dizzy? The lightship will think it's an invitation to dance. I've never heard the likes. Skipper will be livid. Mind you, he's having a kip on his day bed, so he won't know until he reads the log. Right, round we go again – just once more, mind.'

131

The next circuit goes beautifully, and I'm content. Then, I remember my own log. I'm supposed to note down a signal, any signal, from coast station or vessel, every five minutes. These logs are examined by the authorities, then archived, particularly if there has been distress traffic. I've been so occupied in my struggle with the D/F that I totally forgot. I've neglected my legal obligations. But this is my first time in sole charge of a wireless room, and with gear I've not handled before. I sharpen a pencil and contrive fragments of calls from distant foreign coast stations, enough to fill this virginal log page that mocks me. I'm humbled.

Two days and five-hundred sea miles later we creep up the River Scheldt and berth in the vast docks of Antwerp. There are gaps everywhere, piles of rubble, and cleared sites ablaze with fireweed – the tall, waving stems of pink willowherb. The Belgian city is still rebuilding twelve years after the devastation of Hitler's counter-attack after the Allied liberation in 1944. The Germans had hurled their *vengeance weapons*, the V1 and V2 rockets, four-thousand of them, against a port vital for the supply of Allied forces. One rocket struck the Rex Theatre's roof and killed 570 (including 300 allied personnel) who had gathered to watch Gary Cooper in *The Plainsman*. Londoners who had suffered similar raids referred to the V1, a pulse-jet, variously as the buzz-bomb, the doodlebug, or the farting-fury.

It's in the dockland *Buzz-Bomb Bar* that I sample glorious Belgian beer this first night in Antwerp. We occupy two tables placed end to end. The engineers and deck officers relax with globular glasses of blonde Duvel and the darker Rodenbach. We swap stories as the froth slides down glasses shaped like feminine hips.

All is warm and convivial until Ludwik, the elder of the two Polish engineers, announces that the time has come for him to perform his party trick. Stefan, the younger Pole, urges caution. The third mate suggests that Stefan sings the Warsaw Concerto instead. At this insensitive suggestion, Stefan responds with tears for his lost homeland. Ludwik and Stefan had escaped from the 1939 German blitzkrieg on Poland and spent the war in British ships. The war ended fifteen years ago, but the Soviets are now masters of Poland, and these two, like most Poles, are afraid to return.

Ludwik is a bull of a man, with great shoulders and thick neck; he hugs the slender, gentle Stefan, and glares at the third mate. 'You are stupid man. How you sing concerto? See what you do to Stefan? For that you buy two rounds of beer. Go get them now! And for me, get two pickled eggs also.'

When the beer and eggs arrive, Ludwik slaps the table so that the peeled eggs bounce. He picks up a glass and drains it in one great gulp, then takes a vinegar-stained pickled egg and pops it into his mouth. He chews a few times, swallows, then gives a burp. He looks around the table and grins. There's a speck of egg yolk on one front tooth.

'Now I, Ludwik the Great, begins party trick, for enjoyment of shipmates.' He looks around for a response and gets cautious smiles in return. We are all in awe of this huge man. Ludwik drains another glass, then swallows the second pickled egg. He gets up and, despite his bulk, steps like a dancer to the bar. Men move aside to make space. He orders more beer and eggs. By this time, all the customers – seamen of a dozen nationalities, and Belgian dockers – are alert to an unusual event. The raucous conversation has lulled. A waitress hovers nearby, hand on mouth.

We sip our beer and watch, along with men on adjacent tables, as Ludwik counts his way through the sinking of twenty-one glasses of beer and follows each one with a pickled egg. I'm fascinated. He wipes his mouth with the back of his great paw, then stands and addresses all in the tavern: 'Ludwik now finished party trick.' He points to us, rooted to our chairs. 'These are Ludwik's friends! Ludwik fight any man who insult his friends.' There's no response from the rest of the bar, so Ludwik turns to us. Like a bear, he picks Stefan out of his chair and kisses him full on the lips. Next, he picks up the third mate and kisses him full on the lips, then lowers him carefully back into his chair. It's my turn next. I go limp. It's pointless to evade the giant Pole, I weigh ten stone, Ludwik might well be over twenty. I smell the beer, vinegar, and pickled eggs on his breath. I'm gently kissed. Ludwik the Great does this with all seven of us and nobody struggles. He squeezes into his chair and declares: 'Ludwik loves his friends!'

Hughli remains alongside in Antwerp docks for a week. As her holds swallow up crates of French clothing, Belgian chocolate and machine tools, and Telefunken radios and Grundig reel-to-reel tape recorders from rebuilt German factories, I write a letter home, to say I can't be definite, but I hope to see them in a fortnight or so. I write one to Diane (my sweetheart, homeward bound on *Dunera*) at her home in Surrey and wonder if it might be the last. Her own vague letter tells me of her new life in England and how she will be boarded at a school for young ladies. I doubt there's a future for our naive romance. *Dunera* and its memories slip away.

I escape from the rattle of cranes, the din of shunting engines, and the yells of Belgian dockers by walks into town. There are distractions in seaports, and organisations founded to keep sailors safe from the worst pitfalls. The

Missions to Seamen has branches in most ports. The Antwerp mission puts on dances and invites girls of good character to attend. Stefan and I try an evening dance. We find the 'young ladies of good character' to be nice enough, though a little shy. They are keen to practice their English but tend to shrink away if we get too close – though we are careful to be gentlemen. After a few waltzes to the mission's wind-up gramophone, we look for other entertainment.

Downstairs, the mission has a billiard room with a full-sized snooker table. There's a chalkboard on which to book your place. We take our turn at the table and enjoy lining up awkward shots – but disaster comes. A glass of Guinness is knocked over and spilt across the handsome green baize. Others say that I'm responsible. Whatever the truth of it, the dark splodge on that virginal green will probably stain my mind forever.

Rotterdam, Holland, is next. An enormous sprawling dockland lines the river Rotte, a distributary of the Rhine. It's a long walk to the rebuilt city centre. On the way, Stefan and I pass the scaffolded stump of a blackened church spire, bombed-out warehouses, and bustling new constructions filled with the noise of saws and hammers. But in central Rotterdam, in the new plazas and precincts, we are overawed by the night-life on display. People are sitting outside and dining at tables or playing at chess. Uniformed waiters flit among them with trays of food and drink.

The Dutchmen we encounter are dignified but disarmingly friendly. Three, with china-blue eyes and the rolling gait of shipboard life, join us at table and clink glasses of Oranjeboom (Orange Tree) pilsner lager. I point out that in my home port, to clink glasses is said to cause a sailor to drown. 'Ach, not in Nederlandt,' one man says in the Dutch-accented English that I'm coming to enjoy. They make interesting sounds when they pronounce 'd' and 'th', and roll their 'r' in a unique throaty fashion.

A broad-faced Dutch sailor, in a crazed leather jacket, leans across and whispers: 'You vant to know how to get free trink in Hollandt?'

We nod – of course.

'You say, very loud: *Zee oaken keys to Copenhagen Sound are in zee docks of Amsterdam!* And the answer from zee true Hollandter vill be: *Ah sixteen-fifty-eight! Zee golden age of zee Dutch navy. Have a trink!*'

We repeat the key phrase, so as to commit to memory.

The sailor goes on: 'You see, my friendts. King Karl of Sweden, he blockade Copenhagen. No ship get into Baltic. Danes not happy, Dutch not happy. Bad for trade. So Amsterdam send Admiral Obdam with fleet and, with cannon, blow Swedes back into Baltic. Then Hollandt can make money again.'

Though I've never played Shakespeare, I've seen the film *Henry V*, that stars Olivier as the king, and remember fragments of his powerful oration at the siege of Harfluer: *Once more unto the breach dear friends, let us close up these walls with our English dead!* So I declaim the line like Henry V, with energy that I hope would please Shakespeare: 'The oaken keys of Copenhagen Sound are in the docks of Amsterdam!'

A few laughs and a few cheers run around the bar. Glasses are clinked. 'Ja! Zee Golden Age! Have a Trink!'

Moments later the plump and grinning young waitress delivers a tray of foaming half-litres of Oranjeboom. We lift them in salutation to whoever made the gift.

The sailor leans across. 'Do not try again, for one month. Hollandters make strong friends. But limit there is.'

Back in the night air, my Polish friend appears to lose his usual calm and thoughtful demeanour. Though I'm just eighteen, we've become good friends. I think of Stefan as a poetic philosopher. He's about fifteen years older than me and usually offers fatherly advice, but I'm alarmed by his state of excitement tonight. In one bar he learns of a house of entertainment down a side street. He's enthused, but I don't like the sound of it and so station myself a few yards away while Stefan bangs on the locked door. I'm nervous; this area of dimly-lit, damaged and gritty old terraces lacks the gentility and grace of similar places in Japan. It feels dangerous.

Eventually, a window opens two floors up. A woman's head appears and yells something in Dutch. Stefan replies with what sounds like English laced with Polish and ends with a snatch of German. The woman disappears. Stefan bangs on the door again. The head at the window returns, followed by hands that tip a bucket. The water lands precisely on Stefan's head and drenches his best shore-going suit.

It's not dampened his ardour, so he decides to amble back to the city centre where all the bright lights are. I tell him to keep safe and bid him goodnight. I'm tired and my feet ache after the long walk from the docks. But the Port of Rotterdam is vast and I neglected to note *Hughli's* berth. I don't know which way to turn. I've come to rely too much on Stefan for taking charge of such matters.

In the darkness, I encounter a young Dutchman. 'I'm lost,' I tell him. 'I don't remember where my ship is.'

'You remember anything about the buildings when you left your dock?' He speaks a fair English and has intelligent eyes.

I ponder. 'I think there's a burnt-out church close by.'

'Does it have the stump of a tower? And scaffolding?'

'Yes. Which way is it, and how far?'

'I take you. We must walk for thirty minutes.'

I forget my aching feet, in deep conversation with this friendly intellectual, as we trudge through the dark. We pass dock gate after dock gate. I glimpse the liveried funnels of British Clan boats, 'Hungry' Hogarth tramps, elegant and sublime Blue Funnel steamers, among the Greeks, Danes, Swedes, and Finns – every funnel but mine. Eventually, the red Neptune's crown on *Hughli's* smokestack, illuminated by the lights of working cranes, comes into view. My Samaritan brushes aside the handful of guilders I clumsily offer. We shake hands and say goodnight.

13

Collier

From Rotterdam, the *Hughli* crosses the southern end of the North Sea to tie up in the Thames at Tilbury Docks, twenty-five miles downstream of London Bridge. The last of our cargo arrives on lorries and railway wagons. The cargo we take makes us a modern argosy. Crates of whisky and gin are slung aboard in nets suspended from cranes, as are a dozen motor cars. We swallow up railway lines, steel girders and thousands of sacks of goodness-knows-what and crates of this and that. The first mate is in charge of cargo stowage. He does not get much sleep. He must arrange the mass of exports in a sensible order, so that those items for the first port of call, Cape Town, in South Africa, are at the top, and accessible. Those for the final port must be in the bottom of the hold. At the same time, he must have a care for the stability of the ship. To avoid a capsize, he'll insist the heaviest cargo is at the bottom of the hold, and that all in the hold is properly lashed and stable. In heavy seas, moving cargo might be the end of a ship.

Tilbury is a dusty, grey sort of place now, given over to cranes and ships, and a mass of workers' housing that burns coal for heating. Acrid smells issue from chimneys and diesel lorries. In Tudor times all would have been sweet green fields with a fishing village or two. This is the place where the Tudor Queen Elizabeth chose to rally her troops when the one hundred and twenty ships of the Spanish Armada appeared in the English Channel. In plumed helmet and steel cuirass, she declared: *I know I have the body of a weak and feeble woman; but I have the heart and stomach of a king, and of a king of England too, and think foul scorn that Parma or Spain, or any prince of Europe, should dare to invade the borders of my realm; to which rather than any dishonour shall grow by me, I myself will take up arms, I myself will be your general, judge, and rewarder of every one of your virtues in the field.*

None of this concerns me now. Where is my replacement? I've threatened to walk off rather than be bound to this tropical tramp ship for the next two years. We are in the Thames for a week. I frequent the Marconi Office in Tilbury and pester the manager for news of my replacement. He's a dusty, clerical type who is dismissive of my entreaties. 'Look here,' he says, 'We are very short of operators. I've sent telegram after telegram to a man in the Republic of Ireland who has overstayed his leave. If he doesn't turn up, I don't know what we'll do. We've ordered him to relieve you tomorrow, and the day after that we want you in North Shields to sign on a coaster that's loading in the Tyne.'

'A coaster! What about my leave?'

'I'm sorry. We are really pushed for staff. Stay with the coaster for a month or two and then we'll see about getting you some leave. If it all works out, you could have a night at home on your way up to the Tyne.'

I give a grunt. '*Hughli* sails in two days. I'll be catching the train home, whether he turns up or not.'

Late next morning I pack my suitcase, fold up my uniform and lay out my shore-side gear. There's a knock on the cabin door, followed by a cheeky face beneath a shock of red hair.

'Are you the sparks?' The tones are pure Southern Irish. 'I'm Johnny Connor.'

'Come in, Johnny. Good to see you.' I've a few bottles of Worthington pale ale still unopened. I reach for a couple. They fizz confidently when I lift the crown corks.

'Ta! I've been on the run in County Cork, keeping away from Marconi's telegrams. This is to be my new home then?' He climbs onto the bunk and bounces a few times. He jumps down to open drawers in the furniture, then examines the hanging locker. 'Ah now, that's good. A grand piece of solid brass rod. A decent tie rack.'

'It serves.' I respond. I must look puzzled – I've only three ties, and one of those is a bow tie for rare events.

Johnny chucks the smaller of his two cases on the bunk and, with a flourish, throws open the lid. 'Take a look at these, will you?'

The case is filled with layers of multi-coloured ties, variously striped, flowered and checked, and some with nude women in seductive poses. 'Aren't they fine? I collect them. It's a bit of a hobby of mine, you see.'

I need to humour this fellow. 'They're amazing. You'll need plenty of shore time to wear all those. Is that Table Mountain painted on the blue one?'

'It is so.' He laughs. 'I picked it up last time in Cape Town. But I'll not be going ashore there anytime soon.'

'Why's that?' I cringe a little – *Hughli's* first port of call is Cape Town.

He takes a pull from the neck of his Worthington. 'Last time there, I got engaged to be married to the mayor's daughter. Then I did a runner and now I hear he's looking for me. I'm not wanting this ship to be going anywhere near Cape Town.'

I don't respond but suggest I first show him the wireless room and talk him through the gear, then we should nip ashore for a beer before we visit the shipping office.

After a few drinks, my replacement, four years my senior and with plenty of sea experience, has become effusive and regales me with his conquests of the fair sex. I'm bored and just crave to escape to King's Cross and catch the first train north.

At the shipping office, it's with huge relief that I sign off the *Hughli,* and stand aside to watch the Irishman put his name to ship's articles. I have my bags at my feet and a taxi outside. Goodbye, *Hughli.*

(MV Hughli (built1943) will be sold to eastern owners in 1960 and renamed *Nancy Dee.* She will be scrapped in 1971 at Kaohsiung, in Taiwan.)

The giant steam engine pants forward with a series of gasps, out from beneath the soaring, smoke-blackened, arched roof of King's Cross station. Acrid coal fumes and steam tickle my nose, so I slide the window shut. The express gathers speed, and soon the glass domes and arches of Alexandra Palace, that squat on a hill on the left-hand side, fall out of sight and London slips astern. I settle back with relief into the luxury of a Pullman seat and turn my attention to a British Rail pork pie, and the cup of tea that vibrates on the table. I open the *London Evening Standard.* The stop press for 25th July 1956 says: 'Italian ocean liner SS *Andrea Doria* badly damaged in the Atlantic after colliding with Swedish liner *Stockholm* in heavy fog 45 miles south of Nantucket Island.' That sounds nasty, but I'll be home before midnight. I reflect on the turmoil of the day; my only regret is the sadness of my Polish friend, Stefan, as we said goodbye. He was looking forward to us being shipmates for a couple of years. Perhaps we'll bump

into each other, in some port, somewhere in the future. I'll
say farewell to many friends on future ships – friends I'll
never hear of again.

Mam and Dad are astonished when the taxi pulls up and I
emerge. They make a quiet sort of fuss; they are quiet
people, but their delight is obvious. I have a supper of
fried potato and bacon followed by one dreamless night in
my childhood bed.

In the morning, Mam is worried that I'm off to sea
again. She's just heard on the wireless that the damaged
liner *Andrea Doria* has capsized and sank. While 1,660
passengers and crew were rescued and survived, 46 people
have died with the ship as a consequence of the collision. I
promise to take care, then hurry up Warren Road to
Winterbottom Avenue where I catch the red double-
decker United bus to the railway station. The bus is
crammed with working people; the only seats free are
upstairs, amongst the pipe tobacco.

I catch the diesel train north for the thirty-five mile run
to Newcastle-on-Tyne and thence by bus to North
Shields, a little way down river. At the shipping office, I
sign articles for the MV *Corburn,* presently at the coal
staithes in the river, owners Wm. Cory and Sons Ltd. She's
a 2,000-ton collier. This time I make sure to read the
articles before signing; but I need not worry, she's not
going far. *Corburn's* life is humble. She ships black and
dirty cargoes from Britain's coalfields, around the coast to
various power stations. Though my wage will not alter, I
sense I'm coming down in the world.

I find her tied up a little downriver from the massive
black timbers of the coal-loading staithes. The bridge,
engine, and all accommodation are built as one piece on
the stern, otherwise the decks are just a level run of
hatches; *Corburn* is shaped like a long-toed boot. Loading

is complete, and she prepares to sail for the Thames. The mate, a sea-burnt and stubbled little Yorkshireman, is at the top of the gangway. He looks nothing like an officer, more like a deckhand, dressed as he is in baggy trousers and home-knitted woolly guernsey.

'By gum! They've actually sent us a sparks. Skipper's biting his nails wi' worry lest we miss the tide. Pilot's due in three hours. Here, you'd best have keys to wireless room.'

Once again I must become familiar with a set of strange gear. But Marconi Company, who hires out operators like me, also provides their equipment, so it tends to be of a similar sort. All is in fair order, except for the bank of batteries that supply emergency power if the ship's generators fail. The batteries are flat, so I put them on charge. After an hour it's obvious they are not in a healthy state. I'll need to investigate as soon as I've time.

Is that an argument in the wheelhouse? I listen carefully. Voices spill through the little hatchway – the wireless room is part of the bridge structure.

'The pilot's due any minute. Where's my crew?' The voice is cultured.

'They're not yet back from the pub, Skipper.' That sounds like the mate.

'Then go and get them, Mister Beswick. Get up there and order them back! We can't sail with just you and me, a geriatric chief engineer, a cabin boy, and that shaveling sparks who's just turned up.'

An hour passes. There's no sign of the crew, nor of the mate. The pilot is pacing the wheelhouse. He keeps looking at his watch. He's a Tynesider and does not mince his words. 'That's it, Captain Hedley. Your vessel is too deep for the channel at this hour. You've missed the tide. I'll be back at 0400 local time for a dawn sailing. Let's hope you have a crew by then.' He picks up his valise and heads for the gangway. The captain vanishes into his cabin.

I've located the emergency batteries. They're housed in a long wooden box on deck outside the wireless room. I scrape the hinged lid free of layers of coal dust, and lift. The batteries are a sad sight. The electrolyte level is so low it has dropped well below the top of the lead plates. The terminals sport a yellow growth of sulphuric acid crystals. It's a mess of neglect. Part way through my cleaning of the terminals and smearing them with a coat of petroleum grease, the crew come rolling home – a straggled line of ten men, with the mate at their head. I close the battery box lid and go in search of distilled water.

In grey dawn light we clear the Tyne breakwaters and sail into the usual North Sea chop. The journey to the Thames is wet, we are deep laden with coal, and the freeboard is small. I'm used to life in the centre of a vessel and not at the stern. But, it's comfortable enough, though the pitching as she climbs the seas is unusual. *Corburn,* built at Goole, is a mere three years old, My cabin is cosy, a bunk, a settee, a desk and chair, some drawers and a hanging locker for clothes. There's a blue patterned carpet on the deck with only a few stains.

I discover the previous occupant has left me a German beer mug with a Dortmunder logo. I'd noted from the wireless log that *Corburn's* last run was to Hamburg. Perhaps he had a good time ashore. I'd heard tell of the Reeperbahn red-light district. I'm contemplating the empty glass when there's a knock and the captain enters.

'Good evening, Sparks. I hope you haven't taken to drink.'

'No, sir. There's not a drop in the cabin.'

'Glad to learn of that fact. Alcohol is Satan's broth.' He settles his tall frame onto my settee.

I nod and wonder where this might lead.

He gazes at me intently. The brown eyes are a trifle yellowed. Perhaps he's close to retirement. 'Are you a God-fearing young fellow? Do you study the Bible?'

'I've read bits of the Old Testament ... out of curiosity.' I look at the clock. 'I'm on watch in ten minutes, sir. I'd best go and warm up the gear.'

He nods, then picks up my current reading. I slip out of the cabin and leave him absorbed in *The Kraken Wakes* by John Wyndham.

After the two-hour watch, my cabin is empty. The book is on my desk and, by its side, arranged in a fan, a few religious pamphlets published by the Protestant Truth Society.

We intend to discharge the cargo at one of the huge Thames docks at East Ham. The cook has been anxious to know the approximate time we'll tie up; he has our dinner in mind. As soon as the gangway is lowered, Cook sends the cabin boy ashore with a shopping list.

Dinner is served that evening by the cabin boy, a cheeky little monkey, who stands by the hatch to the galley as the cook hands through plates of fried fish and chips. Next comes machine-sliced white bread lathered in butter. We up-end bottles of brown sauce, an essential feature of the British working-class table, and plop vinegary dollops onto our dinners. Cook observes us through the hatch. He wears a satisfied expression as we tuck in. Occasionally he scratches his extensive hairy chest, through the string vest that stretches across his abdomen. I look around at my shipmates. The captain wears a tired uniform jacket with its four gold bands, but sports grey flannel trousers beneath. The rest of us are in comfortable shore clothes: woolly jumpers, non-iron shirts, and crumpled trousers. I work on the meal: a shore-side take-away supper and HP sauce; a far cry from the cuisine of the *Dunera*. There'll be no Baked Alaska on this vessel; but, by my elbow, without a word, the cabin boy, in his rolled-up shirt sleeves, has just plonked down a steaming sponge pudding set in a puddle of fragrant, bright yellow custard.

Next day, while we discharge our load of Tyne coal, I visit the Marconi office. *Corburn's* emergency wireless room batteries are desperate for distilled water. I need at least a gallon. The spares department drags forward a timber crate that protects a glass carboy of five gallons. Excellent, but I'll need a taxi back to the docks.

The manager opens a yellow and blue packet of ten *Player's Weights,* the southern Englishman's equivalent of the *Will's Wild Woodbine* preferred by workmen in the north. 'A taxi to the docks? That's a bit of an extravagance.' Smoke from the cheap cigarette curls to the ceiling of his office. 'It's only distilled water. There's a bus stop just outside the office.'

'You expect me to squeeze a five-gallon carboy onto the bus, then lug it through the docks?'

'Why not? We did it during the war.'

I leaned on his desk. I recalled something we chanted at school: 'A pint of pure water weighs a pound and a quarter,' and paused. 'So a gallon weighs ten pounds. Five gallons is fifty pounds.' The manager nodded. 'Add to that about twenty pounds of glass and crate. Seventy pounds! That's over five stone to haul back to the ship. I'm no donkey, I refuse to do it. And anyway, the war's over.'

He closes one eye against a wisp of smoke. 'I see there's nothing amiss with your mental arithmetic.' He lifts the handset of his heavy black Bakelite phone and rotates the dial several times. I have my taxi.

We sail empty from the River Thames. The crew are steady, now they've got over their escapade in the River

Tyne. *Corburn* is bound for Barry Dock in South Wales where she will load Welsh steam coal. The summer seas are mild, so our track through the English Channel, south of the Isle of Wight, round the Lizard at the tip of Cornwall and into the Bristol Channel, is without event. There are no frills to this little coaster, there's no entertainment, no bar. Free time is spent alone in my cabin, reading or tuning for the BBC on my cheap and portable valve radio. There's little social life at sea on a collier. We meet only at mealtimes. The cuisine is basic; I have my first experience of tripe and onions simmered in milk – yuk!

For diversion, I've brought six bottles of pale ale aboard and intend to uncork a couple each day. There's enough to last the two-day trip. I come off watch somewhere parallel to the coast of Dorset to find a note on my desk from the captain: *Borrowed your beer, will replace it at Barry*. Seems he's given up evangelising to my spiritual needs and now raids my beer. I've noticed the crew don't hold him in esteem. Formerly he was master of a cable-layer and joined continents together. His would be an exacting job to hold course in all weathers in mid-Atlantic, slowly rolling out mile after mile of submarine cable into an ocean abyss two and three miles deep. Sometimes he would need to keep station so that grapnels could be lowered to hook the telegraph cable and raise it to the surface for repair. Alcohol lost him that prestigious job, so now he's master of this grubby little coal boat.

Off the port of Barry, the sea is getting up a lumpy chop. We pick up the pilot from his bouncing motor launch. I admire the agility of these harbour pilots; some of them are no longer young. To enter Barry Dock we must first pass into a sea lock and wait whilst the lock is flooded and the level rises to balance that of the enclosed dock.

I've closed down the radio station and am idling on deck to watch proceedings. We approach the lock at walking pace. Water sprays from the joints of the closed gates. The pilot rings the engine-room telegraph for full astern, so as to bring *Corburn* to a gentle halt. There's no response – perhaps a misunderstanding? We are about to ram the lock gates! I hear shouts from the wheelhouse. The pilot orders the wheel hard to port. There are woeful squeals from sisal fenders as our two-thousand tons of steel make connection with the timbers of the jetty. We come to a halt by sliding along the jetty, using its massive timbers as a brake. The upright timber supports begin to creak, groan, and then snap with dreadful cracking booms. A few sightseers on the jetty flee to safety. (Six years later I'll welcome a Welshman who joins my technical crew in the backrooms of a London TV studio. He'll recount how he picked up his toddler son that day on the jetty at Barry and ran for his life.)

The Cory collier *MV Corburn* passing Portishead
13.9.1967.
Malcolm Cranfield collection

14

Emergency

Our coal boat has wrecked the jetty at Barry Dock. New piles are needed. The ship's owners will be presented with a large bill, but at least we did not ram the lock gates. Now, that would have been costly.

Coal dust smothers the deck, the housing, and my aerials. We load coal destined for a glue factory in Plymouth. From blackened staithes, the best Welsh anthracite is poured into our holds by conveyor belt, accompanied by dreadful crashes and rumblings. But collier ships have reinforced steel hulls so as to withstand such abuse; even in the 18th century their ancestor, the wooden collier bark, was valued for its strength. Captain James Cook chose Whitby collier barks for his three voyages 1768-1776. Cook thought them ideal for the exploration and charting of Australia and the Pacific. He could run them ashore for careening and their strong hulls would not succumb to a stress akin to stranding.

By sailing time the Atlantic has brewed up a storm that will howl into the southern Irish Sea in a few hours. The harbourmaster comes aboard to advise our captain to stay in port until the storm has blown through; the pilot is aboard and he agrees, and our first mate, Mr Beswick, concurs. Captain though, is in an ebullient mood and declares he has handled much worse weather in his time and will therefore put to sea. So out we go, into a rising chop.

Seven hours later we struggle, at eight knots, to break into the Western Approaches, the sea area that begins at the lower extremity of the Irish Sea. Our speed is much reduced with the gale raging full onto the bows. The ship, with its innards crammed with coal, plunges like an enraged leviathan. I've secured my wireless room chair with a storm chain that screws from the seat's base into a socket in the deck; my chair now slides only an inch or two with each heave and pitch of the deck. I'm at the receiver listening to weather reports in Morse. I copy the storm warnings and pass them through the hatch into the wheelhouse. There are identical warnings for sea areas: Sole; Shannon; Rockall; Malin; Fastnet; and Lundy (we are in Lundy now). *Gale force 8, westerly. Increasing severe gale force 9 westerly. Storm force 10 later. Visibility half-a-mile reducing to less than 100 yards in rain.*

I cling to the equipment bench and keep the obligatory watch on the distress and calling frequency of 500 kc/s. I retune whenever a coast station issues a weather report. The eight-inch face of the bulkhead clock is marked with two red zones of three minutes each. All shipping must observe radio silence for three minutes twice an hour, at fifteen and forty-five past. Operators then listen for distress signals in the static-sparkled hush. In my voyages, I've heard SOS calls but they've always been faint and hundreds of miles away. I've not interrupted but listened soberly as ships in attendance replied with their own positions.

I lift off one headphone earpiece to listen to raised voices that spill through from the chartroom:

It's the mate. He seems to make a plea: 'Captain Hedley, we are deep laden. I'm in charge of cargo stowage and I'm saying we are at risk. We need to shelter behind Lundy Island and ride this one out.'

'Are you telling me the cargo is badly stowed, Mr Beswick?'

'No, I'm not! But I've had years on colliers and I've known the best-stowed coal to shift in seas like this. After Lundy we turn south; we'll be on a lee shore with the sea and wind on our beam, and rolling bad. I urge you to shelter behind Lundy Island. It's what coastal masters do in force 10, hereabouts.'

'Mr Mate, I'll remind you I'm not your average coastal master. I've ridden out worse in mid-Atlantic, trailing two-thousand fathoms of valuable submarine cable. Keep Lundy to port and make for open water. I'll be on my day bed. Call me, once we clear the island. Then we'll set course for Land's End.'

I experience a twinge of doubt; this is a diminutive ship, a third the size of *Hughli* and a sixth of *Dunera*, and we are solid with coal. I'll snuggle into my bunk when my watch ends; I'll be no safer, but I might feel more secure.

In breaks between squalls of rain, the cliffs of Lundy Island look vast, threatening, and black. The sea is a heaving mass of marching steel blue, with broken crests and blown skeins of white spume. There are no seabirds, except for a flock of delicate storm petrels that flit around our wake. Hardly bigger than a sparrow, these brown birds with white rumps flutter over the water with wings held up in a 'V' and with feet pattering across the waves. They seem to be picking up morsels of food. Superstitious, old-time seafarers knew them as Mother Carey's Chickens; as the souls of drowned sailors escorted by Mother Carey, the witch-wife of Davy Jones (he of the Locker). They were dreaded portents of storm. But today, I recall from my study of Arthur Mee's *Children's Encyclopaedia* that they nest in burrows on Lundy Island and will now be gathering food for their babies. They'll return to their nests in the dead of night when they're safe from marauding gulls.

I feel queasy gazing over the pitching stern; I don't care for the sight of *Corburn's* propeller lifting free of the water and thrashing the waves. I hurry back to the warmth of the wireless room; although I'm not on official watch at present, the bridge needs radio bearings off the direction finder.

The ship heels and we take a huge sea. We've altered course from west to south-west. The rollers no longer bury our bow as we pitch and plunge. Instead, the seas hit the starboard quarter and pour across the deck, many feet deep.

'Why didn't you call me?' That was the captain. 'It rolled me out of the bunk! What have you done, Mr Beswick?'

'This is the new course you ordered, sir. I thought to let you sleep while you can. There'll be no more rest for any of us.'

Another sickening, screwing pitch and roll. Water floods the deck and buries the hatches. Down below, there are foul oaths and the faint clatter of pans from the galley.

The man on the helm gives a yelp as he loses grip of the wheel. He fights to recover the course.

'This is no good, Mr Mate. This is no bloody good at all.' The captain's words are a trifle slurred. He has a job to keep his feet, but not necessarily due to the motion of the deck. He grabs hold of the compass binnacle and sways there.

'This is the course you asked for, Captain. What do you want now? Too late to get into the lee of Lundy.'

'Then keep her head into the weather. Put her back to due west. Hold her there until we sort things out!' As we lurch onto the new course I hear the captain's cabin door slam shut.

'Right, that's it.' The mate's voice has a tremble. 'Did you catch his breath, helmsman?'

'I did, Mr Beswick. Whisky! Nearly knocked me off the bloody wheel.'

'Hold her steady while I roust out the second mate.'

I look through the hatch to see Mr Beswick hurry from the wheelhouse. He shortly reappears with Jack Knaggs, the second mate, a Sunderland man with bushy eyebrows. The hefty ship's cook lumbers in behind them.

'Now, Jack, you mind the bridge. We won't be long. Come with me, Cooky; you'll be my witness.' The mate and the cook disappear.

Ten minutes later, the first mate is back. 'Right! I've taken command till we get out of this. Skipper's tucked up in his bunk and sleeping like the dead.'

The second mate's eyes bulge beneath his thick brows. 'Suppose he wakes up, comes back and starts giving daft orders?'

'He'll not be doing that.' He pulls a key from his bridge-coat pocket. 'I've locked him in his cabin – for his own safety, him being a bit potty tonight.'

'Do we put all this in the log?'

'Nowt goes in the log; though I'll leave space should things turn nasty. Remember, you're all witnesses to what's transpired.' He looks at me – my face is still framed by the hatch. 'And you too, Sparky.'

Corburn ploughs westwards. The wind climbs to severe gale force 9 (45 knots), waves are twenty foot with dense streaks of foam that lace the water. Spray lashes the wheelhouse windows.

Within the hour we are in storm force 10, followed soon by violent storm force 11 on the Beaufort Scale – a wind speed of 62knots (70mph). The edges of the wave crests are now torn into streams of foam. Our bows charge into hollows, then attempt to climb slopes of forty and fifty feet. Often we fail and simply crash through the marching seas. Sight of the deck is often lost and only the masts stand free of surging water. An oil tanker intersects our course; she will be bound for the refinery at Milford Haven. Her lights rise and fall; they disappear altogether when she slides into a trough. Likewise, we will vanish from her sight. Cook does his best, but dinner is reduced to a bowl of tinned Scotch Broth, heated after a fashion. That's followed by tinned pilchards between thick wedges of bread, to be washed down by mugs of slopping tea.

The radar scanner does its best to deliver images to the wheelhouse, though the cathode-ray-tube display is filled with confusion. The centre of the screen, and our position, is surrounded by reflections off the wave tops, a mass of white blobs known as *sea clutter*. An intermittent echo that resembles a wisp of wool can only be the west coast of Lundy Island. The range-finder indicates that Lundy is now twenty miles astern. A bearing of that 'scrap of wool' says we are heading due west. I can confirm our position by tuning the direction finder to a beacon on the South Bishop light-vessel, and two others, wide apart on the Irish coast. The three bearings intersect to form a triangle called a *cocked hat*. We are somewhere within that triangle. The smaller the *cocked hat*, the more accurate the bearings. Despite the radar churning away, the mate asks for a group of bearings every hour. It's going to be a long night. One hundred and eighty miles ahead is Cape Clear on the southern tip of Ireland, but we cannot detect it yet, the range of the radar is only forty miles and unreliable even at that distance. As night falls, the cabin boy scrambles up the bridge companion-way with mugs of cocoa and fish-paste sandwiches

At 0600, a grey, watery dawn reveals the Irish coast fine on the starboard bow. The storm has ameliorated for us; it will now be exhausting itself among the Welsh mountains. But we still have gale conditions. The first mate orders a change of course from west to southeast. We are doing a dog-leg to the tip of Cornwall. The wind is now on the starboard stern quarter. We do not pitch so much, but the motion has become a screwing roll. The captain is still locked in his cabin; he hammers on the door, shouts for tea and bacon sandwiches. They are delivered, but he's kept locked in.

By evening we are in sight of Land's End at the tip of Cornwall. To round the peninsula and steer for Plymouth will put us in the shelter of land. We are all weary and look forward to that. First though, *Corburn* must pass between the wreck-strewn, spouting reefs of the Scilly Isles and the growling granite cliffs of Land's End. All looks well; men are smiling again, but as we come abreast of Land's End, the engine stops.

The comforting thump-de-thump of our Doxford diesel no longer throbs through the steel bulkheads and deck. We are left with the howl of the wind in the halyards and stays, and the crash and hiss of waves on the hull. In the wheelhouse, just as the mate grasps the hand-cranked telephone, it gives a harsh ring.

The mate answers, 'Bridge.' A pause. 'How long?' A pause. 'We've no helm, and we're two mile off shore. Be as sharp as you can.'

Ten minutes drag by, during which we are without steering. We are broadside on to huge seas and *Corburn* leans as if she cowers with fright from the ocean. I clamber along the alleyway into the wheelhouse. I stand alongside the mate and peer through the spray-lashed windows. Little is to be seen of the deck except for two masts. All is surging sea water as wave after wave rolls over the bulwarks. The able-seaman on the wheel attempts to put the ship's head into the weather, but there's no response from the rudder.

The mate cranks the handle of the phone to the engine-room and shouts above the noise of the wind, 'I need to know how long till we have engines.' I note his knuckles are white. 'I'm broadside on. I've no steering.' His stubbled face is gaunt with fatigue. 'Well, let me know as soon as you can. I don't like the look of this.'

In my mind, I'm composing my first distress signal. To have to key out SOS is not something I've considered before today. The mate staggers to the port window and peers into the gloom. On the next roll, he slides back and grabs the compass binnacle. 'Sparks, you'd best warm up your transmitter. This is bad.'

I can see the dark profile of the Cornish cliffs on the port side, just as well as the mate. They seem to be closer, but between them and us rides a line of surf surmounted by a light. 'What's that?' I point to the lighthouse that gives a long five-second flash every ten seconds.

'That's the Longships, a line of reefs and islets a mile off shore. Power up that transmitter.'

By the wheelhouse door, I turn. 'If it's to be the SOS distress signal, the coast station will want our position and situation. If it's less serious, the next one down is XXX, the urgency signal. If it's to be that, they'll still want the info.'

'Not SOS. We're not in distress yet. Does no good to alarm the owners without good reason, Sparks. The urgency signal will do for now, so warm up the gear while I write out the details.'

Back in the wireless room, I have the Marconi *Oceanspan* transmitter tuned to the distress frequency of 500 kc/s. The *Mercury* main receiver glows alongside its little partner, the fixed-tuned *Alert*. Both are tuned to 500 kc/s.

The mate's face is at the hatch. 'Sparks, you'd best send the Urgency message. Here it is.' He tosses through a scribbled note for me to convert into a signal.

The deck shudders from breaking seas and leans at an uncomfortable angle as I key: 'XXX XXX XXX DE GQMF GQMF GQMF MV CORBURN. BARRY FOR PLYMOUTH. HALF MILE WEST OF LONGSHIPS REEF. ENGINE FAILURE. NO STEERING. SEVERE GALE. REQUEST VESSEL TO STANDBY.' I repeat the message three times and then listen for response.

Land's End Radio station gives immediate reply: 'GQMF GQMF GQMF DE GLD GLD GLD QSL WILL PROMULGATE TO ALERT ALL SHIPS. ADVISE IF SITUATION CHANGES.'

I acknowledge receipt: 'GLD DE GQMF QSL TU'

Land's End Radio is close to the location from which the first transatlantic radio transmission was made in 1901 by a young Italian named Marconi. The Longships reefs we are being pushed towards are unyielding islets of igneous rock, three of them growl at us now: Tal-y-Maen, Carn Bras (on which stands the lighthouse) and Meinek. Legend has it they are fragments of King Arthur's drowned kingdom of Lyonesse. But these are small matters compared to our predicament.

Fifteen minutes pass. The cook lumbers into the wheelhouse with mugs of steaming cocoa. I detect the tang of added whisky. 'Thought you might be needing this.' He stares through the port window at the spouting reef and grunts, 'Bloody Nora.'

The mate cranks the telephone. 'Any joy?' He shouts. Then, 'Don't take that tone with me! I need to know how long!'

There's a tonk-tonk noise and a slight vibration through the arms of my chair, then silence. And again, tonk-tonk. Then tonk-tonk-tonk. It throbs beneath my feet, and the note holds. Ah … the comforting beat of pistons and crankshafts. My spirits lift in harmony. I briefly wonder how the captain is taking all this; locked in his cabin.

The mate gives a whoop. 'We've got steering! Helm, due west. Quick about it. Let's clear off out of here.'

Once around the headland of the Lizard Peninsula, we find milder seas in the shelter of Cornwall. The mate unlocks the captain's door and he emerges as though nothing out of the ordinary has transpired. He paces up and down the wheelhouse, then strides into the chartroom. After inspecting the charts and asserting his authority he stoops his way into the wireless room – he's a tall man – and proffers a message to be sent to the address of a lady in Plymouth.

He leans over me as I transcribe the message onto a telegraph form. It reads: *Plymouth tonight. Hiring car this visit. Hedley.* He taps the side of his nose, confidentially and says, 'That's in the form of a code. It means I want to spend a few hours with her, this time around.'

I count the words and tell him the cost. The telegram is routed through Land's End Radio.

Plymouth harbour opens up before us. The salt-stained *Corburn* chugs discreetly past Royal Navy frigates and submarines to her berth alongside the glue factory. We tie-up next to a coal elevator and soon wrinkle our noses. The stink comes from a twenty-foot tall hill of bones, some with shreds of shrivelled flesh still clinging on. The bones are ultimately destined for the glue works. Meanwhile, rats scamper over and through the hillock; some pursued by feral cats. At least we are out of the weather, tied up and safe. The cook sends the cabin boy ashore for fish and chips for our dinner; the galley is a mess after that passage.

I'm storm-weary and not interested in going ashore tonight. Most of the crew appear to be in sympathy, except for the captain who strides down the gangway in his best shore-side suit. I climb into my bunk with a book and soon doze off to sleep.

I might have slept a couple of hours when I wake to women's shrieks, excited laughter and the sound of high heels running along the corridors of our accommodation. The voices of a couple of our deck-hands come and go among the giggles. It sounds like a party is underway.

Then the shout of the first mate: 'What the hell's going on! What are all these tarts doing aboard?'

I hear the cook: 'They've come from that pub by the dock gate. Captain's holding court up there. He's told the tarts to get themselves aboard for a party. Says he'll be along later.'

'There'll be no party tonight.' The mate, though a lean man without much weight, knows how to bellow. 'Get off this ship now, before I call the police!'

With oohs and ahhs, and tripping heels, the floozies abandon the *Corburn* in favour of the pub by the dock gate.

At breakfast, the next morning, the captain is absent; at least until the brazen cabin-boy, who serves at table, shouts up the stairs, 'Hey, Skipper, do you want your bloody breakfast, or not?'

There's nothing said by the officers at the table or by the cook at the galley hatch who watches everything. How can this behaviour come about in a ship's crew? I have my eye on the mate. He glares as the ship's master descends the stairs to join us at breakfast. The captain looks liverish but manages cereal and milk. A fried breakfast is set before him as soon as the last cornflake goes.

The mate glowers at the captain, who shows signs of hangover and does not tuck into his bacon, egg, and black pudding like the rest of us. The mate pushes back his chair and stands; his knuckles dig into the chequered oilcloth table cover. 'Captain! Last night was a disgrace. You filled this vessel with Plymouth prostitutes. I'm not having it. And I doubt the owners will be much impressed when they learn of it.'

'Oh, don't go on so, Mr Beswick, can't you see I've got a bad head? The owners need not know. It won't happen again.'

'You are right about one thing, Skipper – it won't happen again. There's going to be a sign displayed at the foot of the gangway. It'll say: *No women allowed aboard this ship.*'

The captain gazes at his congealed fried egg and gives a weak nod. But the mate has not finished: 'I want it done straight after breakfast and, Skipper, you are going to paint the sign, and you will set it up.'

15

Hull

Six days later, as soon as *Corburn* clears harbour at 1800hrs, I open the station by informing Land's End Radio that we have departed Plymouth, empty ship, bound for Hull where we should arrive in a day and a half. Captain Hedley must have heard the rattle of the Morse key, for he enters the wireless room and hands me the draft of a telegram. It's to his bank, with instruction to cancel a cheque made out to a professional lady of Plymouth just this morning.

'Get that off straight away, Sparks.' He taps his nose. 'The *car hire* wasn't worth the fee. She won't be pleased, but not to worry.'

I'm astonished at his recovery. It's as though our violent passage from Barry, and our near wreck on the Longships reef, and him all the while locked in his cabin on the mate's orders, never took place. I shudder when I think of what might have happened if the engines had not recovered; we would now be broken corpses strewn among the rocks.

I hear him in the chart-room holding forth on the most economical speed and route up the English Channel; how far to stand off shore to best benefit from the three-knot tide that sweeps in from the Atlantic at this hour, and how that tide should transform our cruising speed from eleven knots to fourteen. How the fuel saved will impress the owners.

The mate has resumed a respectful tone and addresses the captain as *sir*. I'm pleased to overhear this effort to restore the man's dignity. While my sea time amounts to a mere seven months, I already appreciate the need for discipline and how vital to safety is respect for the structure of command aboard ship. I feel more secure now the regime has recovered a semblance of sanity.

The August sun dips astern. We enjoy smooth seas that undulate with a hint of swell, and clear evening skies, as we romp along with our keel riding the tide. As I come off watch, the Jurassic limestone headland of Portland Bill is a mile away on the port side and close enough to discern the quarries that provided the stone for Buckingham Palace and St Paul's Cathedral. The same deathly white stone made the vast number of headstones that mark the graves of our soldiers who fell in Belgium and France between 1914 and 1918.

I sleep well this night, with no sudden bell to shriek at my ear just a few inches away. I've adjusted the sensitivity of the Auto Alarm so that it's not activated by distress calls a thousand miles distant. Now we are in the English Channel, the world's busiest shipping lane, it can be set for a couple of hundred miles only.

On watch at 0800, I see we are abreast of the dramatic chalk cliffs of Beachy Head (despite the name, there's no beach here, it's from the French: *beau chef – beautiful headland*). From those fierce white cliffs, in 1895, the ashes of the German, Friedrich Engels, one of the fathers of communism, were scattered into the sea. My reading of history has aligned me with that thinker's ideals and I consider myself a communist; if I'm anything at all.

At midday, we approach Folkestone in bright sunshine. Even at two miles, the telescope shows the sandy beach of that holiday resort crowded with swimmers and sunbathers. The captain is animated by what he spies on the shore and orders the helmsman to steer closer so that he can get a better telescope image of the girls. I shudder to think of the mate's reaction. It's as well he's in his cabin tussling with the *Daily Telegraph* crossword. He's told us the news that the Egyptian dictator, Colonel Nasser, has seized the Suez Canal. He reckons there'll be trouble.

It's a pleasant afternoon as we pass the entrance to Dover harbour, that busy terminus for cross-channel ferries to France and Belgium. It's the mate's watch. The sea is flat calm as we chug past the breakwaters and across the shipping lane for the ferries.

Precisely in the centre of the navigation channel, *Corburn's* engines fail. We have no forward motion, and hence no steering. We are adrift again, but this time will not be hurled onto a reef. Instead, after frantic exchanges with the engine-room, we drop anchor in calm, shallow water.

The anchor chains have hardly stopped rattling when there's a blast from a ship's whistle. A ferry from Calais is bearing down on us. It blasts again. The mate comes close to screaming: 'Hoist the black ball! Hoist the black ball!'

Two deckhands frantically rig a pair of crossed black discs to the halyard and raise them to the masthead. 'Now the F flag; and the M flag. Hoist them!'

Minutes pass while the sailors rummage in the flag locker and bend flags to a halyard. A white flag with a red diamond is followed up the mast by a blue flag with a white St Andrews cross. The signal reads: *I am disabled and anchored.* I switch on the transmitter; this might be my second urgency signal.

The captain rushes into the wheelhouse. 'What the blazes is going on? Look at those ferries! They're stacked up like London buses.'

I think he exaggerates; there's only one ferry waiting to enter Dover and I see it's already laid out an anchor. But, ah – there's another in the distance, steaming this way. In the harbour interior, something moves above the shed roofs – the funnel of a ferry preparing to leave. The funnel slows and stops. This is embarrassing.

'How long?' That's the captain to the engine-room. 'I'll ask you again. How long? If we don't shift soon, we'll be hauled away by a tug.'

Minutes tick by. The distant ferry from Dunkirk is closer. Soon, he will also need to anchor. But the quiet rhythmic slap of small waves against the hull is broken by a sudden tonk-tonk noise from below. And again, and twice more, and then a shudder as the engine comes to life. There's a pause as the crew listens to the rising note of the engine. We hold our breath until the vibrations settle into the proper rhythm. The captain slaps his hands together. 'Hey ho! Such jolly times we have. Weigh anchor! Let's be off.'

Next day, as we approach the estuary of the River Humber, I make up my mind. I've been thinking about my career. I've concluded, since that unfortunate encounter in Singapore with a shipmate's bottle of VAT 69 whisky, it is in poor shape. Since I discharged from the fine troopship *Dunera,* I've been Shanghaied onto a Jimmy Nourse tramp and had to threaten my way free of two years on her, only to find I'm aboard this crazy coal boat trundling around the *Holy Ghost* (I've picked up seaman's slang for the UK Coast). How long will it go on? I'll put a stop to it.

It's 1600 hours when we tie up at the coal staithes of Hull. I hurry ashore to find a telephone box. Everywhere in Britain the phone boxes are GPO red, but in Hull they are white – the GPO has never had charge of telephones here. I ring South Shields Merchant Navy College, where I studied for my 2nd Class PMG. I'm overjoyed to learn I'll be accepted onto the three-month course in ships' radar maintenance. It starts in two weeks' time. Hurrah!

This news deserves a night out. I stride ashore with a couple of the crew. The pubs are brightly lit and noisy with salty revellers. Hull is packed with cargo steamers of many flags, and the fish docks bristle with the masts of trawlers landing cod from the seas around Iceland. Money pours into the tills of grinning publicans. We happily push our florins and half-crowns across wet and slippery mahogany tops in exchange for bitter beer and pork pies. The spiced-earth smell of hops does so readily bring on thirst and appetite.

After an ale or two in *The Duke of Wellington* and a couple more in *The Empress*, we head down a side street for *The Paragon*, and then to *Polly's*. Apparently, *Polly's* is the place to be. There's a painted image of an Amazon Green parrot on the pub sign outside the entrance. It stands opposite the *Tivoli* theatre where Arthur Lucan died backstage just two years ago. Lucan, dressed as a woman, played Old Mother Riley in uproarious music hall, radio, and film as far back as 1934.

At first, it's impossible to force a way into *Polly's*. The doorway is blocked by a swaying circle of men and women, gathered beneath the parrot. There's heaving and pushing as the fist-fight at the centre comes and goes. Two policemen arrive, whereupon the crowd rushes into the pub. Now we can see the combatants. One is sprawled on the stone flags of the pavement and the other stoops to help him to his feet. The police are asking for names.

The lanky black man now has his opponent upright and supports him with an arm. He addresses the police with a rich American, Southern States accent. 'We want no trouble with ya'll. This guy is ma best buddy.'

A helpful bystander points to a few teeth on the pavement. The lanky man collects them up, carefully puts them in his friend's coat pocket, and turns to the police. 'I'll get these teeth put back in ma friend's head. Now, suhs, if you don't mind, we'll quietly amble back to ar ship.'

In the morning, after a foaming glass of Andrew's Liver Salts that pricks the nose and restores the will to live, followed by tomato juice, and a helping of porridge, I set off for the local office of my employer, *The Marconi International Marine Company*.

The waiting room is full. I detect the fruity odour of *Fair Maid* pipe tobacco. There are about a dozen men seated, in navy macs (it's swishing down with rain today), and a couple standing. I look around at the faces, young and mature. These are men from tankers, deep-sea cargo tramps, coasters, whaling ships and big trawlers; no fancy passenger liners call at the port of Hull. Scraps of slow conversation drift about in thin tobacco fug. I detect a general air of disaffection.

A wooden loudspeaker hangs below the ceiling. It begins to tweet out a British ship's call sign. One man knocks the dottle out of his pipe and leaves the room. Ten minutes later, another burst of Morse, and a man rises.

The conversation wanders. 'Who are you with?'

'Hogarth's of Glasgow.'

'Ah, Hungry Hogarth's. That's a bugger.'

'And you?'

'Harrison's, out of Liverpool'

'Baron Boats! Why, man, that's just as bad. *Two of fat and one of lean.*' There are wry grins and laughs. The reference to the red and white bands on Harrison funnels is well understood.

A chap removes his pipe and begins to croon a parody of Harry Belafonte's latest calypso:

Brown skin girl stay home and mind de baybee
Brown skin girl stay home and mind de baybee
I sail away on de Harrison boat
And if I don't come back
Den you can mind de baybee

Another takes up the refrain but is interrupted by a burst of tinny Morse. Men look around, but nobody rises. Five minutes go by. We read our newspapers; some chaps pencil around the names of horses that will run this afternoon. The loudspeaker comes to life with the same call sign: GTYD. It is keyed very slow, in a fashion we recognise as heavy sarcasm. 'Oh, deary, deary me,' someone mutters. Nobody moves. The call sign beats out again, GTYD, over and over again, fast and furious this time.

After a while, the door opens and the office manager's moustached face peeps in. 'Is *Baron Douglas* here?' There's no response. 'Is Mr Elliot in the room?'

The Harrison man folds his newspaper. 'He is.'

The manager sniffs. 'Can't you recognise your own ship's call sign?'

'I certainly can. And I can key it better than thee does. But, I do have a name. If you want to see me, use the name I had when I joined this bloody outfit.'

After that, there is no more work for the loudspeaker. The manager opens the door and politely asks for each of us by name.

At his desk, he passes a hand over his face. 'September starts tomorrow and I don't know what we're going to do, I've had five resignations already this week.'

He slouches and looks as though he's short of sleep. I begin to feel sympathy for him.

He straightens his back and blinks once or twice. 'So, you intend to resign, Mr Nicholson. Why is that?'

'I'm going back to college to study for the Radar Maintenance ticket.'

'That is commendable. I hope you are successful and I hope you return to Marconi's. We tend to place radar tickets on quality vessels, such as passenger liners that carry Marconi radar.'

'*Corburn* is here to load coal. She'll sail in five days. I won't be on her.'

'I know that. I'm informed you are due paid leave; fifteen days, including those earned by Sundays at sea. There's no point in you staying aboard. We'll get you signed off tomorrow. Your present employment expires at the end of your leave. I hope you come back to us.'

We shake hands, and I walk out with a spring in my step.

(*MV Corburn* was sold to Greek owners in 1972. She was renamed *Aigeorgis* under the Cypriot flag. Scrapped at Brindisi, Italy, in 1979.)

I alight from the red double-decker bus in Winterbottom Avenue, close to the end of a row of prefabs, and sniff the air. There's a temperature inversion over Hartlepool today. The magnesium plant, the Palliser Works, built long and thin, parallel to the sea, on the dunes of Spion Kop, has dropped another of its periodic coverings of white magnesium dust across the council house roofs. As though that were not enough, it has exhaled a colourless vapour; Warren Road reeks of bad eggs. But it is my home, where I was reared, and where my parents live.

As I open the garden gate I notice the dust-blighted privet hedge is in need of a trim. Dad usually keeps it tightly manicured. He grew it from cuttings during the war. He has it topiarised to rise and fall, so as to follow the fancy waved construction of the fence. There's a bit of damage where the local mischiefs have sprawled on it.

Mam fusses around me with tea, and her baking: my favourite, a cake made from ground rice; and curd tarts. My dog, Peter, is looking older, he's got a grey cast to his face, but he's enthused and dances around and around with excitement. Dad is quieter, but he's a quiet man anyway, a touch sombre, the Great War left its mark.

'How will you fare for money, Son – now you've resigned? And can you be sure you'll get your job back?'

'I'll sign on the dole, Dad. The Labour Exchange allows seamen at marine college to claim unemployment benefit. Durham County Council will give me a grant towards travel expenses and suchlike. It's only for three months, and then I'll be back at sea.'

'Isn't it a bit soon? You've only been with Marconi eight months.'

'True enough, Dad. But if I hadn't got off that *Hughli* tramp when I did, you wouldn't have seen me for two years.'

Mam butts in, 'You did right, Son. Two years is too long to be away from home. You'll not know your dad's got angina and a poorly heart. He's had time off work – on the *Sick*. Doctor Gall says she can't give him tablets for his heart because of the angina.'

I look at my dad. Apart from a pink flush about the cheeks, there's a general greyness to his complexion. His pale blue eyes seem more tired than usual. 'How's the job at the yards?'

'It's not taxing me much, though it's a bit of a trail – catching buses to Haverton Hill. There's no riveting to

171

speak of these days, so I'm labouring. I'm a plater's helper. The gang won't let me do much, except fetch and carry, and keep them supplied with tea.'

Daily diesel-train journeys, rattling up and down the coastal route from West Hartlepool to South Shields, are my lot while three months of college roll by. I'm interested in world affairs, so buy the Daily Telegraph each day. Britain, France, and Israel have invaded Egypt to recover the Suez Canal from Nasser and reopen the Straits of Tiran. The British then withdraw with the mission half-accomplished when U.S. President Eisenhower threatens damage to Britain's financial system by selling the US government's holding of Sterling Bonds. The French have no option but to also pull out. (Israel hangs on for a while longer, into 1957, taking time to wreck the infrastructure of Sinai and appropriate useful Egyptian railway equipment.) Meanwhile, Soviet tanks stream into Hungary to crush a popular uprising, and thousands flee to the West.

The radar course at Merchant Navy College is a relaxed affair. There are about twenty of us; all men with sea experience and stories to tell. I become good friends with Brian Marsden, who is on a break from Alfred Holt's Blue Funnel Line. Brian hails from Hexham, further up the River Tyne. He is short and lightly built and is unable to function without his thick-lensed spectacles. He's highly intelligent, with a great sense of comedy. I cannot know how much he will later influence my life, how he will encourage me to enter TV studios when I leave the sea in four years' time, and how I'll mourn when he dies young.

We train on the *Marconi 268*, a radar system built during the war for ship navigation, with priority for submarine detection. It has devices new to us: a cathode-ray tube (pressure on the display face is three-quarters of a ton – so take care!); a heavy resonant cavity magnetron for generating the microwave power pulse; waveguides to carry pulses in and out of the system; racks of unusual valves; strange hydrogen-filled, iron-wire, glass devices called barretters, that regulate valve heater current; and a carbon-pile voltage regulator with a hand-adjusted control to, ever-so-gently, compress a column of carbon granules. This is new technology developed at a frantic war-time rate in great secrecy.

The British magnetron, developed in 1940 by John Randall and 'Harry' Boot at Birmingham University, delivered a microwave pulse one thousand times more powerful than anything possessed by Germany or the USA. It enhanced radar accuracy enough to locate the raised periscope of a submerged U-boat. Winston Churchill agreed that Magnetron Number 12 be shipped, along with other British inventions, across the Atlantic with the *Tizard Mission* in anticipation of American technical help with the war. A USA historian, James Phinney Baxter III, will describe that event: *When the members of the Tizard Mission brought one cavity magnetron to America in 1940, they carried the most valuable cargo ever brought to our shores.*

It defeated the Axis Powers and will give rise to a multiplicity of technologies that range from the mapping of the Solar System down to the humble microwave oven that cooks our convenience dinners.

It's all new and complex, but what we learn will transform us from ship's radio operators and maintenance technicians, into engineers of electronics who will be sought after by wholly new industries about to emerge from the weary 1950s.

The main lecturer is a tall, grey-haired Scot, with a sense of humour in contrast to his demeanour of dignity. He has a crude, monochrome television set in the lecture room.

Before 2 pm every afternoon, he switches it on so that it warms up in time for *Watch with Mother*, a BBC children's television series. He instructs us to close our notebooks for ten minutes while we watch a string puppet programme called *The Flower Pot Men*. The action is set in a garden, at the rear of a potting shed with windows as watchful eyes. Bill and Ben are two mischievous flower pots who come to life, grow arms, legs, and heads, and animate whenever the gardener goes off for his tea. The third character is Little Weed, a sort of miniature sunflower, possessed of a smiling face, that grows between the two flowerpots. On some days they are visited by Slowcoach the Tortoise, and an obscure being constructed of potatoes known as Dan the Potato Man. One or other of the flower-pots is always naughty. The lady narrator, in a quivering soprano, trills: *Which of those two flower pot men did it? Was it Bill or was it Ben?* In sooty black and white, the culprit owns up; the gardener's footfalls crunch on the gravel path; the Flower Pot Men metamorphose into normal clay pots and the blurred credits wobble up the screen. The lady narrator flutes: *And I think the little house knew something about it! Don't you, children?*

The Flower Pot Men gurgle out a version of English called Oddle Poddle, created by Peter Hawkins (who will go on to voice the Daleks and Captain Pugwash). At the close of each episode, they say: *Bye-bye, Bill* and *Bye-bye, Ben,* and *Bye-bye, Little Weed* – *Babap ickle, Weed* – and Weed responds with a wavering *Wee-eee-eed.* It's catching – some of the chaps begin to talk like that.

As far as I can tell, none of this illuminates the mysteries of the magnetron – but you never know . . .

16

The Dance

The long autumn ashore brings enough weekends to renew friendships. On Saturday nights I'm out with my non-seagoing pals, Harvey Blogg and Peter Hicks. We tour the pubs according to which landlord serves good beer. If the quality of a cellar goes sour, or dilution is suspected, the drinkers soon put the word out and that pub is abandoned for a fortnight or two.

The publican in charge of the Volunteer Arms in West Hartlepool's Church Street understands the beer enthusiast's palate and keeps a constant cellar, and here is where we complete our tour of the hostelries. We dive through the door, beneath the suspended sign of a red-coated militia musketman, to sample a beer brewed but a mile away. Four pints of Cameron's *Strongarm*, on top of the weaker Nimmo's ale we've sampled elsewhere, is usually sufficient for any one of our band of teen-aged hearties. We have taken the precaution to lay all that on top of a newspaper-wrapped supper of fried fish in crispy batter, and a portion of chips doused in malt vinegar and salt; a good lining for a Saturday night stomach.

Fingers licked, though still greasy from eating in the street, we settle with foaming glasses of a harsh beer brewed to slake the thirst of local steel-workers and listen to the yarns of pipe-smoking old men who've seen it all.

Amid the reek of Condor and Battleaxe Bar, our outbursts of teen-aged boast and blather are tolerated so long as we keep a rein on them.

Conversation and ribald stories fade when a Salvation Army girl enters the bar. Resplendent in her red-trimmed black uniform and black straw bonnet with blood-red sash, she bears a sheaf of the Salvation Army newspaper, *The War Cry*.

She makes her way around the tables. Men smooth their hair. Her sweet, low voice: '*War Cry*. Who will support the *War Cry*?' melts my heart. Most of the drinkers feed a few pennies through the slot of her collecting tin, a few even drop in a silver sixpence – a sum that would buy half a pint of best beer – for the girl is so pretty and demure. We try to keep our newspapers virginal and innocent of beer stains. It's reckoned to be the mark of a good night out, to fall through the door of home clutching the *War Cry,* but I do wonder how many copies are read. My parents will read it straight through, they have relatives who wear the uniform.

All is dignified while this lovely girl attends each table. The clack of dominoes dies away as strong men become lambs beneath her mild blue eyes. We all feel blessed and renewed by her visit. Though, a few minutes after she leaves, some wag strikes up a parody of a Salvation Army hymn:

I don't care if it rains or freezes,
I am safe in the arms of Jesus.
I am Jesus' little lamb,
Yes, by Jesus Christ I am.
Jesus wants me for a sunbeam,
And a bloody fine sunbeam I'll be.

The landlord bellows through the door, 'You can stop that, now! There'll be no bad language on my premises. And this pub has no license for musical entertainment; not that yours is musical.'

Well-fortified, we stride beneath the streetlamps, through the drizzle, and make for the Queen's Rink, a huge modern dance-hall about a mile distant.

Harvey raises the collar of his mackintosh against the nip from the east. He walks with a long-legged stride. 'Well, hinnies, the beer was half-decent the neet.' He speaks with a slow variant of Pitmatic, the lilting dialect of the Durham Coalfield. Harvey is an apprentice electrician at Horden Pit.

Peter responds in the guttural, flat vowelled Hartlepool he shares with me, 'And that Sally Army lass fair frothed up the head on me pint. She's a toothsome wench.' Peter has a way with words.

I fasten the two top buttons of my navy bridge coat and duck my head; we sport no hats to fend off the rain – hats are for the old folk. 'She's a bobby-dazzler! After seeing her, I've half a mind to take the uniform meself.'

We mount the steps of the Rink with a studied upright and sober demeanour. At any sign of being the worse for drink, the giant dinner-jacketed bouncer on the door will deny entry. There are others, in front and behind: lads from the Headland; from Seaton Carew; and from the Durham coalfield. All breathe out the bitter vapour of hops but contrive facial expressions that imply butter would not melt in their mouths.

The girls will have checked in a couple of hours ago and will be foxtrotting around the floor, led by the elegant legs and arms of a few decent young men who have not been to the pub. I glance around the cavernous dance hall. The girls who throng the walls, in knots two and three deep, appear to grade themselves: well-brought-up at one end, and a less polished sort towards the other. Girls are dancing together, taking turns to lead, there not being enough fellows to go around.

Pretty heads turn above pretty frocks and glance our way as we cram through the doors, our hair carefully combed into a *Brylcreemed* DA style (the duck's arse) and resplendent in our Chicago gangster-inspired draped jackets, Edwardian style drain-pipe trousers, white shirts and slim-Jim ties. The essential comb peeps from each breast pocket.

Some lasses will soon be asked for their first dance of the evening. Perhaps each will meet a new boy; perhaps a boy who will not squash her toes beneath thick crepe-soled creepers. Some might never be asked and will bravely dance the evening through with their friends, pretending not to care. Even so, I know I'll be turned down a few times, and I'll hear little sniggers as I walk away (I'll tell myself: The daft ha'porths don't know what they're missing). I don't blush so much these days, and Cameron's bitter brings on the Dutch courage, so I'm not too bothered.

Mary spots me as I squeeze through the door with the mob. I see her blond hair weave through the crowd and know I'll be straight onto the floor. Mary is not often at the Rink, she favours the Borough Hall on Hartlepool Headland, where I first met her. She's thin-faced, short and sinewy, but bolder than most, and I think she *has her eye on me.* The big band, clarinets, saxophones, drums, trumpets, and double-base, strikes up a quickstep. Mary pulls me into the midst of the circulating crowd of dancers that rotates clockwise around the hall. Her hands are sandpaper-rough; she's a tough little lass, a rivet catcher in the shipyard. Her job is to catch white-hot rivets thrown by the heater-women. She catches them in a bucket and throws them up to the lass on the next platform, who will throw them higher. The rivets must arrive in the rivetter's tongs while still glowing enough to be hammered through holes in the hull plates of the new ship, to be flattened by his mate on the other side. It's no wonder she has rough hands. I dance along and think about all the cream Mary must rub into those damaged palms before she ventures out on Saturday nights. She is not the ideal I seek, but I hope she will find her dream.

I manage the quickstep well enough to make horizontal progress, but Mary prefers to dance close and our quickstep soon degenerates into something akin to a waltz. She has her head on my chest and softly croons a few lines from this year's big hit by Jim Lowe, *Green Door*:

Midnight, one more night without sleeping,
Watching, till the morning comes creeping,
Green door, what's that secret you're keeping?
There's an old piano and they play it hot behind the green door.
Don't know what they're doing, but they laugh a lot behind the green door.
Wish they'd let me in so I could find out what's behind the green door.

As we drift, the tall form of Harvey navigates alongside. His long arms are wrapped around a swan-necked blond (the colour might be out of a bottle). She has a superior air. He winks and gives me the thumbs-up. The lights are dimmed as the music moves to waltz time. A spotlight fires up, to target the slowly spinning ball suspended from the ceiling. Hundreds of glass facets come to life and throw multi-coloured diamond glints among the dancers, around the walls, across our faces. It's magical.

Afterwards, I untangle my dreamy catcher-lass and escort her back to the friend who guards her handbag. I thank Mary, then climb the stairs to the balcony where there is a coffee bar. I join my friend, Peter Hicks, to sip milky coffee and peer down at the dancers below. Peter doesn't favour the DA hairstyle, he sports a crew-cut of the flat-top variety (his hair sticks up like a short brush) he reckons is the latest thing in America. He's wearing his blue-suede shoes, inspired by the rock-and-roll song of the same name. He bought them as brown suede, but coated them in blue shoe polish; the effect works well enough, though I suspect the suede might be a bit sticky.

From our eyrie we scan the girls seated and standing around the walls below. I notice a brown-haired girl laughing with her pale, fair-haired friend. I memorise her position and the autumn red of her dress. The bandleader announces the waltz. I head for the stairs with a slight fear of humiliation. I find her in the crowd and she seems pleased to take my arm. She's an accomplished dancer and light on her feet. I tread on her toes a few times and make apologies. Her name is Beryl Scott; she works in the office at Pounder's Plumbers and Electricians in Stockton Street. She seems sweet and lively – vivacious even. Her happy blue eyes dance in an oval face. I ask if I might have another dance later.

There are shouts from the balcony. An argument? Someone crashes to the dance floor. The band plays on. Despite falling twelve feet and among the dancers, man and fox-trotters appear unhurt. The dinner-jacketed bouncers soon have him by the arms and throw him into the street, unaware that the poor chap has a dislocated shoulder. It's all happening tonight. Things are warming up. In fact, some armpits could do with a dab of talcum powder. I give my own a surreptitious sniff, just to make sure.

I dance with Maggy, a lean girl, tall and above my height. She stoops a little, I assume in an effort to be shorter. Maggy sometimes hovers around the Regal

Cinema, which is on my walk from the bus to the railway station when I'm travelling to college. Then we walk together as far as the station. She has just become a clippy (a conductress) on the buses, so sometimes I travel free. We brave the centre of the floor where the jivers and rock-and-rollers madly flock together whilst the effusive tango dancers make the long orbit around the walls. I like the lass, she is sweet, but she's a couple of inches taller than my five-foot-ten-and-a-half, and I feel odd about that. I guide her through the jive. She reckons she's clumsy but is soon laughing. I remember how she once invited me to her home when her parents were out. It was a simple house in the long Victorian terrace of Belk Street. She wore a pinafore apron over her frock and had been baking. We sat for a long time before the blazing coal fire. She never took her pinny off.

It's strange how shy I am with English girls; after my adventures in Japan I'd assumed I'd be bolder with them. But I'm not. Essentially, they remain a mystery. One attitude I've acquired by mixing with ship's officers is to treat all females as ladies no matter what their background.

Though I'm shorter than Maggy, I can look down on one fellow who is sometimes seen here. He's a dapper little man, with a quiet and calm manner. He tours the hall in evening suit accompanied by a powerful bouncer on either side. When these three evening suits approach, the crowd divides like the Red Sea before Moses.

I also move aside since I discovered the man's name. A few weeks ago, I was with my pals in the gents' toilets. At the wash basins, things became boisterous and water was splashed around. The trio of evening suits soon appeared and the little man ordered silence. I took a step forward in protest, thinking not to take instruction from this small person. A friend grabbed me and pulled me away, with apologies to the evening suit. Once outside the toilets, my friend stood me against the wall:

'You daft bugger,' he hissed. 'Don't you know who it is you were about to have a go at?'

'You mean that little squirt?'

'Him you call a little squirt is Teddy Gardner. He boxed flyweight and bantamweight for Britain, and he held both the European and the British Empire titles. A Lonsdale Belt holder. That's who he is!'

'Oh,' I mumbled. 'Right.'

The next set of three dances are fast. I've found Beryl again, and we quickstep. I manage reasonably well, with simple, long gliding steps, but I give up when the rumba is called, and persuade this pleasant lass to escape to the centre of the floor and join the mob of jivers. I've become pleased with my prowess here. I once paid for dance classes where a serene lady and her polished husband taught awkward post-pubescents the basics. To the hiss and scrape of a gramophone, we fumbled our way through the black-bottom, the boogie-woogie, jitterbug and jive.

Now I'm in the middle of the wild lot in the Queen's Rink and all those painfully tutored steps have mongrelised into the wild abandon that's become rock-and-roll. We step back, step forward, let the feet stamp fast and rhythmic, sway and turn, and attempt moves known as the teapot stir, the windmill, the catapult, and the yo-yo, according to whatever fits the tempo of the band. I hope the carefully combed, wispy curl of the *elephant's trunk* at the front of my DA is making suitable nods as my feet move in what I fancy to be a blur. I make errors, don't signal the next move, and we end up in a tangle of arms. But it's great. She laughs, and I like the way her skirt flares out as she spins.

The musicians are due a break soon, so we beat the crowd and dash upstairs to the coffee bar where we can talk. It's the first time I've bought a girl coffee at the dance. Perhaps I'm interested; she's different to the run-of-the-mill. She has a lovely, open personality and a grace that sets her apart. We talk of many things — even evolution and how things began. She agrees that I might walk her home and that we'll meet again tomorrow to stroll along the shore. It is December 15th, 1956; perhaps I have a sweetheart for Xmas.

Brocklebank's *SS Mahanada* at Gibraltar 1966.
Malcolm Cranfield collection

17

Mahanada

December 1956.

Supported by certificate no. 1180, Maintenance of Radar Equipment on Merchant Ships, issued by The Ministry of Transport, I write for jobs. I've little cash in my pocket now, though Mam keeps me going out of what she's saved from the money allowance I make to my parents when at sea. World shipping currently suffers from a depression, but I'm full of youthful optimism.

The Christian Salvesen whaling company operates out of Leith in Scotland. They have two monsters, the *Southern Harvester* and the *Southern Venturer*. These ships are floating factories that process whales hunted down by teams of nimble catcher vessels armed with explosive harpoons. I've heard the money's good – the crew get a share of the catch. But they have no vacancies. It's a blessing, considering the more sensitive conscience I'll come to develop.

An interview offer comes from Thos & Jno Brocklebank Steam Navigation Co. of Liverpool. They run cargo liners from Liverpool, on the river Mersey, to Calcutta, with calls at ports in the Red Sea and the

Northern Indian Ocean; then back to the Mersey, with occasional diversions to the southern states of the USA. Cargo liners sail from port to port along routes and on schedules published in advance. They transport general freight, raw materials, merchandise, and sometimes a handful of passengers. My new radar ticket might land me a job. As a Brocklebank direct employee, I'd be free of the vagaries of the Marconi Company.

Liverpool is grey and wet, but the Christmas shoppers are happy enough, jabbering away in thick Scouse accents. A newspaper seller outside draughty Lime Street station points me in the direction of the Three Graces of Liverpool. The great buildings stand side by side on the banks of the greasy River Mersey: the Port of Liverpool Building – big and baroque; the two clock towers of the massive Liver Building; and between them the Cunard Building – it has a look of classical Greece. At the Liver Building, I crane my neck to see the famous Liver Birds. Each clock tower carries an eighteen-foot mythical bird in copper and steel. They look like portly cormorants with wings stretched out to dry. Legend has it that whenever a virgin walks beneath, the Liver Birds flap their wings. I've plenty of time, so I watch. The pavement is crowded with folk coming and going, lots of laughing girls in thick winter coats, but the birds don't budge an inch.

Cunard Building is cavernous. The soaring central hall is lined down the centre and along the walls with glorious scale models of Cunard's ships, each in its own sumptuous glass case. They are naval architect's models. Splendid two, three and four funnel liners, cargo steamers, one hybrid of sail and steam, another with side paddles, and a line of lovely square-riggers, all in polished wood and brass. I'm overawed. They'll be worth a king's ransom.

A large man, with a mouthful of erratic teeth, conducts my interview. Even though he looks as though he's been in a fight, Arthur Orum, the company marine radio second superintendent, is a genial man. After sounding me out with questions of a technical nature, he asks:

'Why do you want to sail with Brocklebanks, young fellow?'

'I've heard it's a company that treats its men well. I've no wish to rejoin Marconi.'

He places his hands on the cracked brown leather of his desk top. I notice the robust character of the thumbs and fingers. They have strength. He speaks with a slight growl, 'Brocklebanks has always owned its own gear, and we've never hired staff from Marconi. You do realise our terminus port is Calcutta and only the newer ships have air-conditioned cabins? It can be a bit sweaty up the Hooghli. How are you with the heat?'

'I twice went tropical on a BI troopship. She had no cooling. So I should manage.'

'Much of the fleet is old, but we are rebuilding. We lost sixteen out of twenty-six in the war, but we're almost back to strength.'

'What size is the fleet?' I sense it will be to my advantage to show interest.

'Twenty-three just now. And we've orders placed with the Clyde yards. Are you acquainted with our history?'

'I've heard Brocks have been around a good while.'

Arthur Orum leans back in his chair and folds his hands behind his large, craggy head. 'Most companies carry the house flag on the after mast. If you sign with us you'll notice we fly the house flag from the foremast. Brocklebanks have that privilege, being the world's oldest shipping line. The firm originated with a shipyard in Sheepscut, near Portland, Maine, in 1770, founded by the Cumbrian loyalist Daniel Brocklebank, a master mariner and shipbuilder. In the American War of Independence, Daniel was having none of it. So he moved his enterprise back to his English birthplace, Whitehaven. In 1775 he sailed back to Whitehaven in his own ship, the *Castor*.' His broad face beams. I can see he enjoys recounting this history. '*Castor* became a Letter of Marque, a privateer, an official sort of pirate, a vessel granted authority by the King to attack enemy vessels and bring them before the admiralty to be valued, sold, and the profits shared with the Crown. On Daniel's death his little company was refounded in 1801 by his sons, Thomas and John Brocklebank, with one sailing ship. When the monopoly of the East India Company was abolished in 1813, they began to trade with India and did well. After all those years, even though we're now a branch of Cunard, we're still running up the Hooghli to Calcutta.'

I've inherited my mother's love of history, and respond: 'That's fascinating. I hope I can sail with you.' I quietly recall I've heard tell of the river Hooghli, I've heard it referred to as the *Arsehole of India*. But I'm in need of an employer.

'Good. I've already a decent vessel in mind. She's short of a junior radio officer. You'll sail under one of our best men.'

For a few weeks I've been walking out with Beryl. She's a lovely lass, with a bright personality. I'm sad to leave her, but at eighteen I can't make promises. We agree to write, even though I'll be gone for five months. We kiss farewell, and on 7th January 1957, I sign ship's articles for *SS Mahanada* in Birkenhead. She's a 9,000-ton steam turbine, built in 1943 by Hamilton's yard on the Clyde. I'm excited to be heading east again – this time India!

The European crew is seventeen British officers plus a British carpenter and four helmsmen. There are about sixty Bengalis, a Goanese cook and a handful of sailors from the Maldive Islands. I join a line of fellow Europeans to absorb a cocktail of injections against nasty things we're deemed vulnerable to catch: Yellow fever and the like. They stab us in both upper arms. We'll have bad reactions – swellings. We cast-off tomorrow, so I hope I can manage the Morse key.

Winter in the Bay of Biscay brings green faces. A navigation apprentice/midshipman, on his first trip, has a bad time of it. Through the rain-lashed seas that pile in from the Atlantic we keep a lookout for any signs of a lost ship. The bridge scans the sea surface for scraps of wreckage and flotsam of any sort that might be from the London registered *Nordic Star*. She's a part-welded Liberty ship built in Canada in 1943. She disappeared mid-Atlantic, somewhere west of Ushant, eleven days ago, after a final Morse message that gave her expected time of arrival. She sailed from Philadelphia on December 18th and was due at Le Havre last week. All ships are on alert, but she will never be seen again. Her 7,000 gross tonnage, her 8,400-ton cargo of anthracite coal, and her crew of thirty-four of various nationalities, simply disappear. Perhaps she's a victim of the of the hurricane-force storm whose vestiges we now struggle through. In five months' time an oil-stained lifebelt bearing her name will wash up on a beach on Islay in the Inner Hebrides, and that will be the only trace.

In a year's time, I'll discuss *Nordic Star* with my friend, Brian Marsden. While his ship was in Philadelphia, Brian was approached by the young British radio officer of *Nordic Star*, berthed nearby. His wireless equipment was troublesome. My friend went aboard and did what he could to help. *Nordic Star* then sailed on her last voyage and, after transmitting two standard messages to her owners, went silent and vanished.

There will be similar casualties of the sea. Those Liberty ships were constructed with record-breaking speed to replace losses from German torpedoes. After the war, they were bought cheap and pressed into profit by Greek shipowners, and other outfits registered in Panama and Liberia that fly *Flags of Convenience*. It was not envisaged that so many would still be tramping the world.

Mahanada has two radio officers. We are an Eight Hour Ship: eight hours watch keeping per day, seven days per week when at sea. I keep three watches of two hours each, plus Brocklebank inter-ship schedules at times that can break my sleep. The ships' names begin with *Ma* and feature aspects of the Indian sub-continent. We are named after the Mahanadi River (known as The Sorrow Of Orissa, because of its floods). Others are: *Manipur* (an Indian hill state); *Mahout* (elephant driver); *Mahseer* (a huge Gangetic carp); *Maskeliya* (a Sri Lankan hill town); *Mathura* (a city in Uttar Pradesh); and *Mahsud* (a Pashtun tribe).

The senior man is Tommy Williams, a tall and gentle Welshman in his stout fifties, with a broad forehead and calm blue eyes. He takes one two-hour watch per day, relieves me when mealtimes occur during my watch, looks after the radar and takes DF bearings. He's in charge of the ship's library and I'm expected to help. I take to him immediately. He is kindly and interested in my career so far. His eyes twinkle with understanding and amusement as I offer up my story.

Tommy speaks with that soft North Wales voice. At one point he startles me with: 'You know, Harry ...' He pauses, searching for the right words. 'You're an intelligent lad, but you'd do well to tone down that Hartlepool accent.' I blush and make a resolve to smooth the harsher of my South-East Durham vowels. I remember the

Hartlepool saying that parodies the worst of the local dialect: 'I strip off at werk and hang me shert on a gerder.'

We share one Indian steward, a thin elderly man, who keeps our cabins in good order, serves us at the saloon table, and struggles up the ladder to the wireless room with coffee and sandwiches whatever the weather. He's a quiet, dignified man – it seems ludicrous to refer to him as *the Boy*, but that is the way of things on Indian-crewed ships. It's clear he adores my chief; in fact, the Moslems in our Indian crew all show him great respect. Tommy has an English translation of the Koran on his desk. Our steward will have dusted around it, and told his shipmates that *Burrah* (great) *Marconi Sahib* reads their holy book. I'm only *Chota* (small) *Marconi Sahib*, but the respect they have for Tommy spills over on to me. *Marconi Sahib* is the Indian sailor's name for any radio officer, even though, like us, they might not work for the Marconi company.

The Indian crew (the Lascar seamen) communicate with us by means of a mixture of English and Lascari-bat (lit: sailor talk). I'm amused when they refer to the radar as *Steam Purree Wallah* (the steam-powered look-out man); they appear not to have a word for electricity. Lascari-bat is a collection of simple words and phrases common across many Indian languages. Our officers speak it well enough; there are phrase books on board. I've made progress and can order *thoda cheeni* (little sugar) when I can no longer stomach the excruciatingly sweet coffee Boy brings to the wireless room.

Mahanada clears Cape Finisterre in North-West Spain and leaves the confused waters of the Bay of Biscay. From the bridge, we can discern the spray-shrouded form of a steamship, hard aground beneath the cliffs of Finisterre. I'm told she steamed straight into the cape at night, her officers misled by a faulty radar. I understand why my new radar ticket got me this job.

We run south, well clear of the coast of Portugal, in bright January sunshine. The sea dazzles the eye except where lines of long Atlantic swell roll in from the west. The bridge officer stares into the radar. There are several echoes from vessels well off shore, and a couple that will cross our track intent on the port of Lisbon. But one echo is dead ahead and closing. The master is on the wing of the bridge with his telescope extended, an apprentice by his side. It's the first tripper. He hands the young fellow the telescope.

'I'm glad to see you looking more human since we broke free of Biscay. Now, take a look, lad. You've younger eyes than me. Unless I'm mistaken, there's a dab of something on the horizon. Hold it steady, now. Let's not be dropping it.'

The telescope needs extensive readjustment after the skipper's old eyes. 'Yes, sir. I've got the object. A plume of black smoke.'

'Not the smoke. That'll be some ancient Portuguese coal-burner. We're looking for an oil-fired ship. You'll recall we only make smoke once a day – when we blow tubes. Scan further to starboard.'

'I see it, sir. It might be a dark funnel. There's no trace of smoke.'

'Good enough, you keep an eye on her. If she's *Maskeliya*, then it'll not be long. We don't want to ram her, bow on, Greek galley fashion, do we now?' He trundles his slightly portly shape into the wheelhouse. 'Where's my morning coffee? Late again! I want it eleven-o-clock sharp, wherever we are.'

For two days we have been in radio contact with another of our fleet, a homeward-bound vessel loaded with jute, tea, and manganese ore from Bengal. The master and his opposite number have arranged for us to pass close.

Coffee arrives. As usual, it has the aroma of hot mud laced with condensed milk. The master and the second mate sip and watch the masts creep above the horizon. The white foremast is an 'A' shape; behind it is a banded funnel with a domed cowl on top. She's coming up fast.

The master takes the telescope from the apprentice and lays a hand on his thin shoulder. 'Three short blasts on the whistle, lad. Yes, do it now! Earn your keep, young fellow.'

He gets it about right. Three deafening, sonorous brays come from the steam-powered whistle attached to our funnel. I've never done that and I feel a touch of envy. The first-trip apprentice stands a bit taller now.

Across the undulating sea, three faint blasts come in response.

The mate stands beside the wheel and gives course adjustments to the helmsman. We desire to pass close to starboard, but not stupidly close. We rely on the other ship to also pass on her starboard side. Our combined speeds will be about 28 knots. A collision would be a noisy affair.

The gap narrows until she surges close with a bone in her teeth. Maskeliya ploughs past a hundred yards to starboard. She's only a couple of years old, modern by our standards, and gleams with freshly washed paint; white superstructure above a black hull that carries a continuous white line. Her funnel, like ours: black, with one blue band above a white band, has a great white gull riding the updraft. She makes a proud and elegant prospect as she rides the whispering green swell. She takes each swell like a Grand National thoroughbred at Aintree takes a fence. The crews line the bulwarks, recognise old shipmates, and cheer. Both vessels dip the blue and white house flag on the foremast in salute as we surge past each other. From each ship comes three more blasts in salutation as we bid farewell. She'll be paying off in Dundee, the Scottish jute-spinning town, in four days. We will be away at least five months. The Suez Canal remains blocked after the recent conflict. We have five weeks and 12,000 miles, via the Cape of Good Hope, before we dock in Calcutta.

The author aged 18 in *SS Mahanada's* wireless room. The transmitter on the right is the Siemens SB186 which could deliver radio frequency shocks to the operator's tuning hand.

18

The Red Hand of Ulster

On 14th January, *Mahanada* puts into Las Palmas in the Canaries for six hours; enough time to replenish our bunker oil. White walls and red roofs spread around the margins of a sandy bay beneath low, green hills. The intrepid Christopher Columbus refreshed his own ships' stores at these volcanic islands before risking the unknown. They are off the coast of Morocco, though part of Spain. The Spaniards discovered a primitive people here, who some consider to be remnants of Cro-Magnon man, the artist of the Ice Age caves of France.

We take on fuel sufficient for the long haul to Cape Town, plus a reserve of 25% to cover eventualities. Our vessel is berthed at the seaward end of a featureless oil jetty. A white sun beats down; the breathless air shimmers, so I don't fancy a stroll. Tommy Williams, my chief, is visited by a radio officer from a nearby whale factory ship – the visitor once sailed on *Mahanada*. The caller is astonished to find Tommy still in place after seven years. In fact, he's been with *Mahanada* for thirteen years, since she was built in 1943.

We depart the Canaries with fourteen days and 4,500 miles to go before South Africa. In five mornings, on the glazed ripples of the airless Doldrums, we slip over the Equator, without any 'crossing the line' fuss; this is not a passenger liner; we all have our work. After steaming south through the Doldrums we enter the realm of the South-East Trade Winds and the sea livens up with an occasional white crest.

Two days before Cape Town the quiet monotony of this empty quarter of the South Atlantic is broken by shouts from the wing of the bridge. The sea is the colour of blood! No mistake, it is a bright morning and the sea is deep red. Furthermore, off to starboard, whales are blowing, dozens and dozens of leviathans. Some of them make huge splashes when they break surface, breach and crash back. We line the rails, astonished at the mass of giant baleen whales. The sea is red with a plankton bloom that stretches for miles, and the creatures are gorging. The Meteorological people at Bracknell will be interested to know of this, so the details are included in our scheduled weather report under a section for unusual phenomena

We are an official meteorological ship. We send a Morse message to the British Met Office at Bracknell in Berkshire every few hours. The officer on watch jots down readings taken from the Stevenson Screen, a small weather station on the ship's monkey island (the highest deck of the ship, directly above the wireless room). The Stevenson's louvered chamber contains wet and dry bulb thermometers, a barograph, a mercury barometer suspended in gimbals, and the 'dipping bucket' with thermometer for checking the seawater temperature; plus the all-important book of cloud and sea-state photos. An apprentice hands me the message. It takes me ten minutes to catch the attention of Portishead Radio in Somerset before the signal can skip its way north for relay to the Met Office.

Table Mountain is spread with the famous white tablecloth of cloud on the morning we ease into Cape Town harbour. The city rises gently towards the mountain but ceases at its base. Through the forest of dock cranes, the streets look inviting. I'm probably the first one to venture into town. I've a wallet of money and carry a bag of radio valves packed among towels. They're from the captain's wireless. He has pestered me, on and off, for days to clean the inside of the handsome radio he is manifestly proud of.

'It would be better to leave well alone, sir. Those old valves will be tired and their heaters fragile; disturbance will likely make an end of them.'

He frowns at me from beneath bushy eyebrows. 'Oh aye, Sparks? Your predecessor cleaned the dust out for me. It came to no harm when he did it.' He caresses the walnut veneer of the rounded corner of the cabinet as though it were a woman's hip.

He wears me down. I remove the slotted plywood back and survey the valves huddled beneath overcoats of felted dust. He's watching me.

'Take them out, lad. One by one, and wipe off the dust with a damp cloth. Get the cobwebs shifted. That's what the other sparks used to do for me. He'd give the volume and tone controls a squirt of that switch cleaner jollop you have in your cupboard. Then he'd do likewise with the waveband changer.'

It took me an hour to have the radio in sparkling condition, but it had become completely lifeless. So I'm off into Capetown by taxi. The driver drops me in a side street by a likely looking electrical shop.

The shop is empty except for a pretty black girl about my own age. She's in a thin summer frock and my gaze lingers. I explain my problem, how I must fix the captain's wireless before we sail tomorrow, otherwise he'll be sour with me on the long drag to Ceylon when he can't listen to the BBC on shortwave. I start to unwrap the dud valves on the counter top.

'Sorry, sir, but we don't sell wireless valves. This shop is for light fittings and fuses and other things electricians need.' She goes into a long explanation of the route to another shop that might stock valves. It's complex. I must look dejected, for she smiles. 'In ten minutes it's my lunch break. Then I'll show you the way.'

We set off together, but wait for the crossing lights to turn green. I'm waved down a wide street that bustles with motor cars. We take care to avoid the electric double-decker trolley buses that hum down the road; their poles draw sparks off the overhead wires and remind me of home. It's like a fine English town, even Newcastle-on-Tyne, but with the sparkle of a sunshine you'd only expect in the Mediterranean. After fifty yards the girl is no longer at my side; she's a few steps behind. I stop and wait, but she also stops and then waves me on. After a few more awkward stops and starts, the penny drops. I feel flushed with embarrassment. She declines to walk with me, and won't have me follow her. In this awkward manner, I'm guided to the door of a store that stocks valves. I turn to thank the girl, but she has flitted away. Before today, I'd been unaware of the racial segregation that is Apartheid and ignorant that it was institutionalised in 1948, just nine years ago.

After dinner, with the captain's wireless bright with new valves, and pulling in distant stations to his satisfaction, I stretch out on my bunk. The cabin is built of steel. The leaded cream paint that coats the metal bulkheads does not pretend luxury, it is a wartime built ship after all. But, there's a chair and a wooden desk with drawers, a ceramic washbasin and a polished brass porthole, a narrow wardrobe and a bench settee cum daybed with a long blue cushion. The deck is covered by linoleum, a much-varnished beige. Above my head is a ventilator grill to the deck above. An adjustable nozzle pokes from trunking above the door, it delivers hot or cold air depending on climate; it's often in error or too feeble to make much difference. Screwed to a bulkhead is a rattling reciprocating electric fan that pushes the air around. The bunk is mounted on top of a chest of long drawers. The comfortable mattress is guarded by a wooden board, the fiddle, that's raised in rough weather to stop the sleeper rolling out. Between me and the fiddle is a narrow bolster mattress that lies on its side, this and the wooden fiddle keep me in place. With the bolster by my right side it's like lying next to a silent and impassive woman; in fact, this bolster is known to seafarers as a Dutch Wife (an allusion I suppose to the old enmity between Holland and England when anything false might be termed 'Dutch'.) All woodwork is a mahogany colour that glows – when I'm on watch the 'boy' takes the opportunity to clean and polish. At the end of the bunk, a wooden partition extends to the white deckhead (ceiling); it gives some privacy from the door that might be open to help ventilation.

A head pokes around the blue curtain that covers the door opening. 'Hey, Sparks. Fancy a run ashore?' It's the red-haired, Scottish fifth engineer. He hails from Greenock, a ship-building town near Glasgow. He's inclined to be wild. He seems animated this evening.

'Not for me, thanks, Ian; I've been up to town already today.'

'But, there's a bar where the ceiling is covered in stars, just like the night sky, and it revolves.'

'Sounds interesting, but I'm whacked and just fancy flaking out on my bunk.'

He disappears, only to return with a few cans of cold beer. Within the hour, I'm persuaded and don my shore-going suit and tie. At the gangway, Ian urges more speed. 'Quick, there's a car just pulling away from that Italian tanker.'

'Aye, but it's not a taxi. It's got a flag flying from its bonnet.'

My red-haired shipmate stands in front of the expensive-looking black limousine and gesticulates until it is forced to halt. The uniformed chauffeur lowers the window and scowls. There's a passenger in the back; he looks most dignified in grey suit and finely barbered silver hair.

'Any chance of a lift to town, old chap?' Ian usually rejoices in his Clydeside dialect, but he's also an accomplished mimic. Today, he is a refined Englishman; a Sandhurst officer type.

Before the chauffeur can respond, the gentleman in the back speaks up: 'Take these men to wherever they have in mind.'

Ian takes the front position, by the driver. I sit nervously on leather seats beside the Italian Consul.

The hotel bar indeed has a rotational ceiling, from which the constellations of the Southern Hemisphere wink down on the customers. We are joined at our table by a Cockney, a fellow from London. He is a deck-hand off the *Strathaird,* a P&O liner currently in port; she carries 1200 passengers, mostly British emigrants to Australia. He's attached himself to us for the evening – he seems a bit lonely. It's become clear that my companion, Ian, has been drinking steadily most of today. He's grown a touch tiresome, but he's got a wild eye and I take care not to challenge. Tonight he's assumed an American accent and, with his ability to impersonate, has almost convinced our

Cockney chap that he is indeed American. But he slips up from time to time, whereupon the Cockney pounces on the mistake. I'm getting bored with it.

We three wander deeper into town and repair to a cocktail bar up two flights of stairs. Ian is getting louder. When I next visit the bar for refills, the barman asks if I could please keep my friend quiet. That's reasonable, so I promise to do my best. For half-an-hour, Ian takes little notice of my cautions and becomes a nuisance. A few customers leave. The barman appears at our table, grabs Ian by the collar and lifts him from his chair. The barman is tall but lean. Ian is short and wiry. He struggles. The barman now has him in an arm-lock around the neck. But he's my shipmate, and I won't stand for that. I must have had a surfeit of drink because I rise and take a swing at the barman. I catch him under the chin, and he drops my shipmate.

The double doors to the bar now swing open and three beefy Boers advance upon us. The barman will have had them standing by. Ian seizes a chair and defends himself. Other chairs are knocked over; drinks go flying. I think: This reminds me of one of those saloon brawls in a cowboy film. We are picked up and thrown out onto the staircase landing. Ian is indignant and fights back. I take a few hits. From my viewpoint on the floor, I note that our Cockney friend is prone beside me. I feel as though I'm in a dream. I sense a few blows but they seem like distant soft thuds. Ian is still upright and fighting like a lion. I'm amazed that the huge Boers cannot knock him down. Finally, they resort to throwing him down the stairs. The Cockney is thrown down next. They then reach for me. I bounce off some of the steps onto the next landing. The Boers throw us down the next flight, through the doors, and into the street.

On the pavement outside, we attempt to arrange ourselves into some order. My fingers sense a tender lump emerging on one eyebrow. There's an ache surfacing somewhere around my ribs. Ian's lips are swollen. Cockney seems in reasonable shape, though he might have a black eye by morning. A man in a beige uniform and cap observes us with a sardonic expression. I amble over, in what I hope is a dignified manner, put a hand on his shoulder, and say: 'Officer, I wish to lodge an official complaint. I have been assaulted.'

The 'uniform' steps back. He points to his shoulder where I've deposited a handprint in blood. I stare at it and think, 'Oh! That's interesting. It looks just like the Red Hand of Ulster.' I sway a little while I recall the Irish legend: Two boats race to the shore, each with a chief in the bow. The first chief to touch the land will be King of Ulster. One man senses he will be too late and so chops off his hand and hurls it to the beach. Thus did the O'Neill win Ulster. The red hand is on the banner to this day. It is indeed wonderful what you can learn from Arthur Mee's Children's Encyclopaedia.

I hear a voice. The uniform speaks, 'You waste your breath. You can't lodge a complaint with me – I'm a traffic attendant. But, I do expect you to pay the dry-cleaning bill.' Which prompts me to examine my own clothes. I see that my shore-going suit also needs a dry-clean.

A taxi pulls up. The coloured driver (he might be an Asian) sticks his head out. 'Taxi?' We clamber in. 'Where to? I take you to better night spot than this Afrikaaner dump.'

Ian is still gathering his wits. Cockney speaks up, 'Let's head to my ship and get cleaned up.' (I'm past caring, so acquiesce.) Our London friend takes over. 'Main liner dock, driver. We want the *Strathaird*.'

202

She's a vast white ship of 22,000 tons; nearly three times the size of *Mahanada*. Cockney shouts, 'Follow me!' He runs up the tall gangway with us close behind. There's a uniformed quartermaster on guard at the top. Cockney, whom I'd considered a bit timid up to this point, shoves the quartermaster aside and yells, 'Follow me!' He dives through a doorway. The quartermaster blows furiously on his whistle for reinforcements. 'Quick, this way. We'll take a shortcut to the deck-crew quarters.'

After some twists and turns along alleyways, with whistles in pursuit somewhere behind, we stand before a pair of elegant doors. Cockney pushes them open. We face into the ship's ballroom, full of dinner jackets and ball gowns in mid-waltz . . . or is it the rumba? Anyway, I'm aware there's an orchestra in full blast. 'Follow me!' So we do. As we run through their ranks the dancers stop and peel aside before us, like the Red Sea before the Israelites. We escape through a small door on the far side of the dance floor. Then it's down staircases, around corners, through more doors, until we reach the habitat of the able-seamen.

The crew is seated at a long table complete with glasses and open bottles of South African brandy. I've heard of this stuff. It costs five shillings a bottle and is reckoned to be no more than one month old. It's known as *Cape Smoke* and has a reputation the world over. Distilled to sustain the parched diamond miners of a hundred years ago, it is mentioned in H. Rider Haggard's novel, *Jess:* 'Yes, Baas,' said the Hottentot meekly. 'I was drunk, though not very; I only had half a bottle of Cape Smoke.' I resolve to keep well away from it; though I might have one small tot, just to say I've tried it.

First, though, we must get cleaned up. In the crew washrooms, we rinse away the dried blood and inspect our bruises. It's agreed, 'That was quite a night.' I mutter to myself, 'Never again.'

In the early hours, Cockney bids us farewell at *Strathaird's* gangway; he seems to have squared matters with the quartermasters. It's but a short walk to our own ship. Once aboard, Ian wants to continue our 'session', but I decline. I'm astonished by his capacity. I shoo him from my cabin, fall into my bunk and go out like a light.

I hear hawsers being winched in. The ship moves. Next stop, Calcutta, in nineteen days' time. There's a tap-tap on the fiddle board of my bunk. It's the 'boy' with my tea.

'Morning time, Sahib. Chai comes.'

I peel back the covers and look into the old fellow's kindly eyes. He stares at me. Then his lined brown features crease into a smile. He points at my face. There's a chuckle, followed by a suppressed laugh. 'Ah, ah! Sahib have good night ashore!'

19

Loss

This same morning, *Mahanada* rounds the Cape of Good Hope to enter the Indian Ocean. Vasco da Gama came this way at Christmastide in 1497 in search of a route from Europe to India. He named part of this region *Natal* (Christmas in Portuguese). We probably have the same mild weather as da Gama; it's summer time in this southern hemisphere. January is on her way out; I suppose there will be blizzards at home.

After the Cape, we set course for the Bay of Bengal and Calcutta. Navigating by the south of the vast island of Madagascar, it should take seventeen days to cover the 5,500 sea miles. However, six days later we come to a halt off the island of Mauritius. Within sight of the coast guard station, *Mahanada* suffers engine failure on a placid sea. The coast guard notices that we drift, but we are too far out to identify. His radio operator keys out a general message on 500mc/s: 'VESSEL 5 MILES WEST OF MAURITIUS IDENTIFY. DO YOU REQUIRE ASSISTANCE?' I pass it to the Master.

He sniffs. 'Just ignore it, Sparks. If we respond to that, he'll be straight on to Lloyd's Insurers and I'll have head office on my back in no time at all. Stay dumb and tell him nowt.'

Mauritius calls persistently, but I stay mute. I wonder if we'll end up in need of a tug. But we have an engine-room crew from the Mersey and the Clyde; the very best you could find. I wander outside the wireless room to gaze at the land. The island rises from the deep ocean floor, 700 miles east of Madagascar. It'll be a pity if we don't visit what remains of that extinct, submarine volcano. I'd like to see the home of the dodo, the hapless, flightless, trusting pigeon, 30lb weight and three-foot tall. Sailors found the bird so tasty, by 1662 they had devoured the dodo to the point of extinction. The island is a forty mile egg shape, with a forested spine of basalt. I've read that Malay and Arab seamen visited this remote spot but did not settle. Some have it that a few eroded wax writing tablets found on the shore are signs that the Phoenicians landed. The Dutch claimed the uninhabited island and renamed it after their head of state, Maurice, Prince of Orange and Count of Nassau. By the time the Dutch abandoned the outpost they, and their introduced pigs, dogs, and rats had disposed of the last of the defenceless dodo. Mauritius became the haunt of pirates until claimed by the French, who thought it a fine base for attacks on Britain's India trade. But France lost it to Britain on the defeat of Napoleon.

An hour later, there comes a throb from the engine room. The screw slaps the shallow heave of the water and begins to turn. We soon have Mauritius astern and watch its dark outline sink into a cerise sunset of thin cloud roofed by duck-egg blue. But a black mass advances from the north-east, a sign our calm weather will soon deteriorate.

For a few days, South African weather reports for the Indian Ocean have warned of a cyclonic rotation that developed over the warm seas around the atoll of Diego Garcia in the Chagos Archipelago. Diego is about 400 miles south of the equator and fecund territory for the birth of a cyclone. Cyclones usually crawl their way south-westwards. If Chagos has conceived a cyclone, it could be barrelling straight down our track towards us. The latest report indicates we will be in for a wild ride tomorrow. The master is concerned enough to have the lashings reinforced on our deck cargo. We carry midships a pair of huge, tarpaulin-wrapped steam locomotives destined for Indian railways, one on the port and the other on the starboard side. They strain at their lashings like captive mastodons; I hurry past whenever I make the wet journey to the stern to repair a fault on the Indian crew's radio system.

I talk with other vessels further along our track; it seems we are in for a bad time. Cyclones are identical to hurricanes except that they rotate clockwise, whereas hurricanes rotate anti-clockwise; it all depends on which side of the equator these tropical storms come alive. I'm thinking about this as I stow away all loose objects.

The cyclone has arrived, winds are 70mph and rising. My boss, Tommy Williams, comes to check on me as I begin the evening watch. He makes sure my chair is securely chained to the deck. I watch him take the strain with his legs as the ship pitches. His kind Welsh eyes twinkle. 'This does my varicose veins no good at all. Thirty years on moving decks, Harry, and you'll have them as well. I'm off to have a read in bed. You have a good watch. Send the secunny if you need me.' A secunny is a Lascar sailor who helps on the bridge. He will keep lookout, carry messages, do whatever needs doing should the officers need to keep station. The ship gives a lurch. Tommy staggers as he makes for the door. 'That feels like a change of course,' he mutters as he leaves.

We are on a new track. The seas have become huge. In sheets of rain, the bows climb the slopes of black monsters, fifty-feet tall, rank after rank of them, laced white with nets of spume that stream from their ridge tops. The master is on the bridge and has ordered the helmsman to steer into the seas so that we meet them head-on. The engines are full-ahead, though we might be stationary or even being driven astern. It could be fatal to expose our beam to this sea. Our course is whatever brings safety. Heaven forbid we have another breakdown. *Mahanada's* steelwork creaks and groans as we smash through the crests, but goes quiet in the troughs as we prepare to charge the next watery hill. In the troughs, we are sheltered from the shriek of the wind and there is strange silence. I wonder about the two locomotives on deck, and those crates of Dynamite in the special explosives locker in the tweendeck.

Toward the end of my two-hour watch, at around 10 pm, I pick up a distress signal: SOS SOS SOS DE AQAX AQAX AQAX SS MINOCHER COWASJEE. JAKARTA FOR CAPE TOWN. POSN 25.30S 68.00E, CARGO SHIFTED, SEVERE LIST, RISK OF CAPSIZE. NEED ASSISTANCE. The Morse is clean and firm, though the signal has a plaintive warble, as though from elderly equipment. I switch on the main transmitter then hand the message through the chartroom hatch. An apprentice rushes it to the master in the wheelhouse.

I drum my fingers on the bench by the Morse key as I wait for the transmitter to come alive. I switch on the direction finder – it might be needed. I hurriedly look into my call-sign code book. AQAX – that's a Pakistani call sign. A minute later I have the transmitter tuned and confirm receipt: AQAX AQAX AQAX DE GOFM GOFM GOFM RRR SOS.

He comes straight back with GOFM, *Mahanada's* call-sign. GOFM DE AQAX TU. It is brief because there are two other ships attempting acknowledgement of the distress. I glance through the hatch. The master is at the chart table. With the second mate, he is making calculations. He straightens and comes to the hatchway.

'Sparks. Tell him we are about five-hundred miles north of his position. Tell him we'll come when we can.' I might look puzzled, for he goes on: 'I have to keep her head into this, otherwise we're over. We go nowhere until this blows out.' As if in emphasis, the deck shudders from a giant blow. Captain Newman claws his way back into the wheelhouse.

The transmitter has warmed up. I listen for a break in the distress traffic. Cape Town wireless has acknowledged the distress, and a now a French station on Madagascar does the same. A break comes. I key: AQAX AQAX AQAX DE GOFM GOFM GOFM RRR SOS SS MAHANADA. 500 MILES NORTH OF YOU. WILL COME WHEN WE CAN.

There's an immediate response: GOFM DE AQAX TU. This is a confident Morse fist. I've ceased to be surprised at how operators can sense the character and emotional state of the sender, by his style. It occurs to me that the *Minocher Cowasjee's* man is mature and clear-headed. How do I know this? It is the way he 'speaks'.

The second mate peers through the hatch. He has a pinched look about him. 'You'll no doubt be staying on watch, Sparks. We'll be in this for some hours yet. I'll get sandwiches and cocoa sent through to you. That position we gave is only approximate. We're not sure where we are. We've been driven well off course.'

I'm beginning to comprehend our situation but I'm still young enough to possess the immortal insouciance of youth. 'It'll be a hell of a night,' I venture.

'That's a fact. I just hope those bloody steam engines don't shift.'

The 'boy' slithers a bit as he brings the cocoa. I welcome the hot drink but am unsure about the sandwiches wrapped in a white cloth napkin. I'm used to the routine. Lay them on the bench, watch and wait. Sure enough, a pair of inch-long antenna emerges from a fold in the napkin and wave around. I unfold the napkin and shake out the galley cockroach, and another. They are angular, brown and shiny; not yet the hairy-backs of breeding age. They zip into the gloom beneath the desk before my stamping shoe hits the deck. The sandwiches are tinned sardine. I won't touch them unless I get desperate. I open my elegant tall tin of Anton Justman's Dutch light shag and arrange a clump of tobacco strands into the makings of a hand-rolled smoke; it might be a long night.

There are two ships much closer to the stricken vessel; like us, they are struggling to stay upright; one ship is within twenty miles of the position. The *Minocher Cowasjee* transmits extended dashes. Though accuracy is poor at this distance, I take radio bearings that show his angle from our bow, but not how far away he might be. He keeps calling, repeating his SOS message and keying out long dashes. I exchange a few more transmissions with the operator while his ship increases its list. Sometime close to midnight his signals cease. Has he gone down? Perhaps it's only that the aerial strung between straining masts has parted; perhaps those seven spun strands of phosphor-bronze, oxidised green, are strewn across the hatches; perhaps the aerial is, at this moment, being spliced back together by weary fingers. He may yet call again.

This page of the logbook says 24th January 1957. At intervals, ships and coast stations call the *Minocher Cowasjee* but there is never a response. At one in the morning, I send the secunny with a report to my boss.

Tommy takes over while I have a few hours in my bunk, snug alongside the bolster that is the Dutch wife. My bunk runs fore and aft, so I have a comfortable sleep in this pitching motion even though my head and feet alternate their respective elevations. The cyclone shrieks its way over us in the following hours and dives to the southwest. The rain deluge fades, the wind speed falls from hurricane force to a strong breeze that merely sets the halyards singing; the seas subside, they are only twenty foot and no longer threaten to overwhelm. But we now roll, rather than pitch.

My boss sips coffee whilst listening to the distress frequency. The wireless room filched Oranjeboom ashtray holds his briar pipe.

I glance at the wireless log. 'Morning, Tom. Anything happened?'

'No signals from her. We're back on course for the Ganges.'

'What about the search?'

'There are two ships doing sweeps of her last position, aided by an aircraft. Two Pakistani destroyers are on their way to mount a search. Let's hope they find life-rafts, I doubt boats would have survived.'

'So, we're not involved.' I'm thinking about that radio man. Might he be clinging to a raft?

'Skipper's made a decision based on fuel reserves. We carry only enough bunkers to get us between fuelling ports, plus a 25% reserve. It would take us thirty-six hours to get to the distress position – that's a thousand mile round trip to get back on this course. If we made sweeps we'd run short and be running on vapour before we made Calcutta.'

'Oh. I'd imagined we'd have plenty of fuel.'

'No, Harry lad. We can carry a maximum of fifteen-hundred tons of the stuff, but we never ship more than we need for a particular leg of a journey. If we dragged five-hundred tons of surplus oil around the oceans – oil that was never called for – that would be five-hundred tons less cargo we could ship; bad economics when the company struggles to stay in profit. Though, we did tend to keep her topped up in wartime when we could never be sure where we'd end up.' He shoots me a searching look. 'Those two destroyers are the best bet should there be anyone in boats. They'll be stuffed full of better radar than any merchant craft.'

'She probably capsized.' I think about the crew, about fifty of them, a few in the water, most trapped inside. Down in the hot engine room! I shudder. 'How deep is the sea in these parts?'

'It's reckoned to be two, and sometimes three miles.'

I imagine *Minocher Cowasjee,* upside down, slipping in silence, through mile after mile of black water, slowly crumpling into the abyss.

Seven weeks later, on our way home from Calcutta, I'll stride ashore onto the island of Ceylon. Colombo is a moist, tropical city, the centre handsome with British colonial buildings, the streets lined with palms and dank monsoon drains. Before me stands the white masonry of the five solid floors of the Grand Oriental Hotel, since 1875 known the world over as the GOH. The air-conditioned bar beckons. An ice-cold lager will be just the ticket this sweltering noontime.

Perched on a bar stool I savour the prospect before me. A tall glass full of amber fluid, with white froth on top. Condensation fogs the outside and forms into rivulets that wander down the sides. I take a deep pull and a couple more, then order another Tuborg Gold Label from the white-jacketed, honey-coloured, Singhalese barman. There's a fellow on a stool to my right. We sense we are both seafarers and are soon in conversation. He's British. He says he's the first mate of the *Minocher Cowasjee*!

I ignore my lager. 'But how can that be? She was lost seven weeks ago, 1500 miles south-east of Mauritius.'

'Yes, I've heard. She'll have capsized. I walked off her in Djakarta. She was badly loaded at Vladivostok. I complained but was ignored. She behaved badly en route to Darien in Manchuria, where we loaded soybean. I wanted the cargo taken out and properly stowed, but was overruled. She rolled like a pig through the China Sea. At Djakarta, I demanded the cargo be re-stowed to my satisfaction. I was overruled. So I walked off and made my way here.'

'Blimey! If there's an inquiry, you should be called.' I'm wide-eyed.

'Yes; if there is an investigation.'

'Any other British in the crew?'

'No. The chief engineer is a German – Auguste Gieske. Majority of the crew are Pakistani.'

I notice we speak as though they still live. 'And the radio officer; is he Pakistani too?'

'No, oddly enough, he's an Indian national. He's Anglo-Indian, actually. Name of Thomas Chadburn.'

Forty-six years later I sit on rounded cushions with twenty other writers in the shrine room of a Buddhist retreat centre by Loch Voil in the Scottish Highlands. Mountains surround us; we sit as solid as mountains in early morning meditation. This is a creative writing retreat, supported by meditation. It is going well. This morning my usual distractions, those random wandering thought processes, have faded; there is a profound silence in the mind. I enjoy this zone of refined being; the niggling aches and itches that demand attention, have lost their power – if they are there, my senses ignore them. In this quiet, the subconscious mind sometimes speaks.

I seem to hear Morse signals from long ago. I'm in a heaving wireless room again. Memories emerge from deep places. It is as though the *Minocher Cowasjee* is no longer crumpled on the abyssal plain of the Indian Ocean, but has risen to the surface to renew her struggle with the cyclone. Images rise up. Morse signals. Appeals for help. Rain lashed portholes. Waves that dwarf our masts like black mountains on the march. The drawn faces of the men in the wheelhouse. I become conscious of a painful lump in my throat, and that my cheeks are wet with tears.

The three sweet notes of a gently tapped singing bowl mark the end of meditation. I go for a slow walk alongside the silent, sun-shot gleam of the loch. The air tastes sweet after a night of rain. A sandpiper picks her way across the shingled edge; she samples minute morsels. The nose of a trout breaks surface. It takes a mayfly, and transmits circular ripples outwards across the watery mirror, like radio waves that radiate from a ship's aerial. I reflect on the meditation: these images, are they factual memories, or just fantasies of a mind that craves distraction? Who knows? Yet they remain part of experience. I jot down a few notes.

The vestiges of memory prompt me to research the vanished *Minocher Cowasjee*. There is little progress for three years until, in 2006, I contact Ardeshir Cowasjee, a journalist for the Pakistan newspaper, *Dawn*. He is 80 years old but remains a critic of Pakistan's administration; in his columns, he alleges inefficiency, corruption, and nepotism. He must have upset the Prime Minister; in 1976 Bhutto had him jailed for 72 days without charge. Ardeshir is now the most senior Cowasjee, and patriarch of that family of Parsi Zoroastrians; Parsis are a much-diminished minority in Pakistan. From him, I begin to learn of the *Minocher Cowasjee.*

The ship belonged to the East and West Steamship Company founded by Rustom Cowasjee, Ardeshir's father, and named after Rustom's brother, Minocher Cowasjee. I follow his clues to find that the vessel had several owners and changes of name:

1920 *Parisiana,* Neptune S.N. Co. (Furness Withy)
1923 *London Exchange,* Neptune S.N. Co.
1935 *London Exchange,* Johnston Warren Lines Ltd.
1938 *Benrinnes,* Petrograd Steamers Ltd.
1942 *Benrinnes,* Ben Line Steamers Ltd.
1950 *Fatakada,* East & West S.S. Co.
1955 *Minocher Cowasjee,* East & West S.S. Co.

I get goose pimples when I discover that *Parisiana* was built in Hartlepool. She was built at Irvine's yard, hardly a mile from where I was born, and where my father and his father were both ship riveters. Perhaps they hammered home some of her rivets!

Ardeshir also has a coincidence. Only a week before I made contact, the granddaughter of the lost ship's radio officer emailed him to ask what he knew about the tragedy, and this is fifty years after the event! He gives me her address. She is in Brisbane, Australia. I convey to the lady all I recall, together with two poems I've written about the loss.

Her reply:

Dear Harry,
It's been an incredible journey of discovery for us and you've been so generous to share your personal experience, thank you so much. My

father relived the last moments of his father's life through your poem, and behind his closed office doors, he shed tears.

For nearly half a century he knew only a brief written blurb about the incident in the local paper. We as grandchildren knew little else.
My Grandfather was Anglo Indian, born 13/11/1905. His father was Bertram Chadburn (Scottish) who had a tea plantation in India. His mother worked in the fields and was Nepalese. He was orphaned with his sister at a young age, she died soon after. His upbringing was English. He married 1934, had three children and worked at the telegraph, then as a radio officer, and was called to war in 1942, then returns in 1947. Back working at the telegraph then transferred to Burma in 1948 and returns again to India in 1951 figuring on retiring soon. Apparently, he heard about the radio officer's job from a friend and joined the crew. That's as far as I go with information from my Aunt. Attached are some pictures of my grandfather and myself and family.
Susan Boucher,
Brisbane,
Australia

I stare at the message. Susan's grandfather has 13th November as his birthday – that is my father's birthday.

And again, she writes:
Hi Harry, you have given our family closure as it was my Grandfather, Thomas Chadburn, who was the radio officer on the Minocher Cowasjee, who sent the distress call. Your poems have brought us to tears and yet a sense of peace overwhelms us. You have taken us through an emotional journey of the last moments of my grandfather's life. Thomas's children never really grieved his death and by our contact it has enabled them to do this after 50 years.
I will share these poems with my children, my newborn, my only son, Christopher Thomas, born July 2007, carries his name. Thank you again, Harry.

The poems:

Tramp Ship *Minocher Cowasjee*

Fate was stowed crude
Profit driven, in your holds
At Vladivostok, and your Mate ignored
So that you wallowed in the troughs
And in Jakarta he walked off.

Fifty years are gone
And still I hear your signals
Fill the ether through the howl
Of that terrible rotating storm.

A shaking:
SOS SOS SOS Minocher Cowasjee
25.20 south, 68.00 east,
1500 miles south-east of Mauritius,
Bound Capetown from Jakarta.
Severe list, could capsize.

And my reply:
Reverberating on polished mahogany
Thumped out on a brass, post office pattern key
Heavy, solid, reliable and honest.
Thumped out onto groaning masts:

SS Mahanada
Out of Capetown for Calcutta,
Five hundred miles north of you.

Unable to alter course.
Will come when we can.

That's all I can do,
I am eighteen, how old are you?
Although I cannot see your face,
You live in a stream of intelligence,
And wireless men can read emotion.

You do not see the grim set
Of our captain's face.
I have to keep her head into this
or we're over,
Tell him we'll come when we can.

We have dynamite below.
On deck, two black locomotives strain
At their lashings like captive mastodons.
Our forward hatches are buried.
Astern the screw lifts free –
Spins

Then thuds into the sea again.
You call a few times more until –
In your holds,
Crates of Russian machinery smash
Into sacks of Javan rice.

Topside,
A decorated Serang – steady,
Cropped grey beard – hajji,
Knuckles bloody,
Grapples with the davits.

In the hot oil mist of the engine room,
A clear-eyed engineer
Is mobbed by frightened lascars
Crying out in Bengali
For mother.

And she goes over –
To be filled, to begin
Her bone-snapping
Five-mile journey down
Into the Mid-Indian Basin.

To lay crumpled in the silence
Of the floor of the abyssal plain
And be gazed upon forever
By lamp-headed fish.

Lost Ship

We saw nothing on the wind-glazed surface,
nothing floating in the spume as we steamed
across her track on the chart;
no scrap of cargo, no boiler suit,
nor a crumb of last night's rice.

In the dark we'd talked
in bursts of dots and dashes,
that other man and me.
We'd clung in chairs chained to the deck,
one hand on the tuning knob
chasing each other's warbling signals
as masts swayed
and phosphor-bronze aerials swung out
wild over the troughs;
the other hand thumping a big brass key . . .
in the cyclone.

It was sixty years ago – she flew the flag of Pakistan,
a new country. But the *Minocher Cowasjee* was old,
I now discover – launched as *Parisiana*
by Irvine's yard in Hartlepool, where my father,
back from his war with Kaiser Bill, might well
have hammered rivets into her, hard against
his own dad's hammer on the other side of the plate.

Three miles down they're rusted now, those rivets;
strewn about, forgotten, like Asian mother's tears.
She's just another hull – after all
the ocean floors are flung with ships . . .

SS Minocher Cowasjee at about 1956, the port unknown.
Photograph originally owned by Thomas Chadburn, her
Radio Officer. He has marked himself with a cross.
His grand-daughter, Susan Boucher of Brisbane, Australia,
supplied the image, and holds copyright.

SS Mahanada at Calcutta 1957

20

Bengal

February 1957

Mahanada steams north-east through the Bay of Bengal destined for Calcutta. We are above the Equator once more. February is technically winter here, but it makes small difference on the Indian coast. The cockroaches seem to be invigorated by the proximity of home; they breed without restraint. When I walk the dim passageways at night, they crunch in the gloom beneath my shoes. If I switch on the bedside light in the early hours, I see detachments of glossy brown beings perambulating along the top of the bunk's fiddly board, waving impossibly long antennae. I might stir in my sleep to swipe away a tickle on the cheek. They make me cringe. I grumble to 'Chips', the ship's carpenter about them. He's from Middlesbrough, just ten miles south of where I'm from. He reckons he's not a mere carpenter: he's a cut above that, a skilled shipwright. If needed, he could build a boat.

'I thought you liked insects, Sparks.' His angular features show a half smile.

'That I do. But I draw the line at cockroaches. The entire ship's heaving with the buggers. Once they've finished the grub in the galley, they'll probably come for us.'

'We were supposed to be fumigated in Birkenhead, but it didn't happen.' Chips rummages in the pockets of his boiler suit and fishes out a stale, half-smoked cigarette. He lights it with his petrol-driven Zippo and takes a drag. There's a smell like smouldering socks. He coughs. 'By heck! You can't beat a matured Woodbine.'

'I never saw a single cockroach on the troopship.'

'They're a special feature of the Indian Coast, Harry. You shouldn't let them get to you. I have them in my mess galley, you know. They're crafty little sods. There's even a few that's took to living in the fridge and have grown fur coats.' He has a twinkle in his eye.

'Get away, man. You're having me on!'

'All right then; I'll catch a couple and fetch them to you in a matchbox. I'll put them on your desk.'

'Don't bother – I believe you.'

That evening the officers and cadets sit down to China Chilao, a curry made of minced beef, generously laced with green peas and fried slivers of sliced onion. I dig in with relish. This curry is a favourite. Then my keen entomological eye perceives one strand of brown is not onion. I push it aside with the fork. Yuk! There's something with an odd texture in my mouth. The cockroach appeared 300 million years ago, back in the Carboniferous, whereas my primate kin are hardly a fifth that age. Even so, the texture of a crisply fried living fossil on the tongue is too much. I make an excuse, leave the rest of the officers to their dinner, and rush out to rid myself of the chilao.

I think about the carpenter's cockroaches; those he claims to have evolved fur coats by living in his fridge. Maybe it's true. In the cool Atlantic, these roaches (steam flies, some call them) shelter in the galley, or huddle among the valves and circuits in the wireless room so as to keep warm. Evolution has made them almost indestructible, though we don't see much of them in the radar hut; perhaps they are not immune to all that microwave radiation. But the flit-gun knocks them out. The old chap, my Indian boy, gives my cabin a going over once a week. Pumping the handle of a Flit-gun, he sprays under the furniture and drenches the deck lino with insecticide. The vermin scramble for safety but curl up if they get blasted. If they creep out later, to venture across the lino, they'll pick up the toxin on their feet and die. The chemical has a sickly smell that makes you gag. It's mainly the carrier solvent that stinks. The 5% active ingredient is what knocks down the bugs – it's called DDT. Another thirty years will see it banned; thirty years of Rachel Carson's *Silent Spring*.

Meanwhile, wildlife disturbs my breakfast. A morning ritual in the officers' saloon is to drop a Weetabix or two into the cereal bowl, then give the biscuits a couple of taps with the back of a spoon. Any weevils ensconced in the Weetabix will scurry out and be lifted free with the spoon – they are the size of a peppercorn, with a snout that sports a pair of eyes like a pince-nez on the end of Pinocchio's nose. Next, pour in reconstituted milk from a jug, and wait for any stragglers to paddle to the surface. Scoop them out, and enjoy breakfast. After performing the ritual a few times I decline cereal and dig into sardines on toast. Sometimes there's Kedgeree, a mild curry of rice and flaked fish; the fish can smell a touch ripe – but no matter.

Tucked into the northeast corner of the Bay of Bengal is Sandheads, an area of shallow sea with a silty bottom. A dainty pilot vessel swings casually at anchor here; she provides accommodation for the river pilots essential for the ninety-mile journey up the River Hooghli to Calcutta. The Hooghli is a distributary of the mighty Ganges-Brahmaputra. With a squeal of winches and a rattle of chains, *Mahanada* runs out both forward anchors. Secured thus, we wait our turn to berth in Calcutta. Nothing can be seen of the low coastline of the Ganges delta forty-five miles to the north, it seems strange to anchor so far from land. We anchor in company: there is the lovely old pilot ship to look at; closer to us lies the *Gutenfels,* a smart new West German that sports heavy-lifting gear; further off are a couple of nondescript elderly tramps with slender funnels, and a tanker. We all swing round in unison as the tide changes. The *Gutenfels* sends a Morse signal. It's a challenge to meet them on the Maidan (Calcutta's great park) for a football match and a few beers on *Gutenfels* afterwards. I pass it to the second mate, he's keen on the game.

He strokes his chin. 'Blimey! She's a white crew ship. All those Kraut deckhands to choose from. They're fitness fiends. We'll be murdered. Tell me, what field position do you play, Sparks?'

'I don't! Well, they used to stick me in as fullback at school. I wasn't much good for owt else.'

'Then, fullback it is.'

I shudder when I recall how I threw my body into the legs of attacking strikers in school football matches. Now I'll have to do it again, not against spindly urchins, but against the charge of huge Germans.

With Mike, the senior cadet (a bridge officer in training), I lean on the bulwark for our usual morning chat. He's wheezing a bit more than usual. His finely chiselled face shows some strain.

'Is the asthma a touch worse today, Mike?'

'It is. The closer we get to Calcutta the worse it gets.' He turns away to spit discreetly over the side.

'You'd think all this sea air would do it good.' I glance at his wide shoulders. He's well put together; a better frame than my own.

'It generally is. I'm fine in the North Atlantic. It's this tropical moist air that chokes me up. I dread the thought of a dock strike in Calcutta, a month with a million cow dung fires.'

'Perhaps you should be on the New York run, instead of this.'

'You're right, Harry. Next trip will be the last one of my apprenticeship. Then I'll leave Brock's to study for the Second Mate's ticket. After that, it's the Yankee coast for me, or even the Baltic. Anything but the Indian coast.'

We contemplate the water; it's a muddy yellow-brown here – hardly a ripple; it looks a bit oily and biological as it slowly drifts south into deeper water. It's loaded with silt from the Ganges-Brahmaputra. The Ganges (Ganga – The Mother Goddess) drains the southern slopes of the Himalayas to merge, as she runs east, then turns south into Bengal, with the westward flow of the Brahmaputra (Son of God) at the end of his tortuous course from the highlands of Tibet. 'Interesting silt,' is my thought. But there's no related thought to follow, for at that instant a giant black manta ray leaps out of the sea fifty yards away, spreads its great vampire-like wings and does a massive belly-flop onto the still water. There comes a boom – like a discharged canon. Mike and I smile at each other – there are wonders for the seafarer.

In the morning an American freighter loaded with grain from the USA weighs anchor and heads for the river mouth somewhere over the horizon. She is a wartime Liberty ship, a Samboat. Based on a British design conceived in the town of Sunderland, almost three-thousand were welded together in the USA from prefabricated sections to replace ships lost to U-boats. I'm told the USA is shipping surplus prairie wheat to India as part of an aid programme. India keeps having famines, the USA has a grain glut. These *plain-Jane* workhorses kept Britain alive and fighting; they were coal-fired (Britain was without oil, but had centuries of coal). Now they are part of a huge war surplus fleet mothballed in American rivers; if they were all released onto the market, world shipyards would be bankrupted. Greek shipping magnates like Onassis and Niarchos have built up large fleets of these freighters on the cheap. We see lots of Greek-owned Liberty ships flying flags of convenience: Panama and Liberia, and a couple of other countries whose harbours they'll never see.

Now it's our turn. The pilot launch has left the Yankee and now hooks onto the bottom of our Jacob's ladder. Two Indians ascend – the pilot and his leadsman. Our third mate greets the pilot while his leadsman drops a rope to the launch to haul up the pilot's gear. Chains rattle over the drums of the forward winch, the anchors break surface, dark delta ooze pours off their flukes. The engine room telegraph rings twice, and we slip away from Sandheads.

Three light-ships mark the fifty-mile approach to the river mouth. Out of a faint blue trace on the horizon, the mangrove swamps slowly rise; featureless and dark green, they spread east and west. The pilot takes us between glistening sandbanks and low, jungle-covered islands, into the mouth of the River Hooghli. I recall being shanghaied, tricked, onto a tramp ship of that name, the *SS Hughli*. That was a mere seven months ago, but it seems an age to an eighteen-year-old.

The mangroves end as suddenly as they began. On either side spreads the jungle, with occasional cleared areas and villages. I see people walking along earthen banks that surround paddy fields. The earth is bare except for rice stubble. It's too soon to plant new paddy, that will happen when the monsoon approaches. Instead, men are breaking up the ground with ploughs drawn by buffalo. Here and there the brightly painted towers of Hindu temples poke above trees. At the river margins, out of the shipping lane, brown men in white dhotis work in teams from little boats, casting nets. Shouts rise up and the boats come together. The fishermen begin to haul in the wriggling nets, all the while chanting a work song.

Tommy Williams, my chief, nudges me. 'You'll be enjoying them soon enough.'

'Enjoying what?'

'Bechti. That's a massive Ganges fish. And prawns like you've never seen; as big as a toddler's fist. Both of them make marvellous curry, particularly the Hooghli prawns – five curried on a bed of rice is enough for a prince. The ones we get are fished from the hundreds of side creeks that still run clean. Sometimes I think it's the only reason I stay with this company and the Calcutta run.'

Straw domes drift by on the current. Each hill of straw is supported by a barge that is almost unseen beneath the load. Someone invisible in the stern is operating a steering oar. It's like a scene from a Sunday School Bible. A swollen lump floats past; it rolls over in our wash to reveal four legs and a pair of blue-painted horns. I point. 'A cow. There's a cow!'

Tommy scratches through his vest. 'Not a cow; but near enough. It's a buffalo bloated with gas. You'll see quite a few bodies of the four-legged sort heading for the ocean, and sometimes those with two legs.'

'Human?'

He nods. 'They might have drowned or been chucked in to save on firewood. The Ganges is sacred to the Hindu, he cremates his people on the river bank and scatters the ashes in the flow. It's every Hindu's pious hope to have his funeral by the Ganga.'

'Not a place to go swimming then?'

'You'd have to be daft. There's the sewage of millions, all the way down from Nepal, and there's factory waste from Agra and God knows where else. The kids don't seem to mind though. See the pretty girls? And today is dhobi day.'

The channel has swung close to shore and a tiny village of huts and straw stacks. A noisy hoard of children dives and swims. Older girls are taking their baths, half-dressed in dripping saris; they notice that we watch, and sink down demurely to their necks. A line of Dhobi women are washing clothes, sousing them in river water, then beating the wet garments on flat rocks.

Tom gives his broad Welsh grin. 'While we're in Calcutta, be very careful who you get to do your laundry.'

Standing waves and a warning buoy mark dangerous shallows. Here lies the *James and Mary* sandbar, named after a foundered sailing ship *The Royal James and Mary* of the 17th century. One must admire those early European merchant adventurers who attempted this river in sailing ships in search of the riches of the spice trade. Sixteenth-century Portuguese first, then the seventeenth-century Hollanders, French and English, and later even Danes and North Germans, all attempted to found trading stations. They vied to find favour with the Moghul emperors, make business deals and contract trading licences. They squabbled, sought alliances, turned their cannon on each other's ships. It climaxed in 1690, in Britain's favour when the Englishman, Job Charnock, bought the village of Kalighat, to found a trading post for the British East India Company. Anglicised as Calcutta, it was to burgeon into the second city of the British Empire.

Job Charnock has been described as a silent and morose man – but I wonder. He saw a fifteen-year-old Hindu widow, a Rajput princess, tied to the funeral pyre of her husband. She was about to perform the rite of suttee (widow burning) and be immolated alive alongside his corpse. Job Charnock was smitten by her great beauty. He rescued her by force and carried her away to become his legal wife. They were together for twenty-five years until she died. She bore him a son and three daughters. Job has his grave in Calcutta. Someone should make a film of that story.

Downstream we pause at Diamond Harbour. Here we gently discharge our crates of dynamite; they are not allowed anywhere near the docks of Calcutta.

The Indian coast holds plenty of entertainment for the entomologist. Our lights attract giant brown moths with a full moon 'eye' on each wing. I've not brought my insect collecting gear, but from strips of wood in the carpenter's store in the fo'c'sle, I've fashioned a setting board. I now have a properly mounted moon-eyed moth pinned to a slice of wine cork, secure in a shoe box. We'll soon be steaming deeper into the Ganges delta, through jungle and paddy; now that should interest even a casual bug-hunter.

21

Kidderpore

February 17th.

Thirty-nine days from home. Two tugs push and pull to coax *Mahanada* out of the river Hooghli and into a narrow lock. Dusk gathers. Lights come on all over the docks. The mob of scavenging black kites (*Milvus migrans*, known to us as the *shitehawk*) that decorated our masts and aerials with hungry menace flap away in dribs and drabs, through the Calcutta haze, off to their roosts for the night. They gather as a group, circle a few times, then join with others that rise from cranes and warehouse roofs. They leave in silhouetted lines against streaks of smokey pink and blue. The lock fills, the gate opens, and we are decanted into the greasy waters of Kidderpore Dock, to be nudged alongside a berth where we tie-up next to railway lines. The air is unpleasant. There's a brown tint to the atmosphere from the cooking fires of the poor. They burn cow dung here; on the way upstream I saw how the walls of the country folk are plastered with evenly spaced flat cakes of cow dung, arranged in neat lines to dry. I forget the odour and become fascinated by a troop of monkeys on the ridge of a dockside shed. A shaggy old male guards three females who clutch infants to their chests. Some bachelors on the ridge are giving the old fellow a hard time. He bares his fangs. They'll be rhesus macaques – the sort that laboratories favour for live experiments.

At dawn, the two steam engines we've hauled through sun and storm as deck cargo are lifted by a special crane and lowered onto the railway track. They are drawn away by a shunting engine. Their place is taken by clanking hydraulic cranes. These venerable cranes puff and clatter as they haul nets filled with crates and boxes from *Mahanada's* holds. I'm fascinated by these old cranes, there must be over twenty of them gasping steam as they work the line of ships along the dock. Embossed on their iron sides is *Armstrong Newcastle 1892*; they were brand new when this dock was built. A lovely old steamer, a third our size, lies astern of us – the coal-fired *SS Rayandaman*, built 1922. She has a slight rake to her masts, an overhung stern, and a woodbine funnel. Her open and airy superstructure looks to be teak. The cabin doors open directly onto the deck – a proper tropical ship. She's Indian flagged but born in Glasgow.

SS Rayandaman in River Hooghly at Howrah Bridge

The Kidderpore morning is filled with din. Our holds bustle with brown, bare-foot dock workers, clad variously in coloured lungis and grubby white dhotis. They yell and jabber at each other in Bengali, at such a level it sounds like argument. I note the paler brown of the dockers' foreman. He wears western trousers and white shirt. He boasts proper polished shoes. By his side is a plump tally clerk with clipboard and fountain pen – he demonstrates an air of quiet superiority as he calculates and records everything that is hoisted from the noisy caverns below. A sinewy little man strolls around in khaki shirt and shorts; he sports an Australian style bush hat, worn at a rakish angle. His eyes are everywhere. He carries a dangerous looking staff. His bronze facial colour, his almond eyes with slight Mongoloid folds, mark him out as not from these parts.

I'm watching by the side of Walter Lloyd Williams; he's our second mate, and so takes responsibility for cargo today, the first mate being 'out of sorts'.

'Who is that little chap in the slouch hat?'

'The ship's guard. We always hire Gurkhas in Calcutta; they help to reduce the pilfering. Mostly ex-soldiers, some trained by the British Army, those chaps are solid and reliable – but can be fierce if needs be. They come down from Nepal in the Himalayas to earn a wage as watchmen. You'll see them up town, outside banks, hotels, big stores and the like. The local miscreants are terrified of them.'

The Gurkha approaches. He stops to give us a smart salute, then heads for the stern. As soon the Gurkha is out of sight, a grizzled Indian, in white turban, and a dhoti part-covered by a dusty black jacket that sports brass buttons and three pencils in the breast pocket, ascends the gangway. A little boy with spindly legs follows close behind. He shows a square of paper to the Lascar sailor on duty and is waved aboard. The old fellow picks his way with dignity across the oiled iron deck, across ropes, tarpaulins, and hawsers, and ascends the accommodation ladder. He's stooped beneath a lumpy burden wrapped in blue cloth. He sets it down before us, puts his palms together, and makes a little bow.

'Morning, sahibs. I am Dutt – permitted bookwallah for Brocklebank ship. I bring quality books for you. All clean. Best prices.' He unwraps his load and spreads the blue sheet to reveal a small mountain of books tied with string into stacks of ten. The deft fingers of the little boy arrange the bundles into an attractive order.

Walter glances at the display. 'Got any murders?'

'Atcha, Sahib. The best murders, she come.' He unpicks a knot to reveal a collection of Agatha Christie novels. 'These from Blue Funnel boat. From burrah sahib captain. He buy only from quality London shop. Like new.'

The second mate picks up a paperback, turns it over and flicks through the pages. '*Murder on the Orient Express* – read it.' He picks up another. '*The Murder of Roger Ackroyd*. How much?'

'One rupee, Sahib.'

He picks up two more. 'How much for three?'

'Two rupee, eight anna. Special price for you.'

As Walter gropes into his breast pocket, the epaulettes on his shoulders tilt to show the flash of two gold bands. He pulls out a roll of rupee notes. They look tired and grubby. 'I've had these since last trip. We'll soon be rid of this mucky old stuff – it's decimalisation in six weeks.'

'Atcha, Sahib. Everything new, for the new India.' The bookwallah picks out six bronze coins from his purse and hands them to the second mate.

Walter looks at the eight annas and hands them to me. 'There you are, Sparks. Some keepsakes from days gone by.' Two are square with rounded corners and carry the image of a humped bull on one side and three lions, back to back, on the obverse; two annas each. The four one anna coins have a waved edge; they are worn, but I can make out the image of King George VI. It's ten years since Indian independence from Britain.

'Tigh hi, Sahib. Blitish King George still good for spend. You like quality book? What you like read?'

'Any Zane Grey?' I can't think of any other author.

'No Zane Grey.' He lowers his voice to a conspiratorial whisper. 'But I have special book for you.' He hands me a bedraggled, slim paperback at the end of its life. I see a luscious brunette on the cover; she's leaning forward to reveal a skimpily covered cleavage. She's smoking a cigarette in a nine-inch holder. The title is *Corruption,* by Hank Janson. It boasts *Five Million Sold.* I drop the book back into the pile and instinctively wipe my fingers on my shorts. He hands me another; a thicker book. It's *My Life And Loves* by Frank Harris. I've never heard of it.

Walter laughs. 'You'll enjoy that. Get your circulation going.'

The old book wallah gives a wrinkled smile. 'Very fine book for young sahib. Sahib not buying this in England. It forbidden. Only in India can you buy. Famous book. Only three rupee.'

'I haven't drawn any Indian cash yet. I'll have to see the purser sometime today.'

The mate drops three limp rupee notes onto the stack of books. 'There you are, Sparks. You can owe me.'

Mr Dutt the bookwallah holds up a dignified green hardback. 'This one, best for jig-jig problem with memsahib.'

I take it from his old fingers. *Enduring Passion: Further new contributions to the solution of sex difficulties* by Dr Marie Stopes. Unlike the others, this smells new; India has lots of printing establishments. I'm not ready for this just yet, so I hand it back.

He offers another. 'This famous Hindu book. Tell how rajah have jig-jig.'

Another newish book. I flick it open to discover explicit line drawings dotted through the text. I've never seen anything like them. *Kama Sutra* is the title.

Trade ends when there's a shout from the deck above, 'Agent's just aboard, and he's brought a heap of mail from home!'

I open Beryl's letter first. It was written two weeks ago. She writes sweetly that Hartlepool is having the usual cold winter of rain, sleet, and slush. She's been to a dance at the Town Hall but says it was stuffy and boring compared to the night when we met at the Queen's Rink. The jazz musician Johnny Dankworth, with his *Dankworth Seven,* is booked at the Rink; she hopes her elder brother, Edwin, will take her. Edwin admires Dankworth's alto-saxophone and might be persuaded to lower his standards and visit the Rink for once. She's a nice girl, with a vivid character, and so I suppose she will have loads of admirers. If I stay on this run, we'll see each other just for a couple of weeks, twice a year. I've grown used to my job, ships, and the sea. I enjoy the work and won't be coming ashore any time soon. Besides which, I'm exempt from two years National Service with the military only if I stay at sea until I'm twenty-eight. That's ten more years at sea. Not much of a prospect for a young lady. Ah well. I take down the insulated jug from its fitting by the washbasin, give it a shake and hear it rattle. The 'boy' has recharged it with ice cubes. Good! Time for a gin and tonic swamped with ice.

Mam writes that she hopes I'm not in the gales that are hammering Hartlepool. She describes the waves off the headland as wild and full of white horses, and she says a prayer for me. Dad still has days off work with his angina. He's not enjoying being in the Furness shipyards at Haverton Hill on the Tees. Shipbuilding has changed since the trade unions became so powerful; they down tools if one shop steward discovers another trade union has infringed his own trade's accustomed work. There are arguments about who will drill holes into the new composite materials. A sandwich of metal and wood – should it be drilled by a metalworker or a woodworker? Dad is fed up with them and says he'll never vote for the Labour Party again. I think about dad while I sip the iced gin. He's worn out, like so many who went through the Great War. How long has he got? Mam will be worried. I push the speculations from my mind. I don't want to think about it.

I recharge my fountain pen from a stubby bottle of blue *Quink* and prepare to write replies, but stop when I hear a commotion. Some ne'er-do-well from ashore has broken into the carpenter's workshop in the fo'c'sle. Two taps have been ripped off the bulkhead; stolen, even though they are under pressure. Now water, hot and cold, gouts into the workshop while Chips rushes to the engine-room to have the flow shut off. It's just happened, so the thief won't have got far. In fact, the Gurkha guard has the culprit in an arm-lock; the thief still clutches the taps and a sack of stolen tools. He's Indian but dressed in western shirt and trousers. He looks like a clerk of some sort; I assume that's how he got aboard unquestioned.

Two huge dock policemen, khaki-clad, with well-fed waists, turn up. Their magnificent moustaches bristle as they manacle the thief and put him on a short rope. He's crestfallen as he's prodded down the gangway with sticks.

Once on the dockside the policemen set about the thief with lathis. Those six-foot bamboo staffs are reinforced with an iron ferrule at the tip. The thief gives out a shriek each time the lathi strikes. He's pleading for them to stop.

I watch the beating, my boss at one side. 'Tom, those sticks look murderous.'

'They can easily take a life. The lathi is the original Bengali fighting staff. The cops are skilled at quelling riots with them. They also impress on the miscreant the hazards of thievery.'

'They'll kill the poor bugger.'

'No they won't. I've seen this many a time. The blows will be on his muscular parts. They're careful to leave just enough bruises in the right places to make an impression, in public, before he's prodded along to the station. It's a bit of theatre; a demonstration to other thieves, other *loosewallahs*. There's plenty of them watching; the petty thieves and, much worse, the dacoits. They'll be taking note.'

'What's a dacoit?'

'A distinctly nasty sort of Indian bandit. They're mostly in the countryside, preying on travellers and villages. But they sneak into town now and again. So, you keep well away from back lanes. Stick to Chowringhee after dark – that's the main drag – and you'll be fine. Oh, and always keep your cabin door locked, and the wireless room, and the motor room – everything. When you're out, never leave the porthole open; keep it shut and screwed down. *Loosewallah* sends his little kids in through the porthole, even if they have to shin up a pole from a barge.'

The second mate leans on the rail beside us. 'I've fixed up the football match with the German heavy-lift boat. We play *Gutenfels* at 1000 hours Sunday morning on the Maidan. Not many volunteers so far. I'm having a job getting a team together. All sorts of excuses: pot bellies, ingrowing toenails, dodgy hearts, gin spots, you name it, we've got it.' He looks at my boss, who is close to sixty years old. 'What about you, Tommy?'

Tom straightens; he's a tall man. 'If you can persuade the ship's master to be centre-forward, then I might just come and watch. Him and me had enough exercise dodging the torpedoes the Krauts lobbed at us. Good luck to you, anyway.'

'How will you scrape eleven together?' I ask in the knowledge that I've no excuses not to be in the team, and thinking, with luck he won't assemble enough to field a team. I'm no soccer enthusiast, but I see no way to dodge this.

'Oh, we'll manage. There's always the secret weapon.'

'What's that?'

He winks, taps his nose, then strides away.

The Maidan (literally 'open-field') is a splendid, two square miles of parkland in central Calcutta and the traditional parade ground of the Indian Army. The tree-studded acres are dominated by a memorial to Queen Victoria, Empress of India. The great dome of white Makrana marble towers above trees in the distance as we assemble on one of the football pitches. The Germans line up to formally shake hands with us. They are uniformly well-proportioned and muscular men. Only three are officers, the rest of *Gutenfels'* team are deck crew, accustomed to manual work. Even their officers look as though weight-lifting is their hobby. Our team is made up of six sedentary officers, two nimble apprentices, Chips (the small and sinewy carpenter from Middlesbrough), and two secunnies (Indian sailors). Even though we are all decently rigged in working khaki shorts and shirts, the Germans appear amused by our cocktail of a team. I hear the second mate explain he's been unable to find eleven fit Europeans in *Mahanada's* crew, but that our two young Indian deck hands are enthusiastic to make up the shortfall.

The pitch must be cleared of sundry clutter: some bleating goats, with their minder (a spindly little boy); a couple of humped, sacred cows and attendant cattle egrets; sundry cow pats and the squatting woman in a sari who carries away the dung in her basket. The eye-watering haze, from the cow dung cooking fires of the poor, is hardly detectable here. We make the knots secure in our officers' shoes, then watch the Germans lace up proper football boots. They mean business! My mind is side-tracked when I catch sight of our two secunnies kick off their cheap footwear. They intend to play in bare feet!

We take our positions. We win the toss, and the whistle sounds. The second mate, our team captain, passes the ball to the engineer on his left who promptly loses the heavy sphere of inflated leather to a German winger. In seconds our team is pressed into scrambled defence around our goal. Yells of: 'pass; *reichen*; here; *raus*;' erupt. I take the ball in the midriff; it drops to my feet. I'm winded, but manage to kick it hard in no particular direction, except away from our goal. As one of two full-backs, I assume that's my job. The ball streaks back from a *Gutenfels* boot, is turned by our other full-back and crosses the line. The referee, an off-duty policeman we've hired for the day, blows his whistle. It's a corner kick.

Our goalkeeper, the senior apprentice, puts on a brave, blue-eyed front as the jostling mob assembles before his goalmouth. Excited shouts, in English and German, rise up. There's elbowing and rearrangement of position. We form a wall to block the shot. The referee, a big man with military moustache, paces the distance from the corner arc to our wall. He makes nine strides; the rules say ten yards. We are ordered to shuffle back one yard. He runs to the touchline, stands to attention, and sounds the whistle. The ball describes an arc above our wall. Two men leap to head the ball, clash together, and fall. There's pushing and shoving, a scramble. The ball bounces among a forest of legs. 'Goal!' It's in the back of our net. I limp; some big Bremerhaven boot has squashed my toes.

After thirty exhausting minutes, with the score 2-0 to *Gutenfels,* the ref blasts his whistle to stop play. A colourful Hindu funeral procession, with drums and warbling pipes, is proceeding onto the pitch unannounced. It parades towards the opposition's goal and tenderly lays a litter in the goalmouth. It bears the exposed corpse of a slender young man wreathed in golden marigolds. The referee ushers us to the touchline, explaining that the deceased young man had been, 'Keen player'. We seize the opportunity to sink a few cans of malty Tennent's beer, and sample bottles of crisp German lager, while we observe the funeral service. I enjoy the respite, the music and the chants of a Hindu puja. It takes twenty minutes. A straggle of hopeful beggars approaches to hold out imploring palms. We distribute a few coins and they sit down close by.

At half-time, we lay for the most part under a blazing sun, trying to stave off dehydration with more beer, our faces red with exertion. I recall my boss reciting a line from the days of The Raj: *Horses sweat, men perspire, ladies glow* . . . Well, I'm sweating buckets right now. The second mate is in a huddle with the two secunnies and our two heavily-built Scouse engineers who play midfield. The Germans are relaxed and expansive – they can afford to be – with the score now 4-0 in their favour.

By this time we have an audience of upper-class Indians out for a Sunday stroll with wives, children, and servants bearing picnic baskets. Barefoot rickshaw wallahs have drawn up their conveyances in hope of business. A score of beggars sit in a row; children and women, in faded clothes. The whistle sounds for second half, and off we go again. Here they come – *Gutenfels* is mounting a leisurely attack down one flank. They break through our line and start to pass the ball with arrogant ease, choosing where to strike. Then bewilderment. A cheer goes up. It's hard to see why. But there he is! A secunny has nipped the ball from the attackers and now streaks down the pitch towards a pair of previously unemployed enemy full-backs. They, and their goalkeeper, come forward to meet him, but his lithe form slips around their wall of muscle and, with a flick of a bare foot, puts the ball in the net. The Indian audience is on its feet, yelling with excitement. We join in.

I detect a change in the opposition. There's less pressure on us full-backs. We can take time to breathe. My partner is having a smoke. I reckon the Germans are not so confident. They seem more wary and have even become a touch defensive. Our new plan is to feed the ball to either of the two secunnies so they can strike. Ten minutes later our Indian sailors get us a second goal, and in the last minute we've another bare-foot wonder. The final whistle shows we have lost, 5-3; but that's not so bad.

22

Dear John

Still in Kidderpore Dock, we yield our position alongside the wharf to another vessel that needs cranes. A venerable tug nudges *Mahanada* onto moorings at buoys in the middle of the dock. Our next load of cargo will arrive by a flotilla of barges. Yet more chests of tea will be lifted by our own derricks and winches.

Over breakfast of iced mango juice, toast and marmalade, soft-boiled egg, a kedgeree of fish and rice, more toast, then coffee, the talk in the saloon is mostly about our next orders. We either load up for the UK and head straight home, or we take cargo for the USA before paying off in the UK.

'The clue will lie with all this tea we're shipping.' That was Archie, the chief engineer. 'My money's on the Thames. We'll be home by June.'

'I hope so. I'm expected at a wedding. My own!' That's a junior engineer; they are eating with us now we're in port. At sea, they tend to eat clad in boiler suits in their own, less salubrious mess. In the tropics, the engine-room is a dirty, sweaty place; I've watched men emerge from below, strip down to their underpants, lean over the side, and wring streams of sweat from boiler suits.

The first mate adds his two-penn'orth, 'A wedding? Bear in mind if we are booked for the States you can add six weeks to the trip.'

'Jesus! What do I tell her?'

The mate dabs at a dribble of egg on his chin with his white linen napkin; it has a tiny blue and white flag in one corner – the company emblem. 'Only joking. It's the Royal Docks, London, first stop this time. That's what the agent's just told us.'

There are sighs of relief all round. I'm disappointed. I've not been to the States.

Tied up alongside us is a Russian. She is sea-weary and in need of a coat of paint. On the port side of her rust-streaked hull, amidships, there is a circular dent about ten foot wide. We are soon in conversation with the crew who are mostly from Vladivostok, that USSR port and Pacific terminal of the Trans-Siberian Railway. An English speaker in the crew tells how the dent is from the near miss of a German bomb during the last war.

The crew look fit; in fact each morning they assemble on deck for physical exercises overseen by the ship's delectable lady doctor. She's blond, with the noble cheekbones of the Slav. Well, she looks lovely to us, who've been away a long time.

Apparently, the crew are not allowed ashore; such is the regime imposed by the political officer in the crew. He is one of the mates and walks around in a haughty manner. I have the impression he does not approve of the friendly relations our crews have got going. But Stalin has been dead four years, so things are slightly easier. Nikita Khrushchev took over two years ago and seems to be winding back on the terror politics of Stalin. In the evening the Russians erect a cinema screen on the foremast and set up a projector. This looks worth staying aboard for, so we line up our chairs along *Mahanada's* rails and furnish ourselves with crates of Scottish lager. The Russians have done similar on their own foredeck.

The projector sets off. We start to crack open cans but halt when the first image appears. It's a monumental sculpture of a muscular worker-hero holding the hand of a worker-heroine – she is beautifully sculpted, and topless; the camera moves around the couple to show them to best advantage. None of us focus on the man. Then come long minutes of titles in the blocky Russian script. I know a single word of Russian and that is *nowta;* it's from the few USSR stamps in my collection and probably means 'postage'. I don't see nowta in these titles. After a few shots of marching troops, we watch a dreary scene of someone made up to resemble Joseph Stalin; he points to maps and gives orders to a stout chap in uniform. Stalin is calm. He fingers his pipe and speaks with slow deliberation for interminable minutes. A cut and we are in Hitler's command bunker. The actor does his best to be Adolf, waving his arms about, shouting at his generals and thumping a map with his fist. He looks angry and a touch stressed. He shouts in German, so I pick up a few words. I intuit the word 'Rommel' and something like, 'Anglo-Saxons are fools!' Then: 'Moscow!' He faces the camera and smacks an arm across his chest: 'I'll stand astride the continent of India! Then I strangle America!'

The chippy, with his usual Middlesbrough wit, strikes up a ditty to the tune of the *Colonel Bogey March*, and we join in:

'Hitler! He only has one ball,
The other is in the Welfare Hall,
And Himmler, has something similar,
But poor old Goebbels
Has no balls at all.

Where was the engine-driver
When the boiler burst?
They found his knackers
Ten-thousand miles away,
Floating upon the Hudson Bay,
His penis was found on Venus,
And the rest was found in Spain.'

The Russians are turned our way. They flash grins. The jollity ends when a mass of bombers fill the sky. They rain bombs onto a city that appears already in ruins. At one point we instinctively duck when a propeller-driven fighter aircraft zooms towards us firing twin machine guns. Next shot is a twin-engined aircraft with black crosses on the wings and swastikas on its tail.

The engineer by my side says, 'That's a Junkers 88 dive bomber.'

'What's the fighter?' This engineer is forever asking me to get books on military matters for the ship's library.

'A Soviet Yakovlev. A Yak-1. Wooden wings; a brilliant machine and dead simple to maintain. Those Kraut planes are over-engineered. Crap in a harsh climate.'

The bullets, some of them tracers rip along the Junkers' fuselage until they reach the cockpit. It bursts open and she goes down in a spiral, into the ruins of the city. The engineer cracks open another can, and slurps. He grunts. 'I reckon we're watching *The Battle of Stalingrad*; made in forty-seven.'

I keep losing the thread of the story; the entomologist in me is fascinated by the dance of myriad insects in the projector beam and the assemblage of Bengal moths and beetles that sit on the screen. Is that a wart, or has a big brown noctuid come to rest on the tip of Joseph Stalin's nose? But the cruel, calculating visage disappears and the moth now rides on the turret of a German panzer. Oh, now it's on the ruined wall of the famous Tractor Factory, and now in the middle of the Volga river helping the Russian reinforcements to cross and their wounded to be ferried to safety amid the waterspouts of the Luftwaffe's bombs. It flutters its way to the edge of the screen; I wonder what species it might be.

At the end of the show, apparently that was only part one – part two will be run some other night, the Russian chaps line the rails in a friendly manner. We pass them cans of Glasgow beer. They invite us aboard for a drink; their political officer has gone ashore – probably to the Soviet embassy. We crowd into a cabin where we are plied with blue wine; I've never heard of such a thing – it's from the Ukraine. Then comes the vodka. We learn how to throw it back, link arms, and drink to peace. How they can drink! I'll have a headache in the morning. Though she's not present, I ask about the lady doctor. A chap with reasonable English, a former schoolteacher, explains she looks after all of their needs. 'All of them?' I enquire. 'Yes,' he says. 'All of them …'

In the morning our second mate seeks out the political officer to arrange a football match. The political man is at first reluctant; Russian crews are not usually allowed ashore in non-Soviet bloc ports, lest they defect. If they do desert, their relatives might be punished. But the officer relents, on the understanding we hire a bus and the Russian team is kept together and returned as one. So we have a match on the Maidan and lose handsomely to the Russians. Hey ho . . .

The political officer softens further; he permits us to take a few Russians to The Lighthouse, the best air-conditioned cinema in Calcutta. The film is *Singing in the Rain,* directed by and starring Gene Kelly. Unlike

Stalingrad, it's in full Technicolor. Most of the Russians cannot follow the dialogue, but they all enjoy the song and dance; I suppose it comes across as a sort of ballet.

Another trip out is to The Seaman's Mission, to the weekly dance known to visiting sailors as *The Dingbat's Ball*. Why dingbat? The Oxford dictionary declares dingbat: a stupid or eccentric person; delusions or feelings of unease, particularly those induced by delirium tremens. At Dingbats, music comes from a hand-cranked record player that spins a mix of shellac and vinyl records. A diverse collection of world seafarers, Finns and Swedes, and all sorts, waltz with alluring Anglo-Indian girls, while watched carefully by their chaperone, a lady by the name of Merle-Prince Wright. I have the impression that many of the girls are on the lookout for a husband. Since Indian independence, the thriving community of Anglo-Indians is in decline as they emigrate to other parts of the British Commonwealth. Their community began with intermarriage between British troops, planters, and officials as far back as the 18th century.

The evening goes well, except for shrieks when some wag distributes among the dancers a dozen hopping green frogs he's collected from the mission's garden. Our Russian friends have a great time. An engineer from another Brocklebank ship will meet his future wife at the Dingbat ball. Enid Clump is an attractive girl; she's astonished when, on arrival at Liverpool, she sees British dockers. I'm told she declared: 'My goodness! White coolies!'

Against the background of jaunts ashore, the days drag on while our winches and derricks hoist nets that bulge with chests of tea, marked *Lipton's*, out of barges and into our holds. Whatever happens on deck is noted by the rows of beady eyes along our aerials and the cross-trees of the masts. The black kites miss nothing. Any food on display is swooped on and grabbed by their talons. Many a steward on his way from the galley with meal trays is knocked sideways by an attack. In mediaeval London, a cousin species, the red kite, kept the streets free of offal and suchlike waste.

The Russian ship eventually departs and we wish each other well. After ten days of loading, we will also leave Calcutta. But before we do, I have a letter from Beryl. She writes that she has met someone else, and thinks it best I know as soon as possible. A sick, hollow sensation floods my stomach; even so, I yell out so that the adjoining cabins can hear: 'I've got a *Dear John*!'

In moments Taffy, the third mate, is at the door. 'A Dear John? That means you have to get the beer in.' He yells down the alleyway: 'Boy! *Tunda* beer! *Ek* dozen *tunda* beer!'

The Indian steward soon deposits a crate of Tennent's lager onto my deck and hands me a chit to sign. Tradition insists that whoever gets a *Dear John* throws a party so that his shipmates might commiserate. But he must also foot the bill. A party follows that extends from afternoon into the evening. I keep up a brave front and push aside the empty feeling. There'll be no more sweet letters; I'm bereft; I'll drown this sadness. Men drift in and out to offer sympathy, quaff cold beer, and with arms of comfort around me and theatrical sobs, sing:

'Dear John, when you get this letter, I'll be gone.
I must move on, oh dear John . . .'

Next day, I take to my bunk. I sweat and shiver, have muscle pain, headache, and cannot bear the light. A doctor is summoned. In delirium, I'm aware of a large Bengali gentleman who counts my pulse, takes my temperature, then laughs: 'Ah, ah! The patient has dengue fever! Aspirin for you, my good fellow, and lots of water.' That's all I'm aware of. I remain in a fever for five days, then suddenly I'm well again – though a bit tottery. I must have been bitten by a mosquito a week since. It's my first tropical disease. If things continue this way, I'll soon be an old India hand.

23

Visakhapatnam

We sail tomorrow; time to have the last run ashore and a night out. The carpenter and I clamber into a cycle rickshaw; it's not far to the Lighthouse Cinema. I try not to lean back into the cushions and brocade hangings; last night, in a taxi, a large beetle dropped inside the back of my shirt. I've not forgotten the sensation of its armoured claws and carapace between my shoulder blades.

We soon wish we had stayed aboard for a quiet evening instead. We hear distant shouts and drums, but rickshaw wallah seems unperturbed. He pedals between packed buses and through savoury curry odours from the stalls of street vendors, towards the cinema at a steady pace, until he brakes hard. The road ahead is crammed with marching men, some in western shirt and trousers, but most wear the folded sarong skirt that is the traditional lungi. From the short haircut, together with a tuft at the crown, I deduce many are Hindu. They shout and chant and wave red hammer and sickle banners. We are in their path. More agitators pour from side streets with police whistle blasts in their rear. Our turbaned rickshaw wallah closes the curtains to shield us from view. He puts his finger to his lips: 'Sahibs no e'speak. Quiet. Quiet.'

The Communist-inspired labour unions are on the streets. Today's problem is the new grain elevator built with American aid so that famine relief ships can be unloaded fast. Trouble is, the grain elevator threatens the employment of the mass of labourers who unload grain ships by hand. A mob has attacked the elevator and put it out of action. We stay rigid while the mob floods past. As they march, they shout and bang on the sides of stranded taxis and buses. They thump the side of our rickshaw. It begins to sway as the march swirls around it; our conveyance resembles a rock that divides a torrent. I'm anxious and, from the tight grin on his angular face, I can tell that Chippy thinks we could be in trouble. We agree in a whisper that we might have to make a run for it and we had best stay together. But the rocking stops. A peep through the curtains shows the riot has moved towards the harbour. Police whistles sound at the dock gates. Rickshaw wallah rises from his saddle to stand upright on the pedals; muscular calves, and brown feet in cheap flip-flops, press down, break the inertia of his burden of two well-fed Englishmen, and our conveyance creaks into motion.

At the Lighthouse, in a full auditorium, we settle into a new film, *King Richard and the Crusaders*. George Sanders plays a sardonic Richard the Lion Heart; Rex Harrison contrives an exotic Saladin; while Virginia Mayo yields up a toothsome Lady Edith Plantagenet. The film is appreciated in silence by the sprinkling of Europeans, but the main audience is restless. Whenever the red-cross blazoned crusaders hack into turbaned heads with their broadswords, there are boos and hisses. When the black-cloaked Saladin gives the western knights a hammering, sweeping off heads with his scimitar, there are cheers; some of the audience jump to their feet, gesticulating. I'm reminded of the legendary meeting between King Richard

254

and Saladin and how each challenged the keenness of the other's sword. Richard called for a log of wood. Raising his two-handed English broadsword high above his head, he brought it down with such a thud that the log clove in two. Saladin considered the result, then threw a scarf of the finest silk into the air. He held out his Damascus blade to catch the scarf. As the silk drifted earthwards like a butterfly, it fell across the blade and was silently halved.

After the show, we decant into the street. The flood of locals is in an excited state. In the story we've just enjoyed, the Crusaders are the overall winners. The Indian crowd doesn't like the result, even though half are probably Hindus and not followers of Mohammed. Knots of them give us dark looks. There's a taxi! We jump in. Let's get out of here.

The Hooghli river spits us into the Bay of Bengal, and we rejoice to be free of Calcutta. *Mahanada* has the clean sea once more as she hugs the Indian coast steering south-west for Visakhapatnam. Many of our Indian crew have paid off; they have done their allotted 12 months with us and must now stay ashore for a year. Independent India has contrived regulations that bring foreign shipowners extra hassle. We are obliged to rotate the crews so that available berths are equably shared out among the huge numbers that clamour to sail with British ships (I've calculated that our Indian bosun earns as much as a qualified medical doctor in Calcutta).

To keep the best fraction of our crew for another voyage, our agents pay bribes to the Calcutta seaman's employment office. We've held onto our superb Goanese cook, some of the better stewards, and all the serangs (Indian bosuns). Even so, we have a large proportion of new Lascars (Indian seamen), and some give cause for concern – they come aboard with bloodshot eyes. Are they even genuine Lascars? We suspect some are here on account of bribes paid to the shipping office. Some look as though they're recently down from the hills and have yet to get their first sight of the ocean. For the first few days, we can get little useful work done until their supply of drugs and palm toddy has run out. There's a trickle of these new fellows to the purser's office with the usual VD; he anticipates this and has the treatment all prepared. A couple of youngsters seek refuge from the mate; they are being sexually pestered in the crew accommodation on the poop. The mate and the purser have to sort it all out; I don't envy them. Just give me some racks of friendly glowing valves, a Morse key, and leave me in peace.

On this track, we are close enough inshore to have telescopes trained on the town of Puri, a fishing village that holds the festival of Jagannath. Puri temple is famous for the annual *Rath Yatra*, or the chariot festival of the gods, in which the crowds of devotees haul a trio of deities on three massive, and elaborately decorated temple cars. Each vehicle, as well as the image of the god, supports balconies that hold scores of chanting Brahmin priests. The vast chariots gave us the English loanword *Juggernaut* (immense, unstoppable, threatening entity). Early European observers claimed to have seen thousands of worshippers in attendance. They returned with tales of devotees being crushed under the wheels of these chariots, whether by accident or as a meritorious suicide. Thousands still flock here; modern Hindu priests deny the suicides ever took place. The three gods take to the streets in June. In this present month of March, the divinities Jagannath, Balabhadra, and Subhadra brood in their temples while the good folk of Puri soberly engage in sea fishing.

Down the coast as far again, the approach to Visakhapatnam is protected on the south side by a

256

breakwater composed of scuttled ships reinforced by rock armour. English speakers become weary of attempting the proper name and refer to the place as *Visag*. We pass beneath a cliff to navigate the narrow, dog-leg entrance to the harbour; it has the appearance of a drowned geological fault. The pilot orders a ninety-degree turn to starboard so as to enter the only natural harbour on this coast. A few venerable cranes stand beside steep piles of iron, manganese and chromium ore. Steam engines shunt loaded waggons about the dockland. Hordes of labourers, men and women in ragged clothes the colour of ochre, toil with loaded baskets on their heads. In 1957, Visakhapatnam is a sleepy place, but this infant will grow into a giant industrial city.

The small town is said to be ancient and supposed to be named for Visakha, a talented woman disciple of the Buddha. She would have lived almost 2,500 years ago. Two centuries after Visakha, this region was a corner of the State of Kalinga, destroyed by the Mauryan Emperor Ashoka. Ashoka thus completed his father's empire but was so sickened by the slaughter he witnessed on the battlefield of Kalinga he declared that henceforth he would follow the teachings of the Buddha. Some say he became the wisest and most compassionate ruler the world has yet seen. After his death, India fragmented once more. Only the British Indian Empire managed to restore the sub-continent to a cohesion equal to the achievement of Ashoka. After the Kalinga War (262BC), the bloodiest in Indian history, Ashoka (King Priyadarsi) set up edicts on rocks, and pillars of iron, that outlined how his empire would be governed by empathy for all that lives.

Rock edict no.13 has this: *Beloved-of-the-Gods, King Priyadarsi, conquered the Kalingas eight years after his coronation. One hundred and fifty thousand were deported, one hundred thousand were killed and many more died of other causes. After the*

Kalingas had been conquered, Beloved-of-the-Gods came to feel a strong inclination towards the Dharma, a love for the Dharma and for instruction in Dharma. Now Beloved-of-the-Gods (Priyadarsi), feels deep remorse for having conquered the Kalingas.

Edict on pillar No. 5: *Twenty-six years after my coronation various animals were declared to be protected – parrots, mainas, aruna, ruddy geese, wild ducks, nandimukhas, gelatas, bats, queen ants, terrapins, boneless fish, vedareyaka, gangapuputaka, fish, tortoises, porcupines, squirrels, deer, bulls, okapinda, wild asses, wild pigeons, domestic pigeons and all four-footed creatures that are neither useful nor edible. Those nanny goats, ewes and sows which are with young or giving milk to their young are protected, and so are young ones less than six months old. Cocks are not to be caponized, husks hiding living beings are not to be burnt and forests are not to be burnt either without reason or to kill creatures. One animal is not to be fed to another.*

Legend attributes Ashoka's conversion to a woman who approached him and declared: *Your actions have taken from me my father, husband, and son. Now what will I have left to live for?*

So much I glean from the great Arthur Mee's Children's Encyclopaedia and future consultation with a yet unborn divinity who shall be known as *The World Wide Web*. Knowledge is a wonderful thing, and Arthur Mee will have known much more than Ashoka could hope to absorb. But wisdom, and the turning about of the human heart? Now that is altogether something else.

The Visakhapatnam of 1957 is still part of Madras State, which has a complete prohibition on the consumption of alcohol. Seafarers of sundry nationalities congregate in an extended bungalow on a point just outside the centre of town. The 'club' enjoys a clear view over the harbour and catches the breeze just fine. The alcohol law applies to all except those alcoholics who claim a medical need. At the club, my shipmates and I pay one rupee each and sign the *Confirmed Alcoholics Register,* and associated paperwork, to claim exclusion from the prohibition law. Panther rum, Indian distilled, comes by the bottle; it's rough stuff, but cheaper than the Coke we decant into it.

Next day we prepare to load manganese ore, essential to the manufacture of stainless steel. From the upper accommodation deck, I'm astonished as bamboo staging is rigged alongside the ship. Girls in grubby saris, with skirts hitched around bare legs, mount the staging and, with much incomprehensible chatter, begin. Men on the nearby heaps shovel ore into baskets. The baskets are on a stage, so the girl does not need to bend and lift. She stands whilst a man slides the loaded basket onto her head-pad. She then moves with sublime grace to the staging on the ship's side. The burden is taken by another woman who lifts it into the hands of the woman above. By this means, baskets of ore climb our hull and arrive on the deck to be tipped into *Mahanada's* deep hold. There are scores of muscular women and girls, in steadily moving lines, performing work that I would expect of a crane or a conveyor belt. They are superbly erect and glide like swans on water. As ore pours into the lowest hold, fine dust rises through the hatch opening. The bales of jute and chests of tea are safe in the tween-decks, sheeted over to keep out debris. The women who toil on deck wrap a strip of cloth across their faces. I wonder what the women's homes are like, and their lives. What happens if they get ill?

My boss has arrived at the rail. 'I'll bet you've seen nothing like this before today, Harry boy.' I never tire of Tom's Welsh voice.

'I've not, chief. It's barbaric. There's a steam crane over there; why not use it?'

'That crane's knackered. Has been for years; look at the creepers twined along its jib. Anyway, just suppose there was a modern crane with a big grab – driven by one man; these ladies would be unemployed and their families would know empty bellies. They're earning a wage. The last thing they want to see is a working crane.'

'I hadn't thought of that. I see they've got money enough to chew betel.' One attractive girl, with a ring in one nostril, has just expectorated a long streak of vermilion liquid into the dust of the quayside.

'Well, it's a stimulant and dulls the hunger. It cheers them up and numbs what they must undergo to feed the kids.'

I consider that for a moment. 'A lot of those girls are bonny, and some older women are – what you might call handsome, in a craggy sort of way.' The line has slowed. The women halt in Indian file, beneath baskets of manganese, waiting for the backlog on our deck to clear. There's an accurate volley of betel juice from several pretty mouths. The lips and teeth of the chewers have become as red as the juice. 'What's in that stuff, Tom? Calcutta was awash with it.'

'It's *Paan,* which just means *leaf.* Betel leaf is wrapped around areca nut mixed with slaked lime to hold the wad together. They might add this and that in the way of herbs to sweeten the breath. There's a whole industry churning out the muck.'

'Those lovelies can spit like John Wayne!' Taffy, the third mate, another Welshman, has joined us. He's rolling a cigarette from a pouch of long-stranded Anton Justman's shag – his favourite. He licks the gummed edge and thumbs it straight and neat. 'Make sure to be here at the end of the shift, and you'll see what else they can do.' He snaps the zippo lighter shut and takes a drag. He has an oddly irregular face for a youngish man, a face that folds into interesting creases when he gives his customary wry smile. I can see him playing a weather-beaten trail rider in a western movie. But perhaps his ears stick out a bit too much for him to become a heart-throb.

At the end of their shift, the dusky ladies gather around a fire hydrant and, without removing their saris, take a cold wash in full view of those of us who, like me, have nothing better to do but gawp at the proceedings. One bold girl makes eye contact across the jetty and calls out, 'Lifebuoy?' Immediately, a bar of toilet soap is thrown towards her by one of our engineers. She catches it with the skill of a cricketer, opens the packet to inspect the coral-coloured soap and sniffs its light perfume. She then unwraps her dripping sari and stands proudly for five long seconds to reveal a magnificent wet body. Another girl takes a pace forward. 'Lifebuoy?' she calls, in sweet, musical tones. She catches the bar just as adroitly as her workmate. Glistening with hydrant water, her body is as alluring as the first. Some wag throws a bar of green carbolic laundry soap, of the roughest sort. A girl catches it and throws it back. Several more bars of our shipping company's *best soap for officers* are plucked from the air before this bit of theatre starts to lose its novelty. I have an awkward sensation that this cannot be right. We are intruders, yet it's a scene of our making. We have come here with eight thousand tons of ship, and some boxes of pink soap, to collect the means of making stainless steel, but these bare-footed women might be little changed from their sisters who lost menfolk at Kalinga. The world is out of joint.

Our purser/chief steward strides past — he always strides. His blond hair is in neat natural waves; he dresses impeccably and his catering is high quality; out of earshot he's referred to as *The Duke of Bootle* (Bootle is a crowded working-class, ship-building district of Merseyside flattened by the Luftwaffe). He shouts to a sweaty engineer in a greasy boiler suit who clutches three bars of

Lifebuoy: 'If I were you, mate, I'd go easy chucking that about. There's not a lot left in my store. When it's bloody well gone, you're all on carbolic.'

We have three more days in port whilst this laborious loading takes place. It's time we visited the beach. With two apprentices, I join a colourful throng on the floating platform of a chain-ferry. Our bare legs below our shorts are tickled by goats, at risk of bruises from a cart pulled by restive bullocks, and grinned at by country folk returning from market. Best of all though, is the elephant that chews contentedly on green stuff her mahout feeds into her mouth; meanwhile, her trunk explores whatever it can reach, bare knees included. With much clanking and puffing, the engine house on the far bank hauls in the chains to pull us across the harbour's narrow entrance.

We tramp two miles, via a steep cliff, through a smiling village, across a headland, then down the cliff onto an empty stretch of pale sand. It was worth hauling the cans of beer, even though they are now as warm as tepid tea. We swim a bit, lay in the sun, explore the tide margin, investigate the empty shells of sea urchins, shift our towels whenever a platoon of inquisitive hermit crabs sidles up. The air is pure; scented by the sea, mixed with unaccountable perfumes from shore. We young fellows, who take weeks to blunt a razor, share an Indian interlude far from the beggared mayhem of Calcutta.

24

Sunburn and Home

We steam out of Visakhapatnam on 13th April and reach Colombo, on the island of Ceylon, three days later. I've not brought my stamp album to sea, thinking it a boyhood distraction. Even so, when posting letters home beneath the soaring Victorian ceiling of Colombo's central post office, I cannot resist the stamps on display. I hand over a few rupees and buy a commemorative set that celebrates an event called *Buddha Jayanti*. They were issued last year, 1956, and mark 2,500 years since the birth of Gautama Buddha at Lumbini, in what is now Nepal. They are handsome stamps that feature an eight-spoked wheel. Forty years will pass before I understand the significance of that wheel.

We'll be in Colombo for ten days. It's in the bar of the Grand Oriental Hotel that I meet the former mate of the lost *Minocher Cowasjee,* but I've dealt with that haunting coincidence in an earlier chapter. An image of the distressed ship keeps returning and will do throughout my years. Meanwhile, there are diversions on this beautiful island.

I have my mind deep into *The Deceivers* by John Masters, written in 1950 but set in 1830s India. It's a chilling novel based on the suppression of the Thuggee. The English word *thug* is derived from the Sanskrit *thag,* which means deceiver. These sadistic dacoits were overcome by a Cornishman, William Henry Sleeman of the Bengal Army. The Thugs were a cult of murderous highway robbers and ritual stranglers devoted to a debased form of the goddess Kali The Destroyer. In Masters' novel, the thugs infiltrate and befriend bands of travellers, only to murder them in their sleep in an orgy of ecstatic strangling. It's filled with heart-stopping menace and affects my dreams. The hairs on the back of my neck are erect. I sense a presence behind me, and hold my breath.

'Fancy a run ashore, Sparks? A few of us are off to Mount Lavinia for a swim.' It's Taffy, the third mate.

'What's Mount Lavinia, when it's at home?'

'A famous posh hotel, on a headland above a fine beach. A place not to be missed. You'll like it, boyo. An easy bus ride down the coast. Come on, chuck that book aside, grab a towel and take the chance to top up your sun-tan ready to impress those Geordie bints in Monkey Town.' His Welsh banter is persuasive.

The pre-war Bedford bus sways and rattles south for eight miles along the coastal plain. We've distributed twenty-four cans of Tennents of Glasgow lager about our five persons and, to surreptitious piercings and slow fizzes, are already lightening the burden. Passengers come and go with bundles and baskets. We are immersed in the odours of armpits and spices. Even so, some of the Singhalese maidens are delightful to contemplate; a pity we are here for only a few days. Although the slats of the wooden seats press into the backside, I'm glad I came. The road is a ribbon of villages sprinkled with temples and churches, schools and markets; there's even a happy elephant being washed in a pond by his mahout and a gaggle of children.

We make for the Mount Lavinia Hotel which stands imperiously on a rocky promontory above the shore. It's a steaming hot day and we crave cold beer. At the grand and columned entrance (the place was built in 1806 as a residence by Sir Thomas Maitland, the British Governor) a stout, topee-headed flunky bars our passage. I sense he has us pinned out twenty fathoms beneath the tip of his nose. 'Hotel full. Closed one month.' His moustache bristles. The fellow sports epaulettes that would shame Mussolini.

Ken, the *Mahanada's* Scouse electrician, is not impressed. 'Get away with you, whacker; the joint can't be closed and full at the same time.'

The flunky sticks out his chest. 'Lavinia hotel booked by Mr Sam Spiegel of America, for making big film.'

'Oh, aye? And what film might that be that keeps drought-stricken seafarers away from the bar?'

'*Bridge on River Kwai* it name. Last month, Prime Minister Bandaranaike come to see bridge blown up.'

'Never heard of the film, or that fancy pants Bandyknickerleg bloke either! Fetch the manager! We want cold beers.'

'How might I be of assistance?' I'd noticed a suave fellow in a beige suit observing us from a distance. Now he stands by Ken's arm.

Ken tucks his Hawaiian palm-blazoned shirt into the waist of his baggy khaki shorts. 'We desire to visit your esteemed air-conditioned bar. This bold, bejewelled fellow declines to let us pass.'

'Normally, I'd be delighted to welcome you to the Lavinia. But currently, we have William Holden, Jack Hawkins, and Alec Guinness as guests, together with a huge film crew and all its paraphernalia. Mr Spiegel has reserved the entire hotel for the purpose of his production.'

265

Ken takes hold of the manager's sleeve. 'Jack Hawkins! He was in *The Cruel Sea*. I saw that one. He had to depth-charge a load of swimming survivors – a merchant crew in the water, just to get at the U-boat hidden beneath. A smashing, but sad picture.'

Taffy butts in, 'He acted in *Angels One Five* as well. Amazing action between Hurricanes and Messerschmidts; I saw it in Birkenhead. And Alec Guinness did a scary old Fagin in *Oliver Twist*. Saw that at the Llandudno Palladium when I went on leave. Sat at the back, in the doubles, in the courting seats, with a cariad bach. Lovely, she was. Can't remember too much about the film, though.'

The manager loosens Ken's grip on his sleeve. 'You might also recall William Holden won an Oscar for his role in *Stalag 17*. I suspect you'll enjoy *Bridge on the River Kwai* when it's released. It's about the Burma Railway and how those dreadful Japanese treated our prisoners-of-war. I understand Alec Guinness is superb as the deranged Colonel Nicholson.'

'Deranged? My name's Nicholson.' I fix the manager with what I consider a hard stare. 'I've never heard of him. Where's he from?'

'He's from nowhere. The story is a work of fiction – based loosely on the Burma campaign. Now, gentlemen, there is a bar on the shore where you can purchase cold beer, and where you might even meet some of Mr Spiegel's make-up girls; they tend to favour a dip in the sea.'

As we descend the steps to the palm-lined beach, I pause to read a noticeboard that tells of a dancer, and a secret tunnel that the British Governor had constructed so that he could visit the nearby house of the dancing girl he had become enamoured of. The girl, a lovely mestizo mix of Portuguese and Sinhalese ancestry, was Lavinia Aponsuwa. London became aware of the liaison and, in

1811, transferred Sir Thomas to the Mediterranean island of Malta, and later to Corfu, where he died a bachelor. In 1920, the tunnel was sealed. 'Poor sod,' I mutter and hurry to the shore to join my mates.

The beach is superb: soft coral flecked yellow sand; coconut palms; and a stall that sells charcoaled fish curry. After a swim in a tranquil sea, still stripped down to dripping khaki shorts we join a band of local lads and help to kick around their football. We keep a lookout for Spiegel's make-up girls but there are none to hand. The sun beats down all afternoon, but we are oblivious. Despite our deep tropical tans, we have overdone it and are becoming boiled lobsters even on the bus back to the ship.

I've never known such fierce sunburn. It's difficult to sleep. Next day, we appeal to the purser/chief-steward for medication. He laughs, says we are stupid buggers, and gives each of us a bottle of calamine lotion. The lotion has a cooling effect, but cannot repair the damage. My forehead and shoulders are blistered and peeling. The skin wrinkles and slides off to expose weeping flesh. My once bronzed body is now a mess of hanging strands. In five weeks' time, we'll sail into the Thames and I wonder if I'll have enough time to grow new skin.

Four weeks ago, in March 1957, Colonel Nasser declared the Suez Canal fit for traffic once more. But there remain wrecks from the British/French/Israeli attack still to be cleared; they would be a hazard to all but small vessels. We are to reverse our outward journey and go home via the Cape of Good Hope. It will be routine: twelve days to Durban in South Africa, to replenish bunker oil; a further sixteen days to Las Palmas in the Canary Islands for more bunkers; then six days at sea and we should reach Tilbury Docks in the Thames. Pay off: train to Fenchurch Street, twenty-two miles; lug my gear via the Underground across London to King's Cross; then the train home on leave. Hurrah!

And so my train steams into West Hartlepool late on 31st. May 1957. Friday is a prime day to begin five weeks of leave. I already know that Elvis Presley is making the running with *All Shook Up;* I look forward to a few pints of Cameron's Strongarm with my mates in the Volunteer's down Lynn Street, and seeing what mad fashions they've cultivated since I left five months ago. I put the mangled copy of *The Daily Mirror* that I found on the train, into a waste bin. Nothing much in the paper apart from the news that Britain has tested her first hydrogen bomb above some inoffensive atoll in mid-Pacific, and there's been a fuss at the French Lawn Tennis championships when a chap in the mixed doubles fell into an argument with the spectators and invited a few onto the court to fight it out.

I'm pleased to see the fluted brass doorknob on the front door of 55 Warren Road; I think it rather noble for a rented semi-detached owned by the North-Eastern Housing Association, rent seven shillings and sixpence per week. The knob gleams with a fresh polish. It gets a good going over with Brasso on Mondays, but when my telegram arrived today, she'll have done it again. Mam, who looks to be a touch stouter around the middle, gives me a hug and a kiss, and Dad gives a warm handshake. Peter, my mongrel dog, dances around, his flag of a tail thumping on chair legs.

'Did you have a good trip, Son?' Dad looks grey and tired. He'll be sixty-four in November. I wish he did not need to trail to Haverton Hill, to that Furness shipyard on the Tees, every weekday. He survived the battle of Ypres – he should have his feet up by now.

I decide not to mention the lost ship; they'll only worry whenever their own sky goes dark with threat. 'A grand run to the East, Dad. Though it made for a lot of empty sea and long trudge there and back because Suez was shut. But Brocklebanks is a fine company; they treat us well and feed us like fighting cocks. It's not the most comfortable experience, tied up in Calcutta for upwards of six weeks, so the company is keen to keep the men sweet lest they drift away to better runs, South America, Australia, and the like. I'm to rejoin the same ship, first week of July, but this time we'll use the Canal – if the feckless Gypos have it properly cleared.'

Mam sets out knife, fork, and spoon on the table. 'What have you had to eat, Son?'

'A cold pork pie and loads of British Rail tea.'

'You'll be famished. What about egg and chips, with black pudding. Then date and apple pie, with custard, after?'

'Lovely, Mam. That'll be lovely. I've not seen black pudding for months, and I have missed your pies.'

'When your telegram came, I went straight down to the smokehouse and got some big kippers; you can have one for breakfast.'

'That's smashing, Mam. I'll be getting gout at this rate.'

Dad is in his armchair, by the fireplace. He's shaving the edge of a block of Walnut baccy ready to fill his pipe. Peter is by my chair; he occasionally nudges me with a wet nose to remind me to slip him another morsel of food off my plate. I wipe the eggy plate with a slice of bread and butter, then drop a hard corner of crust into Peter's jaws. Mam swaps the plate for a dish of pie swimming in bright yellow custard. She lays a newspaper cutting on the oil-cloth table cover and points with a forefinger; I notice how the nail still grows distorted even though it's fifty years since she was burnt as a child.

'Do you know about this? It's old news now, but isn't she the lass you went out with over Christmas?' Her palm gives one stroke to the back of my head; only one – we are not a demonstrative family.

I pick up the cutting, and lean back as I read:

NORTHERN DAILY MAIL, Saturday, April 27, 1957. West H'pool climber still in hospital. Miss Beryl Scott, the 19-year-old West Hartlepool girl who fell 225 feet down a Lakeland mountain on Sunday is still in Keswick Hospital. An X-ray has shown that Beryl, who lives at 6 Caxton Grove, Rift House, has cracked a small ankle bone. She is expected home tomorrow. She was climbing Kern Crag in a party of four when her West Hartlepool boy friend Stewart, dislodged a rock ahead of her. This struck her a glancing blow on the shoulder, and knocked her off balance. As result, Beryl plunged 75 feet down the face of the cliff and rolled a further 150 feet down scree. Stewart helped her walk to Styhead Pass where she fainted. On top of the pass was a stretcher post belonging to Keswick Mountain Rescue Team. Members of the Scottish Climbing Club carried her the two miles to Seathwaite, where a waiting ambulance took her to hospital It was Beryl's first climbing expedition. She often goes rambling.

Beryl's photograph is included. She's wearing a tightly buttoned-up coat, as though against the cold. She's in profile and wearing a tam o'Shanter. The picture looks to be an old one. She's probably about sixteen in this image, but is definitely the pleasant girl I met at the dance. In silence, I read it twice more. 'No, Mam. I didn't know about it. She sent a letter to Calcutta saying she was seeing another lad. I've heard nowt since.'

'It's a miracle she survived that fall; it can't be her time. Who's this Stewart lad she was with?'

'No idea. Never heard of him.'

25

Casanova

I'm home for five weeks. Five weeks of being fussed over by Mam. Five weeks of Sunday suet puddings steamed in a muslin cloth and served with thick onion gravy. There's the inevitable, solid supper of leftovers: a patty of potato mixed with peas and swede, and fried hard so that it has a crunchy brown crust. On the side might sit my favourite, a slice of corned beef pie packed with aromatic onion and sage. Nothing is wasted. We pour dollops of brown sauce onto whatever else will not keep much longer on the cold shelf in the pantry – the house has no refrigerator. Judging by the ample waistlines of the middle-aged, the handsome paunches beneath the dark waistcoats of Sunday suits, paunches that make such a splendid surface for the display of watch chains, most of the town go to bed on suppers like these.

Lunch is unheard of in this working class town of heavy industry. Men take their dinners to work – never their lunch. In the grit and grime of the shipyards and steelworks they devour their sandwiches and lumps of cold pie at midday break, and at the end of the shift, return home to something hot. Sunday is the time for a family dinner, served at midday. We load up with a copious meal, one that in good times includes a joint of meat, carved by father and served by mother. Father, head of the house and breadwinner, will be given the choicest cut. It's roast pork today. I note how Dad takes care not to break up the crispy crackling.

Mam often forgets the condiments. As she unties her pinny to sit with us, Dad scans the table and says, 'Salt, Lass.' She bustles to the cupboard by the hearth and returns with salt cellar and pepper pot. I watch this and think how little has changed. The same moments, the same snippets of gruff but loving speech, the same uncomplicated way of being. Thirty-three years married; five children, of which only my sister and I survive. My parents are become more grey and more stout. They are quietly devoted; only once do I recall raised voices and that was years ago when Mam put on her hat and coat and left him for one night. I thought the World had come to an end.

'How's the Yorkshire?' Mam nods to the pudding made from a batter of flour, egg, and milk. It is golden-brown, soft on the bottom and crisp around the raised edge. The results can be variable depending on oven heat and all sorts of mysterious vagaries that only women have knowledge of. The pudding can rise and inflate like a balloon, and then might slowly collapse in a second once out of the oven. Today, I can see it has behaved perfectly. It has taken the form of a steep-sided dish and fills Dad's plate like a lotus leaf. In this house it is always served as a savoury first course, with onion gravy, before the main dish of meat and three veg.

Dad pours a stream of gravy into the centre of his Yorkshire pudding, carefully cuts a slice so that the gravy floods out in a controlled manner through the breach in the pudding's wall. He chews, swallows, turns to Mam. 'It's champion, Honey. Never better. My mother's were handsome enough, but they'd never hold a candle to yours.'

Mam smiles happily. She brushes a wisp of hair away from her eyebrow, the undamaged one. She passes me the gravy boat, after giving it a stir to ensure I get some onion. 'Son, have you remembered it's your birthday on Friday? Seventh of June. I'll get a nice bit of fish for your tea.'

Dad looks up from his plate. 'Aye! You'll be all of nineteen. Will you be celebrating?'

'I'll meet my mates and see if I can persuade them to buy me a half ...' My utterance tails off. Dad is not so fond of pubs. His own father indulged to excess and made Grandmother's life difficult on pay days.

Mam sighs, 'If only Kenneth had lived, then you'd have had an older brother to go out with.' She dabs her eyes.

Dad puts his hand on her shoulder. 'Now, now, Lass. Don't let your dinner spoil.'

I make myself useful by digging over a triangular patch of garden that has become infested with couch grass. Dad formerly grew splendid potatoes here, and long, straight carrots, in the sandy soil of what was once consolidated sand dune before it became pasture and then housing estate. He now cultivates just a few patches in the back garden. It's getting beyond him. I feel ashamed at the prospect of all these weeds. I do my best to remove the jointed white roots, wickens and stolons of the couch grass; leave one fragment and the monster sprouts anew. This patch has never been properly cleared of the couch grass since Alojzy Pokorsky dug it over near the end of the

273

war. He dug well, turned over the soil, but did not remove the roots; the couch came back with a vengeance. Alojzy was no gardener, (His name anglicised as Harry - so that's how we knew him) but he had escaped Hitler's advance into Poland when his Polish warship, the destroyer *Burza,* in the company of two others, slipped out of Gdynia, raced through the Baltic at high speed, and joined the residue of the Polish navy at Leith in Scotland, to fight through the war as part of the British fleet.

I'm thinking of that platinum-haired Polish officer as I dig. He was blue-eyed; had an angled, handsome face with noble Slavic cheekbones. His destroyer, the *Burza,* sailed 100,000 miles, escorted 29 convoys, attacked seventeen U-boats, sunk one and damaged four. She was attacked by enemy aircraft a score of times and shot down two. She rescued about 500 survivors of sunken ships, and three times she was severely damaged.

After his long duty at sea, in 1944 Harry Pokorsky's ship was sent to Hartlepool for refit, and this is how he met my sister, Dorothy. He would often visit our home and enjoy Mam's Sunday dinners – he praised the mint sauce she made from Dad's bed of that invasive herb. He came with gifts: chocolate and nylon stockings. He gave me a black puppy from the litter produced by the ship's dog; a shame the little fellow did not flourish.

After the war, he was offered repatriation to his own country, but the Russians dominated Poland, so he refused. All that remained of his family at home, was an old aunt. Most had fallen to the Nazis; but his brothers, officers in the Polish Army, lay in mass graves in the Katyn forest along with half the Polish officer corps; 8,000 officers imprisoned during the 1939 Soviet invasion of Poland (Hitler and Stalin had agreed to carve up Poland between them). They are buried with 6,000 police officers and those Polish intelligentsia, officials, and priests, that the Soviets deemed *hardened and uncompromising enemies of Soviet authority.* The mass murder was approved by Joseph Stalin. Rather than risk the depraved justice of the NKVD, the Soviet secret police, Harry found temporary work as a forester in Northumberland. That rough work did not suit him – he was a refined and sensitive man. His romance with my sister had come to an end, so he took a job on a merchant ship bound for Australia. Upon arrival, Harry Pokorsky walked ashore to find a new life. He writes fond letters to my mother, which she treasures. He now owns a motorcycle repair business near Brisbane. Harry tells the rest of the world that he's German; he's not yet legal in Australia and would rather be deported to West Germany than communist Poland.

While I sift through the turned earth for wickens and the fleshy roots of dock and dandelion, I calculate I've only three weeks leave remaining. I've been home two weeks and I've not made contact with Beryl. Her accident was six weeks ago. She probably won't want to hear from me now she has a steady boyfriend, even though he's the clown who dislodged the rock. But we were friends; perhaps we should say a final goodbye. I decide to make a phone call. There's a telephone box outside the new shops, a mere two-hundred yards up our road.

The tiny switchboard at Pounder's 'Plumbers and Electricians' puts me through to the office where Beryl is a clerk. She comes on the line with an anxious voice, and I recall that private phone calls are frowned upon. 'Hello?'

'It's me – Harry. I'm home on leave. I read about your accident and wondered how you are …'

We meet outside Burn Valley Gardens. The June midday sun is warm; the long and slender park is radiant with blossom. Beryl is lovely in a navy-blue blazer and full, flowered skirt. We decide to take a slow stroll to a shaded park bench. She has a soft plaster cast on one leg and moves with a hint of stiffness.

'How did you come to fall off a mountain? In the Lake District, was it?'

'Four of us went hill walking near Keswick. It poured torrents of rain as we went up Great Gable. Two went back, but I encouraged Stewart to keep going as we were so near to the top, so it's my own fault. He was ahead as we climbed. The ground was sodden with all that rain. The boulders were loose on the last slope. Stewart tested one with his boot but it came loose. He shouted, 'Below!' It came bounding down the mountain at me. It would have hit my head, but I leaned to one side and it bounced off my shoulder. That's when I fell.'

I'm awkward with this girl, it's five months since we last met, though it feels right to be with her now. 'The newspaper says you fell seventy-five feet and rolled fifty yards, it's a wonder you survived.'

'I tumbled and bounced for ages. I must have fainted because I was relaxed when I hit a squelchy bit of a grassy slope. Then, I was just conscious of rolling over and over downwards; each time I rolled, the rock bounced over me. I came to a stop at a stretch of scree just before the edge of the next precipice. Stewart came charging down, thinking I might be dead. I blurted out, 'My mother will go mad at me,' which cheered him up a bit. I managed to limp as far as Styhead Pass, but then I froze with shock. Stewart went for help. I was gathered up on a stretcher and taken to Keswick hospital by a mountain rescue team who were out training – lucky for me. Stewart's father brought Dad to see me. Stewart's father has a car. On the journey, Dad took up smoking again. So I get the blame for that.'

Just as I realise that we are now holding hands, Beryl unwinds her fingers from mine. She almost whispers: 'I'm engaged to be married.' But I sense it's without much conviction.

I take her hand again; she does not flinch. 'Are you sure you're ready for that?'

'I'm not sure at all. You see, after my fall on the mountain and all the fuss that followed, our two families got close. Stewart had new stones fitted to my grandmother's ring and said he would ask Dad if we could become engaged. I told him: "Don't you dare!" But he did. Then it all got out of hand, with everybody making arrangements for a wedding.'

'You might not be over the shock of the accident. Perhaps it should be delayed until you're sure.'

'I've had niggling doubts from the start, but I'm carried along by all the rigmarole the families make. He sends me flowers every Friday. I feel overwhelmed by it all. But Dad and Mam are all for it. Stewart's an electrician and his father owns a grocer's business.'

'A much better prospect than a rough seafarer, then. Even though your mother married one.'

'Dad was an engineer, but a ship's officer just like you.'

'Then, I suppose he'll reckon to have the measure of me.'

'You're not like him at all. I'm glad you still send me letters sometimes. I got one in hospital amongst all the Get Well cards. I kept it till last, and I thought at the time that was significant.'

After more talk, she becomes anxious that her dinner break nears its end.

I shuffle my feet. How will this unfold? I've a twinge of embarrassed responsibility, but I can make no promises. 'Shall we meet again?'

'If you'd like to. Stewart and I are going to Scarborough tomorrow for the weekend. I'll tell him on the bus, on the way there, that I don't want to be engaged after all. It's all paid for, so we might as well go.' She glances at her hands. 'We've booked separate rooms.'

My sister, Dorothy, is here this Sunday; she is staying with her husband's parents in West Hartlepool. I'm upstairs in my bedroom, the one I grew up in. I'm considering asking Mam to iron a shirt ready for tonight – though I'm not sure where I'll be going. I'll wear the very narrow tie I bought yesterday – they are all the rage just now.

I hear a tentative knock at the front door. My sister opens it. Dorothy shouts up the stairs, 'Hey, Casanova! There's someone to see you. She's brought her bike.'

It's Beryl. She looks up the stairs. Her eyes seem to focus on the tattoo on my forearm. I roll down the shirt sleeve. 'I'll be down in a minute.'

Dorothy says, 'Will you come in, pet?'

'No thanks, I'll just wait here.'

We set off up Warren Road, to the new part. When I was in short trousers this was a rutted country track between hedges of unkempt but glorious hawthorn. I often wandered this way with my dog; he would sniff for rabbits whilst I searched for bird's nests. It was known then as Lover's Lane, but now we walk on tarmac, lined with new houses that have fanciful Dutch-style arched roofs. We pass the wall of Howbeck Hospital – it used to be a Victorian Workhouse where the poor spent their last days. I try to avoid looking at the roof of the mortuary that peeps above the wall; as urchins, we knew it as *The Dead House* and would run past it as fast as we could.

'How did it go?'

I'm on foot, she is wheeling her bike. I've offered to do that, but she's declined. 'I told him, on the way to Scarborough, that you were home on leave. I told him that I still wanted to see you. He took it well enough. He suggested we should go straight home again; told me he'd climb the Wainstones to get it all out of his system. But I thought we should try to have a nice time since we had gone all that way. I had my fortune told on Scarborough pier, by a Gypsy in a tent.'

'And what did the Gypsy say?'

'She said I had a choice to make, and if I chose the one who went to sea I would rue every hair of my head.'

'Oh dear!'

'The Gypsy might have noticed that I'd moved the engagement ring to my other hand. She probably saw the mark on the finger where it had been. But just after that, the stones Stewart had paid for, to be set in my grandma's ring ... they fell out.'

We meet the next day, on Monday. We are in Bianco's in Tower Street; it's a smart and modern Italian ice-cream parlour – the table tops are Formica. Beryl's bicycle is outside. She's just delivered the firm's takings to the bank and is stealing an extra fifteen minutes – she'll say there was a queue.

She sips her milk-shake through a straw, then her lovely blue eyes lift. 'There's an awful fuss at home. Stewart's mother rushed to see my parents, wailing and going on. My sister, Kathleen, floats around the house singing, *I'm just wild about Harry, and Harry's wild about me, dah, de, dah, dah.*'

There's a plump lady on the next table, spooning into a knickerbocker glory. Despite the fine day, she's wearing a silver fox around her neck. The animal's ears flop and its glass eyes look as though they've been dull for a hundred years. But not her's – she's taking it all in.

I whisper, 'I sail in three weeks' time. I'll be gone for another five-month stretch – six months if we come back via The States. Is there any chance you can take a holiday from work?'

Beryl mimics my furtiveness, 'I've already asked my boss, Mr Portis, if that would be allowed. He said Miss Papple can manage on her own for a week. I can start on Friday, as soon as we've made up the men's wages.'

'That's wonderful. We can go for short walks. We can take the train to Saltburn, have fish and chips, and sit on the cliff top among the flowers. If you've got your head for heights back, that is.'

'I'd like that. But not too far just yet. I get my plaster off this week, though I get the odd twinge in my back sometimes.'

We take the bus to Crimdon Dene and walk to the shore where my father and I collected seacoal washed up after winter storms. The little stream that meanders through the Dene is black and without minnows; a sign the coal pits beyond Hesleden still work. But the dunes are sublime with pink burnet roses set against a background of rustling blue marram grass. We hide among the sheltered dunes and talk, and kiss. The crystal air off the North Sea has a salt tang; this is a long way from the foetid reek of Calcutta.

Another day we walk beside the railway line towards Bluebell Wood. There's an abandoned railwayman's cottage by the line. We can still make out where he grew his vegetables. The raspberries are rampant and no longer pruned, but they have sweet fruit. His pink rose hangs in wild abandon above the old fellow's front door. Still green, that door – though not painted for years. In the back garden, a hen house sags. My mother brought me this way once; I'll have been about four, but I've a vague memory of holding her hand while Mam spoke to the old chap in this same garden.

Beryl in the polka-dot scarf.

In the wooded valley, it's too late in the year for bluebells. But there is a riot of white shepherd's purse, pink willowherb and, if you look carefully, there are tiny wild strawberries ripe and ready for the tongue. I show Beryl the ash tree from which I rescued a baby tawny owl. Some fiend had suspended the creature on a length of string – I grew her on until she could fend for herself.

On the cliffs at Saltburn with Beryl

Beryl at Saltburn, June 1957

At Saltburn, near the top of Hunt Cliff, we sunbathe among the flowers and gaze across the North Sea. Denmark and Holland are out there somewhere. The Danish Vikings made a bee-line for this place. They settled here, called their new home *Land of Cliffs*, or *Cliffland*. It is still known to us as Cleveland. We don't know this, but in the fields behind us sleeps a Saxon princess, her body bedecked in enamels mounted in gold. In fifty years' time, the archaeologists will find her, and all her kin buried in a great circle, with the princess at the centre.

The sea is mild and a mirror to any thin cloud that happens along. In this balmy afternoon, we have stripped as much as we dare. Beryl has removed her top and fashioned a sort of bikini from a scarf to hide her bra. She wears pale blue shorts. The white polka-dotted, red bandana bikini top completes a vision that I'll carry abroad.

The end of Volume One.

I must now begin Volume Two – please wish me a following wind . . .

Printed in Great Britain
by Amazon

56782394R00165